ON TRIAL!

Law, Lawyers, and the Legal System

ON TRIAL!

Law, Lawyers, and the Legal System

Benjamin M. Becker
David L. Gibberman

Philosophical Library
New York

Library of Congress Cataloging-in-Publication Data:

Becker, Benjamin Max, 1909—
   On trial!

   Bibliography: p.
   1. Lawyers—United States.   2. Practice of law—
United States.   I. Gibberman, David L.   II. Title.
   KF297.B43   1986   340'.023'73   86-12234
ISBN 0-8022-2512-8

Preface

On Trial! takes a rich, perceptive look at "lawyers"— what they do and how they think—and provides a remarkably clear analysis of our legal systems, both federal and state, and how they work. The book develops the role law and lawyers play in our lives, our communities, our businesses, our employment and our society. The authors, both lawyers, avoid the twin pitfalls which plague the works of the typical lawyer turned author: the book is neither overly technical nor filled with meaningless "war stories." It is not only easily readable but also enjoyable reading.

Every attorney will find much of himself and his own experience in the law in this collage of what lawyers know but may not think about frequently. I recommend it to my fellow lawyers and judges as a refresher. I recommend it also to law students, and especially to those contemplating the study of law. For them it will give an overview of what the life of a lawyer is like, whether as a member of a large firm or as an individual practitioner. In many ways, *On Trial!* can serve as a primer in the "real law" and as a supplement to legal education by the case-book method.

v

Non-lawyers will also enjoy this book, as it washes away the misconceptions of law and lawyers created by television and movies. It gives them an easily understood and realistic insight into what appears to most laymen as confusing and suspicious mumbo-jumbo.

Seymour Simon
Justice, Illinois Supreme Court

Contents

Introduction

During the half century that I have practiced law, I have come to realize that few people understand what lawyers do and how the legal system operates. This ignorance makes them fear the legal process and discourages them from using law for their own benefit. More important, this ignorance makes them feel powerless to make needed changes in the legal system.

When, as a newly licensed lawyer, I entered practice in 1935, the law profession generally was considered an honorable pursuit. But times have changed. For the past few decades, lawyers and the law profession have suffered increasing criticism and disenchantment on the part of the general public. Such people as President Jimmy Carter, United States Supreme Court Chief Justice Warren Burger, Derek Bok, president of Harvard University, and others have complained about lawyers who are incompetent to practice law, who encourage litigation and clog the courts, who charge excessive fees, and, in the wake of the Watergate affair, lawyers who engage in unethical and criminal conduct.

Throughout my life, I have felt a responsibility to use my legal talents for public service. For many years I have thought about writing a book to help people understand how our legal system can work for them, but there never seemed enough time for such an endeavor. Three years ago I decided to make the time, and I was fortunate to be able to interest another attorney, David L. Gibberman, in bringing a younger perspective to such a work. Although this book uses some of my experiences as examples, David is a co-author in the fullest meaning of the term. Whatever merit this book has, the authors share jointly.

In *On Trial! Law, Lawyers, and the Legal System*, we have tried to explain what the average person can and should expect from lawyers and the legal system. Individuals interested in law as a career can read this book to discover whether they are suited to be lawyers. They will learn about the reality of practicing law, the intellectual challenge in practicing law, and what is wrong with the law, lawyers, and the legal system. Experienced lawyers can read about issues they may not have time to think about during their busy daily practice.

This book is not a collection of "war" stories about famous cases or clients. Nor will it satiate anyone's craving for scandal about lawyers and the legal system. Instead, it is intended to be a reasonable review of situations and problems confronting lawyers during their practice, with guidelines and suggestions about how lawyers and the general public can improve the practice of law and our legal system.

Finally, let this be the legacy of a lawyer who has had the good fortune to have enjoyed the fulfillment, stimulation, challenge, and rewards of a half-century in what for the most part is a great and honorable profession.

ON TRIAL!

Law, Lawyers, and the Legal System

Chapter 1

Our System of Civil Justice

The blunt, inexcusable fact is that this nation, which prides itself on efficiency and justice, has developed a legal system that is the most expensive in the world, yet cannot manage to protect the rights of most of its citizens.

Derek C. Bok, formerly Dean of Harvard Law School and now President of Harvard University[1]

Our system is too costly, too painful, too destructive, too inefficient for a truly civilized people.

Warren E. Burger, former Chief Justice of the United States Supreme Court[2]

1

When people think of our system of civil justice, they tend to think only of our court system. But courts are only the most visible portion of the iceberg. The vast majority of all disputes either are never settled or are settled without resort to a lawyer, and most disputes that do reach a lawyer are settled without need for a trial. Each dispute that has to be decided by a judge or jury actually represents a failure of our system of civil justice since there is a much greater chance of achieving "justice" when the parties work out their own solutions. Our legal system is so complicated, so expensive, and so prone to making "justice" accidental that most people going all the way through it are bound to wind up as losers.

Before people began relying excessively on courts and law to resolve their conflicts, quarrels were settled by armed struggle between the disputants or their champions. Institutionalizing this private combat as court trials between adversaries championed by lawyers marked an important advance in resolving disputes. Not only could civil peace be more easily maintained but a rough form of justice was substituted for "might makes right." Courts began to look for principles of law that they could use to resolve common disputes, and these rudimentary laws were an important step towards doing justice.

Many philosophers and some lawyers probably would object to my differentiating "justice" from "might makes right" since it has become popular in some circles to dismiss "justice" either as the ideology of the ruling class or as a concept so vague that it is meaningless. "Justice is the first virtue of those who command, and stops the complaints of those who obey," according to Denis Diderot, an 18th century French philosopher.[3] Karl Marx argued that "justice" is merely a mask for capitalist exploitation of the workers.[4]

To Jeremy Bentham, "justice" is a state of mind. It means "that a man is firmly persuaded of the truth of this or that moral proposition, though he either thinks he *need not*, or finds he *can't* tell *why*."[5] Alf Ross, an eminent Danish jurist, viewed "justice" as more emotional and irrational:

"To invoke justice is the same thing as banging on the table."[6]

"Justice" may be irrelevant to some philosophers, but it is important to the average person. True, most people never articulate what they mean by "justice." To some, "justice" may be reciprocal action—an eye for an eye. To others, it may mean unquestioning conformity with laws, human or eternal. Or it may mean preserving or expanding an individual's rights (e.g., right to own property, right to speak freely, maybe even a right to have a job). Some look at "justice" more from the perspective of society in general instead of from the perspective of the individual. To them, "justice" may mean promoting certain social goals such as assuring a more even distribution of money and property among all people or inculcating certain attitudes in people, a goal of the Soviet system of justice. People have a sense of what is right and what is wrong and want to believe that justice can exist in this world—and maybe in other worlds to come. "Justice" may have no precise meaning that can be mechanically applied to every factual situation, but, given a set of facts, most people can agree on what would be a "just" result.

We measure "justice" by looking at both the process of determining "justice" and the results. Both measures are implied by the letters carved into the portal of the Supreme Court Building: EQUAL JUSTICE UNDER LAW. Some people have questioned whether "justice" derives from human institutions or whether it measures human institutions. I do not look on this as an either-or answer. How an institution dispensing justice is structured can affect what decisions are made. And what those decisions are can be used to determine whether the institution is accomplishing its task.

How then does our system of civil justice stack up against these measures of "justice"? Not very well, I am afraid. Everyone has heard horror stories about crooked judges, incompetent lawyers, and unjust laws. I have run across examples of all of them during my years of practice. But what concerns me more than these human frailties and errors are institutional flaws in our system of civil justice. Human frailties and errors will always be with us, but fortunately these can be minimized and corrected. It is the institutional flaws, which bring out the worst in human nature and make "justice" nigh impossible, that we must seriously consider and correct. These flaws are discussed in detail throughout this book.

What do I mean when I talk about our "system of civil justice"? The physical structures are the courts of law located in each state. Some of these courts are municipal courts. Others are state or federal courts. There are various types of courts since there are various sources of law. For example, federal courts handle cases involving federal law. They also hear cases between citizens from different states—what lawyers refer to as "diversity of citizenship" cases. Federal courts were given that power because there was a fear that state courts would tend to favor their citizens over residents of other states.

The checks and balances of our federal system of government mirror and complicate our legal system. Certain complications arise when a case involves both federal and state law—complications that delight law professors, put extra food on lawyers' tables, and vex litigants. There are also problems deciding whether one segment of our federal system has the power to do what it did or wants to do or whether such an action exceeds its powers. The powers of states and municipalities are circumscribed by state constitutions and the United States Constitution, and the federal government's powers are limited by the U.S. Constitution. To minimize mistakes by the courts, there are courts to correct errors, courts known as appellate courts.

It is popular to say that we are ruled by law and not by people, but that statement is misleading. When people make this boast, they mean that we are governed by commonly accepted principles and not the whims of a particular person. The statement is misleading because it implies divine sanction for those laws, but the reality is that those laws are made and administered by people—and can be changed if that suits peoples' needs. This myth that laws are somehow sacred and beyond change is reflected in American preacher Henry Ward Beecher's wry observation that "It usually takes a hundred years to make a law, and then, after it has done its work, it usually takes a hundred years to get rid of it."[7]

The legal system provides a framework for making sure that people's expectations are met. The traditional basic functions of law have been to settle disputes and maintain order. There are tales of a Persian custom of decreeing anarchy for five days after a king's death so that people would then be able to appreciate rulers and law.[8]

Fast becoming a basic function of the legal system is the regulation of what *is* and what *is not* proper behavior in society. In the Soviet Union, law is considered more important for guiding people toward the Communist ideal than for serving as a set of principles to resolve private disputes. Law in the Soviet Union is for the benefit of those in power and not for the benefit of the individual. In Aleksandr Solzhenitsyn's *Gulag Archipelago*, a person protesting how his trial has been conducted is told by the Soviet judge: "The *law* will crush you, smash you, destroy you!"[9]

How the functions of law are fulfilled is also important. It is not enough to settle a dispute arbitrarily or to end disorder. People want to believe that the settlement will be "fair" and that their basic freedoms will not be sacrificed for "order." People also have to be able to understand what their obligations are. Unfortunately, laws are often poorly drafted and cannot be understood. Poor draftsmanship can also lead to unintended results. Consider the Belvedere, California ordinance that "No dog shall be in a public place without its master on a leash."[10]

As trials became a substitute for private brawls, judge-made law evolved. This is what lawyers refer to as the "common law," sometimes mistakenly thought of as "a brooding omnipresence in the sky."[11] Judge-made law consists of principles applied by judges to settle disputes on trial. As you might imagine, this early law varied from judge to judge and town to town. William Blackstone, an 18th century English judge, made the first attempt to bring order to this chaos by publishing his *Commentaries on the Laws of England* from 1765 to 1769. Blackstone began to lecture on English law at Oxford because he was unsuccessful at practicing law. Before he began lecturing, English law was not considered a proper subject for English youth to study.

Many Americans were hostile towards English law after the Revolutionary War, and several states made it illegal to cite any English law developed after July 1, 1776. Blackstone's commentaries on English law, published in the United States in 1771, became America's chief link with English common law. Each state developed its own distinct body of common law, and even now judge-made law frequently varies from state to state.

Two disadvantages of judge-made law are 1) that it is made by judges, who may or may not reflect the will of most people, and 2) that it is made with reference to how it will affect the parties to the dispute and not necessarily with consideration for how it will affect society in general. When he commented that "hard cases make bad law,"[12] Supreme Court Justice Oliver Wendell Holmes, Jr. was concerned that judges can be swayed by emotionally appealing facts.

The second objection would not be much of a problem if the effect of a judge's decision were limited to the disputants, but it is not. What a judge decides not only serves as precedent that will be relied on by other judges confronting similar situations but it also influences how people will settle their differences short of trial. Judges may be able to decide what will be a fair result in a particular situation, but society might disagree. For example, in recent years there has been a trend toward no-fault laws because legislators have decided it is less important to decide who was at fault than it is to compensate the victims of accidents.

We still have judge-made law, but more and more laws are passed by legislators, who at least theoretically have greater access to information than judges and are better able to reflect the views of the majority of Americans. Being able to reflect the views of the majority is considered a disadvantage when it comes to protecting civil liberties, particularly the civil liberties of the minority; for that reason we have a constitution that reins the power of the majority to tyrannize the minority and that is interpreted by judges who are insulated from the pressure of the majority.

The United States Constitution provides a broad framework for the operation of our society. It outlines how our government should function and what its relationship should be to the people it governs. Many people mistakenly think that the Constitution is the ultimate authority on the rights of the individual, but that power is reserved to the nine United States Supreme Court justices, who are the final arbiters of what the Constitution means. Over the years they have changed that meaning to adapt an 18th century document to 20th century life. As Chief Justice Charles Evans Hughes observed: "We are under a Constitution, but the Constitution is what the judges say it is, and the judiciary is the safeguard of our liberty and of our property under the Constitution."[13]

People are quick to blame lawyers for needlessly complicating matters. Some do. But much of the needless complication is due to the way laws are written. One of the great myths of our system of justice, unfortunately perpetuated by participants in the system, is that laws are clearly written and static. The myth gives an aura of respect to the system, but the reality is that many laws are vague and/or not clearly thought through, can be changed easily, and often are. It might be nice to have static laws, but it is unrealistic to expect laws to cover all the complications and variations of human relations.

The myth that law is static perpetuates the status quo and discourages us from evaluating laws to make certain that they are still meeting our needs. As Supreme Court Justice Harlan F. Stone once said, "The law itself is on trial, quite as much as the cause which is to be decided."[14] Clarence Darrow had the same idea when he said, "Laws should be like clothes. They should be made to fit the people they are meant to serve."[15] Many of our laws are complicated because they carry the baggage of history and have not been reevaluated in light of modern conditions.

Some people have argued that writing laws to make them fairer would make them more unpredictable and difficult to obey. They make that assertion because they equate fairness with discretion and believe that increasing the circumstances to be considered will increase uncertainty about what the law is. For example, a law holding a homeowner liable for injuries sustained by someone while on the homeowner's property is clear. But such a law may not be fair. Most people would not think it fair to hold a homeowner liable for the injuries of a guest who acts recklessly (e.g., by entering a room marked "Danger—Keep Out") or a trespasser (e.g., a burglar). Many would change their minds, however, if the trespasser were a child or someone forced to go on the land because of an emergency. The more exceptions there are to the rule the more difficult it is to predict whether it has been violated (e.g., what is reasonable or reckless behavior by a guest?).

I certainly do not favor uncertainty, since that would drastically increase litigation, but I do not accept the implication that laws cannot be both fair and easy to obey. As a former instructor of legal drafting, I am convinced that the problem lies more in poor draftsmanship than in any irreconcilable conflict between fairness and certainty.

Over the past few decades, our society has increasingly relied on statutory and judge-made law to regulate every aspect of our lives. There was a time when people would wistfully say, "There ought to be a law." Now there usually is. Consider the International Falls, Minnesota ordinance making it illegal for a cat to chase a dog up a telephone pole, the North Carolina ordinance making it illegal to sing out of tune, the South Bend, Indiana ordinance prohibiting monkeys from smoking cigarettes (but not cigars), the

Normal, Oklahoma law prohibiting people from making faces at a dog, the Miami ordinance prohibiting cats from molesting alligators, the Florida law prohibiting sexual relations with a porcupine, or the Urbana, Illinois ordinance prohibiting monsters within the city limits.[16]

Increasingly we believe that right and wrong have to be defined by law instead of community morality. We react to perceived problems by enacting a law or filing a suit instead of working together to find an amicable solution. Litigation now is used even to resolve political disputes, once considered off-limits to the courts. Richard Neely, former Chief Justice of the West Virginia Supreme Court of Appeals, even has argued that American democracy could not work without courts eliminating structural deficiencies of other governmental institutions (e.g., before courts ruled the practice unconstitutional it was possible for one town with twice as many people as another to have the same number of representatives).[17]

Overreliance on "legal" solutions reflects a breakdown in the social fabric holding our society together and a loss of mutual trust. The early Puritans of Massachusetts believed it was unchristian to litigate and instead resolved disputes through arbitration and mediation. Later immigrants also avoided the courts and instead let the community help people settle their arguments. Community resolutions not only helped immigrants preserve their ethnic identity but also protected them from discrimination practiced by prejudiced judges and jurors.

As community bonds loosened, the courts replaced the family, religious institutions, and local communities as institutions for settling disputes. In recent years, our laws have multiplied so rapidly that they have become a burden for the wealthy, who may have to spend a small fortune to comply with all the governmental regulations, and yet are no help for the many who cannot afford a lawyer.

Making laws fit people like clothes would not assure "justice" since that would still leave the problem of assuring that the laws are fairly applied. Another myth of our system

of justice is that laws can be mechanically applied by
judges and jurors. In reality, it is often difficult to decide
what the facts are and whether a law covers a particular
situation.

Some people deliberately lie about what happened; others
unintentionally confuse the facts, maybe because they are
not good observers or listeners or because they badly want
to believe that something happened a certain way. No matter the reason, it is often difficult for judges and juries to sort
through all that is said and decide what the facts are. As
Judge Jerome Frank wrote: "A wag has it that courts decide
cases according to the 'preponderance of the perjury.' "[18]

Facts are not distorted just by the disputants and their
witnesses; facts also can be distorted by jurors and judges.
Jurors may not listen carefully to what is said or may not be
able to understand what is said or may bring their own
biases to bear and believe the wrong story. Even if jurors
receive and grasp the facts, they may not understand the
law—judges do not always help jurors understand the
law—and may resort to applying their own standard of
fairness instead of the standard incorporated into the law.

Judges have the same problem as jurors in ferreting out
the truth but are not as trusted as jurors to do it right. People
have mixed feelings about judges. The black robe and
solemnity of the court proceedings give judges a mystique
that demands respect. But throughout history there have
been reports of dishonest judges. There is even a Russian
proverb saying that "The thing to fear is not the law but the
judge."[19]

I have heard of a few dishonest judges, but most "bad"
judges are incompetent rather than dishonest. Although
the United States has had its share of incompetent judges,
on the whole appointed judges have been fairly competent.
That has not necessarily been the case with elected judges,
but in recent years political parties have become more selective about their candidates for the bench.

I well remember the days when political hacks were
selected by the political bosses. Of course there was a price

to pay for selection—payable in cash and/or favorable treatment for the political boss and his party. The gangsters would push their own candidates and woe the judge so selected who did not give the mob total loyalty. I remember two judges from Chicago's west side who were known to hold court on a street curb. Night courts were frequently a time to release questionable characters associated with the mob. There was one case many years ago that I thought my client would win hands down. We didn't. I later learned that opposing counsel had made an arrangement with the local political boss to advance to the appellate court the trial judge deciding against my client.

We like to think of judges as wise people dispensing "justice," stern yet compassionate, unbiased and never succumbing to boredom. But judges can be as biased as jurors. A judge may favor the little guy or big business or be influenced by personal experience to discount or discredit certain testimony. Judges with marital problems may discount certain complaints by spouses. Judges who have had bad experiences with certain types of people may be inclined not to believe what those people say. A good judge will control those biases and fairly apply the law.

The delay in bringing cases to trial affects what "justice" is available. Delays are not new. Even Hamlet complained about "the law's delay."[20] The party at fault is encouraged to drag out a dispute as long as possible to avoid payment for as long as possible. People suffering serious injuries are encouraged to take less money than they are entitled to rather than have to wait years to get any money. The longer that insurers can delay payment, the longer they can make money on funds rightfully belonging to the injured party. Unfortunately, as British political leader William Gladstone observed: "Justice delayed is justice denied."[21]

The cost of litigation also affects what "justice" is available. Despite alarm over the number of suits filed each year, many disputes do not get into court because any potential benefit is outweighed by its cost. Some people cannot afford to sue, particularly if the maximum amount they can expect to win is less than the amount they would have to pay in legal fees and expenses. The cost of litigation can, however, help people suffering minor injuries extort more money than they deserve since they know it will cost the defendant more money to defend a suit than it would to pay a premium for settling a dispute.

Complicating the process of pulling "justice" out of our courts is the adversary system, which pits people in competition to win the favor of the judge or juror. In this system, "justice" becomes an inadvertent byproduct, which suits most disputants since they are concerned only with victory. During my more than fifty years as a lawyer, I have represented and assisted lawyers in representing many people before judges and juries. Not once has a victorious client conceded that the judge or jury was wrong. And not once has a losing client conceded that the judge or jurors were right.

This preference of people for victory instead of justice has been a familiar complaint of critics of our adversary system. There is an old story passed from lawyer to lawyer about a victorious lawyer who cables his client that "justice has prevailed." The client cables back: "Appeal immediately." Nor did this fact escape H. L. Mencken's wit: "Injustice is relatively easy to bear; what stings is justice."[22] Or Will Rogers: "We are always saying, 'Let the law take its course.' But what we mean is 'Let the law take our course.' "[23]

In our adversary system, only one side can be the "winner," but sometimes "justice" lies somewhere in between. Both sides may have meritorious claims, but once a dispute gets to trial there can be only one winner, and that winner is too often the person with the more capable lawyer or the most money to spend rather than the one with the more deserving claim. Many cases need to be settled, not decided by the courts. Revenge may be satisfied in court, but people who wish to maintain amicable relations have a better chance of doing so if they avoid litigation and settle disputes by themselves.

People spend all the money they can afford to gain the least competitive advantage. When I went to law school in the 1930's, we learned how common law pleading rules could be manipulated to trap adversaries. Those types of games stopped when legislators and courts simplified the pleading requirements and made it easier to discover information pertinent to a case. But that did not stop the games lawyers play. A federal judge once complained to me about the excessive amount of time used to harass an opponent. Lawyers have told me, "We'll deposition the hell out of them (their opponents)." That adds to the lawyer's hours and increases the lawyer's fee.

When judges and jurors determine a "victor," they do not help people resolve disputes; instead they merely say that one side is right and the other wrong. Legal issues can be resolved by courts, but they rarely are able to resolve the root cause of peoples' animosity. And a determination by the courts may take years. Most people abhor uncertainty in their lives because it makes them feel vulnerable; but relying on the adversary system to settle a quarrel can mean uncertainty for the years it takes to wend the dispute through the court system.

The result usually is an increase, not a decrease, in animosity. Which makes courts particularly inappropriate for resolving disputes between people who have to deal with each other after the dispute is resolved (e.g., family members, neighbors, landlords and tenants). Generally, clients resent it when their attorney is friendly with opposing counsel, but lawyers do that because they have to deal with those people on a daily basis.

Chief Justice Warren E. Burger, the mere mention of whose name will anger many lawyers upset at what they consider his unjustified swipes at lawyers and the legal system, summed up criticisms of the adversary system when he said:

> We Americans are a competitive people and that spirit has brought us to near greatness. But that competitive spirit

gives rise to conflicts and tensions. Our distant forebears moved slowly from trial by battle and other barbaric means of resolving conflicts and disputes, and we must move away from total reliance on the adversary contest for resolving all disputes. For some disputes, of course, trials will be the only means, but for many, trials by the adversarial contest must in time go the way of the ancient trials by battle and blood. Our system is too costly, too painful, too destructive, too inefficient for a truly civilized people. To rely on the adversary process as the principal means of resolving conflicting claims is a mistake that simply must be corrected.[24]

My experience over the years has been that there is more justice when people are encouraged to work out their differences by themselves than when they rely on the courts to settle matters. Abraham Lincoln was giving particularly good advice when he told lawyers:

> Discourage litigation. Persuade your neighbors to compromise whenever you can. Point out to them how the nominal winner is often a real loser—in fees, expenses, and waste of time. As a peacemaker the lawyer has a superior opportunity of being a good man. There will still be business enough.[25]

Those who are able to work out their own differences have the satisfaction of knowing that they had final say over their settlement. Those who leave resolution to the courts abdicate responsibility for settling their own grievances and risk becoming "losers."

Unfortunately, people trained to participate in the adversary system can become so engrossed in the combat that they overlook less destructive alternatives for settling disputes. As Chief Justice Burger has observed:

> The entire legal profession—lawyers, judges, law teachers—have become so mesmerized with the stimulation of the courtroom contest that we tend to forget that we ought to be healers of conflicts.[26]

Another reason some lawyers may overlook less destructive

alternatives for settling disputes is that trials can give them publicity and extra business.

In recent years, people have observed the increase in litigation and have wrung their hands over what they perceive as an increase in contentiousness among Americans and a breakdown in the traditional method of resolving disputes—mediation by family members, religious organizations, or local community members. Chief Justice Burger has complained about what he sees as the "inherently litigious nature of Americans."[27]

If one looks at some of the types of cases that have made the news in recent years—children suing parents for poor upbringing, students suing professors for providing inadequate education or a wrong grade, football fans suing to overturn a referee's call, someone suing a groundhog for mistakenly forecasting an early spring, and a man suing a woman for standing him up on a date—one has to wonder whether people have become litigation crazy. Other support for that view is the nearly five-fold increase in the number of cases filed in federal courts since 1940.

Although there has been a boom in cases handled by federal courts, it is important to remember that federal courts handle only a small fraction of all court cases. Virtually all (estimates say up to 98%[28]) cases are handled by state courts. A state like New York will handle more than two million cases a year.[29] The number of cases filed in state courts has been increasing faster than the population growth in recent years but not nearly so fast as federal cases. There has been a tremendous growth in federal court litigation because so many new federal rights have been created since the start of the New Deal. Federal litigation also has been encouraged by the Supreme Court's failure to give other courts clear guidelines about what the law is (e.g., when police may make a search without a warrant).

A study by Marc Galanter, professor of law at the University of Wisconsin Law School, noted that current per capita rates of litigation have risen in recent years but have not reached an unprecedented level and in fact are still below that of other countries and even lower than at other times in American history.[30] As recently as 1960, Charles Breitel, then a New York judge, actually complained about a decline in litigation and wrote how he regretted that more people did not take advantage of the courts.[31] Galanter has argued that it has been an increase in injuries produced by society and an increase in the complexity of society, not any "eruption of pathological contentiousness or a dangerous and unprecedented loosening of needed restraints," that has caused the recent rise in litigation.[32]

Although there may not be an unprecedented number of court cases per person, there is much more legal work that has to be done in this country now than when I started practicing law. There has been such a profusion of laws and regulations that many businesses need a lawyer overlooking most decisions. The average person risks violating some local, state, or federal law or regulation each day.

The problem with overregulation is that compliance uses time and energy that might better be devoted to other activities. Derek C. Bok has criticized the "massive diversion of exceptional talent into pursuits that often add little to the growth of the economy, the pursuit of culture, or the enhancement of the human spirit."[33] He has observed that

> far too many of these rare individuals are becoming lawyers at a time when the country cries out for more talented business executives, more enlightened public servants, more inventive engineers, more able high-school principals and teachers.[34]

Even though people's lives are more touched by law now than at any time in history, almost two-thirds of the public either never consult a lawyer or do so only once during their lives, according to Barbara Curran's report on the legal needs of the public.[35] The same study found that lawyers are consulted for few legal needs other than wills and marital matters.

It really should not be surprising that people are reluctant to go to lawyers. Even lawyers frequently neglect their own legal problems. For example, lawyers are notorious for not drafting last wills for themselves. Some attribute the lay person's reluctance to consult a lawyer to the high cost of legal services—or at least to the fear that any legal services will be costly. Others think it is a combination of the expense of lawyers and the legal "ignorance" of the general population. Unfortunately, many people do not realize when they have a legal problem. This legal "ignorance" is a real problem since it has been repeatedly shown that many people who do seek the advice of lawyers do so only following the encouragement of friends.[36]

Many people have been concerned about lack of access to the legal system. President Jimmy Carter complained that "[n]inety percent of our lawyers serve ten percent of our people."[37] Derek Bok has complained that "[t]here is far too much law for those who can afford it and far too little for those who cannot."[38] Earl Johnson, Jr., a California state judge, has said: "Poor people have access to American courts in the same sense that the Christians had access to the lions when they were dragged into a Roman arena."[39]

Denying access to the courts violates Judge Learned Hand's admonition that: "If we are to keep our democracy, there must be one commandment: Thou shalt not ration Justice."[40] Access to the legal system is necessary to guarantee our various freedoms. If political rights cannot be affirmed in court because of the costs involved, then those rights become meaningless.

It is particularly important for the poor to have access to legal services since their lives tend to be more regulated by laws than other groups in society. Unfortunately, poor people, who usually are undereducated, tend not to know how to resolve problems by themselves short of litigation and cannot afford a lawyer to give them needed assistance. In contrast, wealthy and middle class people are better able to make their way through bureaucratic mazes to resolve problems short of litigation. The need for access is indicated by an Eviction Defense Center survey finding that 85% of

tenants with lawyers won their cases but only 10% of those
without lawyers were able to defend themselves successfully.[41]

Some people have been quick to make lawyers responsible for assuring everyone access to legal services. Certainly
lawyers have a moral obligation to help the needy. But
lawyers should not have to bear the entire burden of delivering legal services to all members of the public. Farmers do
not have to pay for the food stamp program, and doctors do
not have to pay for the poor's medical care.

Legal aid for the poor is not a new idea. In 1495 King
Henry VII signed a law providing counsel for the poor. The
contingent fee, whereby a lawyer agrees to take a percentage of any winnings but nothing if a client loses, has been
the American legal community's most important contribution towards giving people access to legal services, but it
only works if a lawyer thinks enough money can be won to
make his or her effort worthwhile.

For some years now, our nation has been providing min-
imal legal aid for the poor. Prior to Lyndon Johnson's Great
Society, poor people had to rely on charitable organizations
for legal assistance. The first legal aid society for the American poor was organized by the German Society of New
York City in 1896. One or two experienced, volunteer lawyers, with the assistance of law students and perhaps one or
more staff attorneys, depending on the financing available
to the group, would help people with problems relating to
immigration and citizenship, landlords, and children in
trouble with the law.

In larger urban communities, particularly the big cities
dominated by political machines—New York, Chicago, and
Kansas City (some will remember the days of Tammany
Hall in New York, John "Bathhouse" Coughlin, Ed Kelly,
and Pat Nash in my home town, Chicago, and Tom Pender-
gast in Kansas City)—lawyers affiliated with the precinct
political machine would help voters with their legal problems, usually gratis. In time, those lawyers might be
rewarded with a judgeship. Most people at that time

believed that it was up to private individuals and groups, not the government, to provide legal services for the poor. Leaders of the American bar for years have been urging lawyers to spend more time working for poor people without charge.

Despite the American Bar Association's acknowledgment in the 1920's of a need to give special assistance to the poor, many legal needs of the poor have remained unmet. In 1965, the Office of Economic Opportunity began to fund legal services for the poor in civil matters. In 1975, this responsibility was assumed by the Legal Services Corporation, which is independent from the executive branch.

The Legal Services Corporation funds local legal service organizations that provide legal services for the poor. The corporation's initial goal was to provide two lawyers per 10,000 poor people, and over its first five years this goal was essentially met.[42] Under President Reagan's administration, however, this ratio has been halved.[43] Legal aid groups in big cities now handle a tremendous number of cases each year. Common problems involve disputes over benefits under various local, state, and federal aid programs, landlord-tenant disputes, divorces, and various consumer problems.

Since the Legal Services Corporation does not have the resources to handle all the legal problems of the poor, legal aid lawyers have rationed their time and resources by giving priority to cases they feel will have the greatest social, political, and economic impact on the poor in general instead of dealing with matters that only affect a few individuals. Those favoring this type of priority have argued that cases affecting a great number of the needy are cost-effective because they solve a lot of people's problems at one time.

Opponents have argued that the choice of cases has reflected the middle class, liberal bias of lawyers more anxious to erode the free enterprise system than to help meet the immediate needs of the poor. Critics have particularly resented legal challenges against public officials and other

political activism by legal aid lawyers, such as the use of
Legal Services Corporation funds to lobby for or against
certain legislation. They also have objected to the government's funding of suits against itself. They feel that, to
discourage them from overusing the services, the poor
should have to pay something for the legal aid.

Some of the cases critics have objected to have been: a suit
to force Connecticut to pay for a sex-change operation; a
suit on behalf of Indians to reclaim two-thirds of Maine;
suits to protest jail conditions; and a case fighting a University of California program to develop farm machinery
that could be operated by fewer people.[44] Cases conceived
by poverty groups with a liberal bias particularly have
drawn the ire of state and local officials, who resent suits
challenging their treatment of the poor.

No doubt there have been some questionable cases lit-
igated by Legal Services Corporation attorneys. But these
controversial cases have represented a small portion of all
cases funded by the corporation. Eliminating all funding
for the corporation would avoid the questionable cases but
would also reduce poor people's access to the legal system.
Better controls can minimize the number of controversial
cases handled by the corporation, but some controversy is
inevitable if the rights of the poor are to be championed.
Working for the poor may necessarily involve political controversy since almost any assertion of a right to benefits is a
political question.

The Legal Services Corporation is not the only watchdog
over people's rights. Over time, a special type of lawyer has
sprung up, a lawyer who will take cases involving public
causes, such as alleged violations of freedom of speech and
controversial criminal allegations, such as those against
Nicola Sacco and Bartolomeo Vanzetti, Eugene Debs, and
Julius and Ethel Rosenberg. Organizations also have
sprung up as watchdogs of people's rights. The American
Civil Liberties Union is one example. Another is the
National Association for the Advancement of Colored
People—Legal Defense Fund, which over the years has
handled thousands of cases involving minority rights.

The poor are not the only ones who cannot afford legal services. Over the past two or three decades middle class America has been especially disadvantaged by increasing legal costs to the point that many are now denied them. Barbara Curran's report on legal needs of the public disclosed a gap "amounting to a chasm" between the ideal and the reality of the average citizen's access to legal assistance.[45]

The average American typically needs legal help to buy a home, start or purchase a modest business, prepare a last will, get a divorce, help a child in trouble with the law, settle a quarrel with neighbors, obtain unemployment compensation or workers' compensation, contract for home improvements, and resolve problems with merchandise.

These Americans are not eligible for free legal services, and many cannot afford to pay for them. Most do not have a regular lawyer. During good times, they may go to a neighborhood lawyer, perhaps to a lawyer friend, and receive legal services at rates lower than those charged by "downtown" lawyers. There is often a more informal atmosphere at the offices of neighborhood lawyers. These lawyers often live in the neighborhood where they practice and are active in the community. They tend to handle real estate, probate, personal injury cases, domestic relations matters, and problems of small businesses.

Since 1977 when the Supreme Court ruled that lawyers can advertise (advertising was permitted in the 1800's but was banned in 1908), there has been pressure on lawyers to charge lower legal fees. Added pressure to curb legal fees also has come from the tremendous growth in the number of lawyers and a growing resolve among clients to limit their legal expenses. When I started practicing law, there were fee schedules prepared by local bar associations, but now rates vary among lawyers with the same level of skills. Many bar associations have set up lists of lawyers willing to do work for lower than usual legal rates.

The United States Supreme Court's decision to permit advertising has encouraged the growth of neighborhood legal clinics. The largest of the for-profit legal clinics is the one founded in 1977 by Joel Hyatt. The first legal clinic was opened in California in 1972 by Leonard Jacoby and Steven Meyers. Lawyers in legal clinics are able to provide routine legal services at a lower rate than other lawyers since they systematize their procedures, reduce a lawyer's involvement, and rely on high volume to cover their overhead. In a well run clinic, people other than lawyers do much of the work. A receptionist will give clients a questionnaire to fill out and will then show clients a film answering common questions about a particular type of legal matter. Lawyers will then answer any other questions a client might have.

Gaining the right to advertise for the large number of clients they need to become profitable has been only one of the substantial hurdles that legal clinics have had to overcome. Initially, the quality of legal services rendered by legal clinic lawyers was suspect. But a study by the University of Miami School of Law has indicated that clients of legal clinics are more satisfied with their attorneys than clients patronizing traditional firms.[46] Although there have been financing problems in operating on a large scale, and it has been difficult to render quality legal services at lower than prevailing legal rates, it is clear that neighborhood legal clinics are here to stay.

Group plans organized for employees are helping millions of employees get needed legal services. Working much like group health insurance plans, these plans were encouraged by the Tax Reform Act of 1976, which provided that the benefits would not be considered taxable income for employees. Such plans typically cover housing matters, domestic disputes, traffic incidents, consumer problems, adoptions, last wills—the matters that an average person might need a lawyer for.

Prepaid legal service plans are available for those not covered by a company plan, but many people are not interested in such plans because they do not think they will need a lawyer. For a set fee each year, participants are entitled to have a lawyer help them write a simple last will or review certain legal documents, such as simple leases, real estate agreements, and various other purchase agreements. Participants usually also are entitled to free consultations about various other legal matters.

As a rule, however, such plans pay for few legal services other than general advice. Participants in such plans should realize that they still will have to pay for most legal services, although they may be entitled to a discount on some matters. For example, usually there will be extra charges for a divorce, a more complicated last will (such as one with a trust), or a suit against someone, such as one to recover damages for a personal injury. People thinking of joining a prepaid legal plan also should realize that their choice of lawyer may be limited to a plan attorney.

Many have resorted to being their own lawyer, and a whole industry has developed to help them. Non-lawyers can be trained to handle such legal matters as routine real estate sales, uncontested divorces, administrative agency matters, tax returns, debt collection, and probate. But it is difficult for those untrained in the law to know what their rights are and to identify whether they have a problem that can be handled by the legal system. Do-it-yourself books can take a lay person step-by-step through common legal problems, but they will not help people with special needs or problems. For example, the average person can write a simple will, but the task becomes riskier if there are sufficient assets to bring taxes into question or if there are special needs of family members. It is unfortunate that the law is often more complicated than it needs to be. Some people see this as a conspiracy by lawyers to keep themselves in business, but I am more inclined to attribute needless complications to fuzzy thinking, poor writing skills, and too much deference to ancient ritual.

The average person needs to become more educated about the law. Such knowledge not only can help avoid legal problems (e.g., many legal problems could be avoided if all people realized that usually they cannot change their mind after signing a contract) but also can help people better deal with a lawyer and become more involved in improving our legal system.

One potential benefit of legal advertising is that people

may learn what some of their rights are. Another source of information about legal rights and remedies is the "Dial-Law" recordings at libraries in urban communities. It is now possible to call up the local library and receive taped answers to common legal questions involving such things as leases, last wills, employment rights, Social Security, and family law.

Preventive law is another way of reducing legal fees and improving access to legal services. By "preventive law" I mean the taking of steps to avoid potentially costly legal problems. It is wise to have a "legal checkup" when planning to marry, when buying or selling a home, or when starting a business. A last will can avoid needless complications for loved ones.

Various reforms have been advocated to improve the delivery of legal services. But many of these reforms merely tinker with the system and do not make the overhaul needed to assure access to "justice." Some reformers advocate putting more money into the system on behalf of those currently denied access. Advocates of these reforms assume that more litigation will be beneficial. But increasing the amount of litigation will not assure people greater access to "justice." As I mentioned earlier, I believe that litigation marks a failure of our system of civil justice.

The problem with litigation is not just its cost. Litigation takes too long to resolve a dispute, often does not result in justice, can lead to adverse publicity, and can damage the psyche of litigants, who may become saddled with years of uncertainty and heightened animosity towards people labeled "opponents." The only "winners" in the end are lawyers, who take a goodly share of each litigation dollar. A 1977 government study of product liability cases concluded that it costs 77 cents in legal fees and expenses for each 65 cents received by the victim (and that figure did not include the government's cost to hold trials or the time lost by jurors).[47]

More promising than reforms that increase the amount of litigation has been the development and encouragement of alternative methods of dispute resolution, such as arbitration, mediation, rent-a-judge programs, mini-trials, summary jury trials, expanded small claims courts, and neighborhood justice centers. With arbitration, people ask a neutral third party to decide which side is right. With mediation, by contrast, a neutral third person helps people to resolve disputes by themselves. As the name implies, rent-a-judge programs involve hiring a judge, usually retired, to try disputes at an earlier date than would be possible through the court system. Mini-trials, born in 1977, are expedited, nonbinding, private trials designed to encourage disputants to arrive at a settlement.[48] Summary jury trials, started in 1980, are nonbinding, court-supervised trials.[49] Like mini-trials, they give litigants a good idea of their chances of success and encourage settlement. In small claims courts, there are simplified procedures so that people can represent themselves in court. The person being sued usually can be represented by a lawyer but need not have one. Waiting time for a court date is much shorter than for a regular trial. Neighborhood justice centers were established in the 1970's. Mediation and arbitration are emphasized, with small claims court used as a last resort. Alternative methods of dispute resolution are discussed in more detail in Chapter 7.

It is important that people not only recognize the shortcomings of our system of civil justice but also believe that they have the power to fashion a system that can satisfy our evolving definition of justice. As Chief Justice Burger has said:

> The story of justice, like the story of freedom, is a story that never ends. What seems unrealistic, visionary, and unreachable today must be the target even if we cannot reach it soon or even in our time. If we ever begin to think we have achieved our goals, that will mean our sights were set too low or that we had no concern for our profession or the public interest.[50]

Chapter 2

Criminal Justice

> *The quality of a nation's civiliza-*
> *tion can be largely measured by the*
> *methods it uses in the enforcement*
> *of its criminal law.*
> Illinois Supreme Court Justice
> Walter V. Schaefer[1]

> *The American criminal justice sys-*
> *tem is corrupt to its core: it depends*
> *on a pervasive dishonesty by its*
> *participants. It is unfair: it dis-*
> *criminates against the poor, the*
> *uneducated, the members of minor-*
> *ity groups. But it is not grossly*
> *inaccurate: large numbers of inno-*
> *cent defendants do not populate*
> *our prisons. Nor can our system*
> *fairly be characterized as "re-*
> *pressive."*
> Alan Dershowitz, professor at
> Harvard Law School[2]

Much of the public's disenchantment with the legal profession can be attributed to the lawyer's role in the criminal
justice system. Because some people tend to assume that

anyone charged with a crime is a bad person, they tend to conclude that anyone helping a defendant avoid punishment is therefore an accomplice to a crime. Defense attorneys frequently become stained by their victories. This result will be inevitable as long as the public and lawyers have different expectations for criminal justice.

Courts and lawyers have borne the brunt of criticism for failures of our criminal justice system, but they constitute only one portion of the system. Most of the money expended for criminal justice is spent for police to deter crime and apprehend criminals and for the prisons that remove criminals from society and occasionally rehabilitate them. Courts have become the lightning rod for criticism because they have imposed restraints on how police and prison officials can perform their jobs and because the results of their work are open to public inspection.

Segments of the general public tend to believe that courts have not been tough enough on criminals, but prisons are overflowing with prisoners who have been given long sentences. Some critics have complained that judges in fact are too tough and too inclined to support the police and prosecutors. No matter how tough judges are, they cannot solve crime by themselves. Long sentences by themselves will not deter crime. Nor will giving free rein to the police do it. Instead, greater effort must be made to inculcate moral values in young people, and that moral structure must be enforced by a criminal justice system that not only will catch offenders but also will impose a punishment severe enough to make the chance of escaping punishment not worth the risk.

Each state and the federal government has its own criminal justice system, but all must respect the rights afforded an accused by the United States Constitution. Each state's criminal justice system is in turn limited by that state's own constitution and laws. Some crimes can be punished by both state and federal law (e.g., bank robberies and many drug offenses).

Only about a third of all crimes and less than half of all

violent crimes are reported.[3] Once a crime has been reported, a law enforcement agency has to identify and apprehend a suspect. Very often no suspect is identified or apprehended. After a person has been arrested, a decision is made whether or not to prosecute the person. United States prosecutors represent the public when they prosecute people for crimes. This is in contrast to the old European attitude towards crime, which treated it as a wrong against an individual and forced the victim to seek justice through private prosecution.

After the police arrest a suspect, the prosecutor coordinates how the government will respond to the crime. Cases may be dismissed if there is insufficient evidence that can be used in court, witnesses are reluctant to testify, or the prosecutor decides that witnesses would not make a convincing impression in court. Sometimes prosecutors have a policy of not prosecuting certain types of cases (e.g., possession of small amounts of marijuana).

Anyone charged with a crime must be taken before a judge or magistrate, who decides whether there is probable cause to detain the accused. An accused gets another chance to avoid being charged with a crime when a second probable cause determination is made by either a grand jury or prosecutor.

After the accused is indicted by a grand jury or the prosecutor issues an information (a document accusing the person of a crime), the accused is arraigned, which means that he or she is told what he or she is accused of having done, is advised of various rights, and is asked to plead guilty or not guilty. If the plea is guilty and the plea is accepted by a judge (a judge may reject a plea if, for example, the judge believes the accused was coerced into pleading guilty), then a sentence is imposed. A person pleading innocent has the right to be tried by a judge or jury.

Discretion is exercised throughout the criminal justice system. Police have discretion whether to investigate certain charges or enforce various laws. Prosecutors decide which charges to file or whether to prosecute at all. Judges set bail or conditions for release, accept pleas, dismiss charges, and impose sentences. Correctional officials decide which prison a person will be sent to, what privileges a prisoner will have, and how a prisoner will be disciplined for infractions. The parole authority determines when a prisoner will be paroled and under what conditions.

Over the years, people have debated what causes crime. Some have looked at factors beyond an individual's control, such as the environment or biological makeup. Those blaming society have focused on poverty, ignorance, unemployment, inadequate housing, and health problems as causes of crime. Those looking for a biological basis for criminal behavior have looked for "criminal" genes. Others have taken a less deterministic view and instead have focused on the individual's propensity and incentive to commit a crime. Under this view, the environment and genetic makeup may increase an individual's propensity and incentive to commit a crime, but the individual is still considered responsible for his or her actions.

The theoretical underpinning for modern criminal law is that the individual is responsible for his or her actions. Another key concept is that the individual should be criminally responsible only for misdeeds he or she intended to commit. We believe that people normally can exercise free will and that they can be guilty of a crime only if they are to blame for committing a certain illegal act. This concept has not always prevailed. In pre-Norman England, it was the result that counted, not intent, and accidental killings, killings in self-defense, and murders were all punishable by death.[4]

Because of this belief that people must be to blame for committing a criminal act, insanity evolved as a defense in criminal actions. Insanity was recognized as far back as the blood feuds in England.[5] Insanity did not absolve people from liability, but it did affect the punishment. The insane person's kin were given the burden of compensating victims and making sure the insane person caused no more trouble.

An early test of insanity was the M'Naghten rule, developed by the British House of Lords in 1843 and still in use today. Under this rule, a person is considered insane if, because of mental disease, he or she either did not understand the nature and quality of the act or could not distinguish right from wrong.

As new psychiatric theories were developed, people began to recognize that people may be able to tell right from wrong and yet not be able to keep themselves from committing a wrongful act. To take this into consideration, the M'Naghten rule was modified by some states to include "irresistable impulse" as a type of insanity.

Many states use the broader test of insanity developed by the American Law Institute:

> A person is not responsible for criminal conduct if at the time of such conduct and as a result of mental disease or defect he lacks substantial capacity either to appreciate the criminality of his conduct or to conform his conduct to the requirements of the law.

This was the standard used in the trial of John Hinckley, Jr., who was acquitted by reason of insanity of attempting to assassinate President Ronald Reagan.

Cases like Hinckley's have infuriated the public and caused even advocates of the defense to reevaluate its proper scope. Its advocates point out that the defense is rarely raised and rarely successful and that it is necessary to maintain moral justice (i.e., advocates argue that it would be immoral to punish people for behavior they could not control). But the broad definition currently in vogue has become an embarrassment to the psychiatric community and has given a black eye to the criminal justice system.

The American Medical Association has called for the elimination of the insanity defense.[6] Instead, the AMA has advocated the use of evidence of a defendant's mental problems to prove whether or not the defendant had the requisite state of mind (mens rea) to commit the offense. That is how alcoholism and drug addiction are treated. Only mental illnesses that clearly impair a person's understanding of reality would be considered. A mental disease or defect that makes it difficult for a person to control his or her actions would not be a defense for a criminal act but might be taken into consideration when sentencing the individual.

Because psychiatrists disagree about what is "normal" self-control and cannot objectively measure impairment, any testimony about the defendant's capacity to control his or her behavior is likely to be contradictory. Indeed, psychiatric theories about self-control are at odds with the fundamental notion of our system of criminal justice, which is that people are individually responsible for their actions. Psychiatrists tend to view human behavior as determined by factors other than free will.

What the AMA and other medical organizations, including the American Psychiatric Association, have recognized is that the current state of knowledge does not allow us to measure people's ability to control their behavior. Members of the general public have been wary of the defense because they feel psychiatrists can be fooled by clever defendants. And they can. Witness the case where a man convinced several psychiatrists that he was suffering from post-traumatic stress disorder stemming from his combat experience in Vietnam.[7] He escaped prosecution for sixteen robberies because it was not until after his insanity defense was accepted by the prosecutor that the prosecutor discovered that the man had never been in Vietnam.

Because psychiatrists cannot agree about when a person lacks substantial capacity to control his or her actions, insanity defenses raising that issue turn into an expensive battle of the experts, with one side trotting out psychiatrists willing to say that a person cannot control his or her own actions and an equal number of psychiatrists willing to say just the opposite. Hundreds of thousands of dollars were paid to hire opposing experts at the trial of John W. Hinckley, Jr. The spectacle only succeeds in undermining the public's confidence that the goals of criminal law will be met by the criminal justice system.

Criminal law, like civil law, attempts to encourage conduct that will benefit others in society. The main goal of criminal law is to prevent harm to people's health, safety, morals, property, and general welfare. Unlike civil law, violation of a criminal law carries the moral condemnation of society and the possibility of imprisonment.

This punishment is designed to fulfill several goals. One goal of punishment is to deter people from harming others in society. Punishment is also meant to remove criminals from society, exact retribution, and rehabilitate offenders for reentry into society. Unfortunately, rehabilitation can be inconsistent with the other goals. For example, a penalty significant enough to deter people from committing crimes may not allow for the possibility of rehabilitation.

When meting out punishment, we also consider it important to make the punishment fit the crime, to treat similar crimes the same way, and to consider prior criminal behavior when considering the severity of a sentence. In the 1970's, people who felt that judges had too much discretion in imposing sentences pointed out that the discretion had eroded the deterrent effect of the punishment by reducing the certainty of sanction and had resulted in a disparity in the severity of punishment for similar crimes. Reforms in the 1970's and the 1980's have restricted judicial discretion.

Most criminal laws were developed by judges.[8] Murder, manslaughter, robbery, burglary, arson, and rape were all considered crimes by the 17th century. Conspiracy became a crime in 1664, forgery in 1727, and attempts at crime in 1784. It was not until the 1930's that it became illegal to file a false criminal report. Now criminal laws are codified by statute.

Criminal laws originally were enforced by the victims of crimes instead of the government. Until the Middle Ages, sanctions for criminal acts were imposed by the victim or the victim's family. In later years, certain criminal acts, such as murder, rape, and robbery, were considered crimes against all members of the community and were prosecuted by the government. As governments stepped into the role of prosecutor, victims became overlooked by the criminal justice system. That has started to change in recent years, when attempts have been made to give victims justice.

Because we place a high value on freedom, a governing principle of our system of criminal justice has been that people are innocent until proven guilty beyond a reasonable doubt. Sometimes this governing philosophy has been expressed by the statement that it is better for ten guilty people to be freed than for one innocent person to be convicted.

Unfortunately, there have been cases of people jailed for crimes that they did not commit. Such instances probably are unavoidable. We guard against this possibility by requiring all jurors to be convinced of a defendant's guilt beyond a reasonable doubt before punishment may be imposed. If even one juror doubts that the defendant is guilty, then that person will go free. But just as in civil matters, jurors and judges often are asked to weigh conflicting testimony and decide who is telling the truth. This is not an easy task, and mistakes are bound to happen.

It takes a special person to become a criminal defense attorney. Much as defense lawyers like to trumpet the innocence of their clients, the fact is that most of the people they defend are criminals. As Alan Dershowitz, who practices criminal law, has written: "Any criminal lawyer who tells you that most of his clients are not guilty is either bluffing or deliberately limiting his practice to a few innocent defendants."[9]

Fortunately, I never had to depend on criminal cases for my livelihood and only handled a few matters for relatives of clients. Before accepting those cases, I investigated the circumstances to assure myself that the person probably was not guilty. I support the principle that everyone is entitled to a defense, but I know that I could never defend someone I believed was guilty. My conscience would never forgive me for helping someone escape punishment and go on to victimize others. Many lawyers hold the same view, but many more would view my attitude as shirking responsibility.

Criminal defense attorneys are obligated to use their best effort to help people avoid punishment. At a minimum, that requires them to challenge the wording of laws and the methods used by the government to uncover evidence of a crime. Many also interpret their duty as requiring them to make truthful witnesses appear mistaken or untruthful. Such use of a lawyer's superior verbal skills seems particularly unfair when the witness is a child testifying about abuse.

Defense attorneys are faced with difficult moral dilemmas—and often deal with them differently than the average person would. For instance, should the attorney call the defendant as a witness even though he or she suspects that the defendant will lie? Most defense attorneys would answer yes, even if it is not merely a suspicion but a genuine concern. Many duck the issue by discouraging clients from telling them that they are guilty. If a client clearly is guilty of the crime charged, then lawyers are taught to appeal to the jurors' sympathy by saying nice things about the client and his or her family and bad things about witnesses for the prosecution.

Should an attorney give legal advice if he or she knows that the advice will encourage the defendant to lie (e.g., advice about defenses to a criminal act)? This answer is more clearly yes since the alternative would be to keep the defendant in the dark about his or her predicament. But the results are still morally unsettling. The defendant is far more likely to tell the truth right after being arrested than after speaking with an attorney and learning what needs to be said to escape punishment. If a defense attorney knows that a prosecution witness is telling the truth, should the attorney still do all possible to make it appear that the witness is mistaken or lying? Again, most defense attorneys would answer yes, saying that it is their obligation to test the veracity of witnesses and the duty of the judge or jury to make the final judgment.

The attorney-client privilege greatly contributes to the defense lawyer's poor public image. Professional ethics make it appear that lawyers are part of a criminal's conspiracy by permitting them to hold a client's secrets inviolate, even if it means failing to prevent a violent crime. Criminal defense attorneys have earned particular opprobrium for concealing knowledge they obtain about a crime, such as the whereabouts of a client's victim or murder weapon.

Because of what they do and whom they associate with, criminal defense attorneys are viewed by many people as either criminals themselves or at best amoral people willing to pull any trick in the book to put a criminal back on the streets. As Roberta Roper, whose daughter Stephanie was repeatedly raped, struck with a chain, shot, burned, and left in a swamp with her hands severed, has commented: "It's a defense attorney's ingenuity, and not truth and justice, that prevails."[10] The two men convicted of murdering her daughter were made eligible for parole after only twelve years.

Defense attorneys particularly anger the public when they seem to take pleasure in successfully defending guilty people. Unfortunately, like any adversary contest, defense work can begin to seem like a game challenging an attorney's skill and ingenuity instead of a search for truth and justice. The lawyer can become so engrossed with the challenge that he or she does not consider the moral implications of what he or she is doing. Victories become a testament to a lawyer's ability and a good advertisement for more clients. It has to be a great boost to one's ego to acquit someone who is guilty. Usually this attitude is submerged, but not always. Consider this 19th century ad by Major Hopkins, an Arizona lawyer:

Come to Major Hopkins to get full satisfaction. I win nine-tenths of my cases. If you want to sue, if you have been sued, I am the man to take your case. Embezzlement, highway robbery, felonious assault, arson, and horse stealing, don't amount to shucks if you have a good lawyer behind you. My strong point is weeping as I appeal to the jury, and I seldom fail to clear my man. Out of eleven murder cases last year I cleared nine of the murderers. Having been in jail no less

than four times myself, my experience cannot fail to prove of
value to my clients. Come early and avoid the rush.[11]

Modern defense attorneys rely more on press reports and
word-of-mouth than on ads to promote their legal skills.

Defense attorneys defend their role by pointing out that it
is important to do all they can to keep the government
honest. Those accused of committing crimes are pitted not
only against the great resources of the government but also
against the public perception that they must have done
something wrong if they have been accused. In theory, the
government seeks justice, not convictions. Towards that
end, a prosecutor has discretion whether or not to investigate and prosecute someone for a crime. In reality, however,
there are prosecutors more interested in building a name for
themselves than in meting out justice.

There is a tension in the criminal justice system between
the search for truth and the desire to protect individuals
from governmental persecution. Defense attorneys come
down in favor of the dignity of the individual and will do all
they can to help their clients, even if that means frustrating
the search for truth. As Alan Dershowitz has written: "It is
the job of the defense attorney—especially when representing the guilty—to prevent, by all lawful means, the 'whole
truth' from coming out."[12]

Wealthy defendants have the money to hire the best lawyers and best experts either to further or frustrate justice.
Few defendants can afford to hire lawyers willing to devote
the time to match the government's effort or experts to
counter experts hired by the prosecution. This is a particular problem since police crime labs are notorious for making
errors. Instead, many defendants have to rely on public
defenders, who usually are overburdened with cases and
may begin their preparation only hours before a case comes
to trial.

Public defenders have a thankless task. As Laurance
Smith has written about his experience as a public defender:

If you don't do the job well enough, you may be ridiculed by your professional peers, perhaps even sued or subjected to professional discipline. But if you do the job very well—as any regular viewer of *Sixty Minutes* can tell you—the public's reaction may be strongly negative. That reaction will quickly translate into attempts by politicians, seeking public approval, to get rid of you or make you impotent.

. . . .

A public defender is barely tolerated by respectable society and is often dismissed as a "dump truck" by clients.[13]

There is also a tension between our desire to protect individuals from government and our desire to protect society from criminals. People emphasizing the need to protect society from criminals tend to characterize rules designed to protect individuals as "technical violations" or "loopholes." But, as attorney Gerry Spence has said: "What looks like a loophole to you as you watch your neighbor on the legal spit is a sacred right when it's you who's turning slowly over the hot coals."[14]

Over the years, the United States Supreme Court has established rules to protect the innocent from being unjustly convicted. For example, in 1963 the court decided that people have the right to a lawyer when they are accused of a felony. The third degree, popularized by old movies as a means of obtaining confessions, once was widespread but no longer is. The United States Supreme Court has emphasized that ours is an accusatorial, not an inquisitorial system, meaning that the government must establish a person's guilt with independent evidence, not by coerced statements from the defendant.

The Fifth Amendment privilege against self-incrimination, characterized by Justice Walter Schaefer as "a doctrine in search of a reason,"[15] has developed a bad reputation because it often has been invoked by notorious criminals. It also flies in the face of everyday experience. When parents or teachers feel that a child has done something wrong, their natural inclination is to question the child about their suspicions—and not accept a child's silence.

The two best arguments for the privilege are that it preserves governmental morality by forcing the prosecution to prove its case without a defendant's help and that it protects an individual's privacy. As Justice James Stephen has written, the privilege "contributes greatly to the dignity and apparent humanity of a criminal trial."[16]

Like other privileges, it impedes the search for truth. But unlike other privileges, such as those between husband and wife, doctor and patient, lawyer and client, or priest and penitent, it does not promote a valuable social relationship. Instead, the people protected are those who either have committed a crime or believe that they have committed a crime.

The privilege originated to protect people from *accusing* themselves of a crime, not to allow them to avoid giving any evidence that could place them in a bad light.[17] It evolved into its present form as a defense against abridgment of freedom of expression.[18] People accused of religious or political crimes were the first protected by the privilege. Such expression can now be protected by the First Amendment.

Since criminal defendants tend to be uneducated and no match for the sharp questions of a prosecutor and since by testifying defendants give the prosecution license to bring out that person's entire criminal history, there still is a need for the privilege. But, as a practical matter, the prosecution is not hurt by a defendant's failure to testify since jurors tend to infer guilt from a defendant's silence, particularly after years of watching reputed mobsters exercising the privilege during televised hearings.

Probably the most controversial of the Supreme Court's procedural requirements for the criminal justice system is that illegally obtained evidence must be excluded from trials. This rule, referred to as the exclusionary rule, has been popularized (and made infamous) in the public consciousness by the required Miranda warnings.

The exclusionary rule furthers objectives that are unrelated to the guilt or innocence of people accused of a crime. It reflects the philosophy that it is more important to deter certain governmental conduct and protect the privacy of the individual than to use reliable evidence to send a guilty person to jail. Cases applying this rule necessarily arouse the ire of people concerned with keeping criminals off the streets since the rule is only applied to exclude evidence of a crime. Innocent people whose privacy has been invaded by the police cannot benefit from the rule because they have done nothing wrong and have nothing to conceal.

It is not certain what effect this rule has had on law enforcement. Critics of the rule decry the number of criminals freed by the rule and have pointed to a study funded by the National Institute of Justice finding that approximately 5% of people arrested in California for committing felonies but never charged with a crime were not prosecuted because of potential problems with the rule.[19] Critics have also decried the drain on judicial resources caused by the many motions to suppress evidence.

There is evidence that the exclusionary rule has encouraged police to become more professional and efficient in investigating crime, but it is not clear how much police misconduct actually has been deterred. If the rules about what is and is not police misconduct were clear, then the rule might have more effect on police behavior. But many rules are maddeningly complex, so complex that it is not unusual for judges all the way up to the Supreme Court to disagree whether the police violated the Constitution in a given situation. If after much reflection judges cannot agree whether the police acted correctly, how can police untrained in the law be expected to guess right? And should the public be punished for that wrong guess? In recent years the Supreme Court has tended to give police more of the benefit of the doubt but in so doing has further complicated the rules of proper police behavior.

Most countries use all evidence, even if it has been illegally obtained, and then have proceedings to punish the police for any illegal actions. A few countries weigh the seriousness of the police officer's misconduct against the cost of letting a criminal go free and will suppress evidence

if the misconduct was serious. Here in the United States we
rely on the exclusionary rule to deter police misconduct, but
it is society in general, not individual police officers, who
are punished by the release of criminals. The exclusionary
rule does nothing to help innocent people victimized by
police misconduct since those people will not be brought to
trial.

Ironically, as defendants have been given more procedural protections, the added cost of those protections has
encouraged prosecutors to press defendants to forego them
through plea bargains. Plea bargains are agreements
between prosecutors and defendants whereby defendants
plead guilty to one or more charges in return for the dismis-
sal of other, often more serious charges. Over the years, our
criminal justice system has become dependent on guilty
pleas to properly function.

Although we think of the criminal justice system as an
adversary process pitting the government against the individual, most of the "justice" is dispensed by plea bargains.
An estimated 90% of all criminal convictions are the result
of guilty pleas.[20] Plea bargains save overworked prosecutors time and guarantee them a win. Defendants avoid the
cost and uncertain outcome of a trial. Innocent people may
plead guilty to avoid the bother and expense of a trial (e.g.,
traffic tickets). For people unable to afford bail, it may pay
to plead guilty to a minor offense rather than spend months
in jail, particularly if the maximum sentence they could
receive is less than the time they could spend in jail waiting
for trial. Cost is a particular problem for people charged
with misdemeanors. As Professor Malcolm Feeley wrote in
The Process Is the Punishment:

> In essence, the process itself is the punishment. The time,
> effort, money, and opportunities lost as a direct result of
> being caught up in the system can quickly come to outweigh
> the penalty that issues from adjudication and sentence.[21]

Judges may encourage people to plead guilty by establishing a policy of imposing stiffer sentences following a

trial than following a plea bargain. This threat of differential punishment greatly encourages plea bargaining. Criminal defense lawyers may encourage people to plead guilty. Many lawyers have a financial incentive to make a bargain since they can make more money when an average client pleads guilty than when a case goes to trial. This is true since lawyers normally take a flat fee for their services and having a client plead guilty requires less work for a lawyer than a full blown trial.

Plea bargaining distorts criminal justice by making cost a factor in addition to culpability. The desire to avoid the expense of a trial affects both the defendant and the prosecution and may give a bargaining edge to wealthy people accused of a crime. In return for selling their constitutional right to a trial, defendants may avoid the costs of defending themselves and the risk of severe punishment. This secret bargaining promotes a public perception of corruption and can make defendants believe that they have gotten away with something. It also deprecates the importance of criminal sanctions by making them something that can be traded for economic advantage.

Paradoxically, however, plea bargaining may result in more convictions of guilty persons than an ideal system giving everyone the resources for a trial since criminal "justice" can be bought as easily as civil "justice" under the adversary system. Because the adversary system can distort the truth, people able to afford the best defense are more likely to evade punishment for their misdeeds.

Most European countries place symbolic importance on trials and require trials when there are serious charges even if the defendant admits guilt. Plea bargaining is tolerated in this country as a necessary evil. Defenders of the practice have argued that we cannot afford to give all accused persons their day in court and that the system would overload if all cases were forced to go to trial. But Albert W. Alschuler, when he was professor of law at the University of Colorado School of Law, estimated that the extra cost of eliminating plea bargains in felony cases would not exceed $1 billion.[22]

Some proponents of plea bargaining have argued that its abolition would only force the practice underground. But as Professor Alschuler has responded:

> This theory offers a dark view of the legal profession. It sees America's men and women of the law as lawless, and it proclaims without evidence, without hesitation, and even without blushing that large numbers of these people not only would break the law to achieve their goals, but also that they would lie about this violation.[23]

The adversary system distorts criminal justice as much as civil justice since truth can be obscured by each side's desire for victory. But as long as we place a higher value on individual freedom than on protecting society from criminals, the adversary system will be the best way of assuring that no one's freedom will wrongly be curtailed by misguided governmental action.

Over the years, there have been a few highly publicized cases raising doubt whether the defendants really were guilty. I am thinking of such celebrated cases as those involving Nicola Sacco and Bartolomeo Vanzetti, Bruno Hauptmann, Alger Hiss, and the Rosenbergs. There have also been less publicized cases of people being railroaded into jail and cases where it was later proved that the wrong person was convicted. On the whole, though, our system has done substantial justice. Judges and jurors should particularly be praised for resisting the government's use of our criminal laws to punish unpopular political opinions and actions.

Criminal "justice" requires not only protection of the individual but also protection of society from criminals, and where we strike that balance determines what kind of people we are. Overprotection of the accused can restrict lives through fear. This seems to account for the new urban myth of vigilante justice. But underprotection of the accused means sacrifice of freedoms that we have fought hard to maintain. The choice is ours to make.

Chapter 3

Public Image of Lawyers and the Law Profession

Never in my half century of law practice has there been such widespread criticism of lawyers and the legal profession as during the past decade. But criticism of lawyers is not new. Carl Sandburg wrote in "The Lawyers Know Too Much":

> In the heels of the higgling lawyers, Bob,
> Too many slippery ifs and buts and howevers,
> Too much hereinbefore provided whereas,
> Too many doors to go in and out of.
>> When the lawyers are through
>> What is there left, Bob?
>> Can a mouse nibble at it
>> And find enough to fasten a tooth in?[1]

Charles Lamb, an English essayist and critic living in the 18th and 19th centuries, also did not have a high opinion of lawyers: "Lawyers, I suppose, were children once."[2] According to a Russian proverb, "When God wanted to chastise mankind, He invented lawyers."[3]

Dishonesty has so often been associated with lawyers that St. Ives, the patron saint of lawyers, was praised because he "was a Breton and a lawyer, but not dishonest—an astonishing thing in people's eyes!"[4] Benjamin Franklin was no more kind: "A countryman between two lawyers is like a fish between two cats."[5] Nor was Thomas More, who excluded lawyers from his Utopia.

One of the few to speak kindly about lawyers was the French aristocrat Alexis de Tocqueville, who in 1835 wrote in his classic *Democracy in America*:

> As the *lawyers constitute the only enlightened class which the people does not mistrust*, they are naturally called upon to occupy most of the public stations. They fill the legislative assemblies, and they conduct the administration; they consequently exercise a powerful influence upon the formation of the law, and upon its execution. (emphasis added)[6]

He did not mention the public clamor in 1786 to abolish courts and suppress lawyers in New Hampshire and Vermont.

A newspaperman once told me that an attack on the legal profession is always good for an article or two. Certainly there is no lack of criticism in the press. For example, the following headlines have appeared in recent years:

"Those #*X!!! Lawyers—Like Shakespeare's Kate,
    Hard to Live with—and without"
                                                    Time[7]

"Too Much Law, Too Many Lawyers, Not Enough Justice"
                                        The Wall Street Journal[8]

"If You Dislike Lawyers, Read This"
                                        The New York Times[9]

"Breitel [Chief Judge of the New York Court of Appeals]
Tells Lawyers that Greed Is Undermining Their
Profession"

The New York Times[10]

"The Trouble With Lawyers"

The New York Times Magazine[11]

Not a pretty picture of lawyers and the legal profession. But
in fairness we should keep in mind that dog-bites-person
stories are not news because they are too commonplace. If
most lawyers really were dishonest, conniving, and incompetent, then only the few honest, aboveboard, and competent lawyers would make news.

In *Woe unto You, Lawyers*, Fred Rodell, when he was a
professor of law at Yale Law School, advocated a world
without courts and lawyers. Countless others have quoted
Shakespeare with approval: "The first thing we do, let's kill
all the lawyers."[12] National public opinion polls consist-
ently have ranked lawyers low in public confidence. *The
Wall Street Journal* has described Utopia as a world without lawyers:

What would life be like if the great law firms and the solo
practitioners stayed home, clogging the golf courses and
tennis courses of America? It would be Paradise Regained.
The normal intercourse of life would flow smoothly, unchecked by the law's and the lawyer's limitless capacity to
complicate and tangle things. Disputes would have to be
resolved by common sense and mutual trust, rather than on
the basis of who could hire the fastest gun. The wheels of
commerce would turn more swiftly as people without special
training in obfuscation and logic-chopping made clear and
understandable agreements. Individuals with disagreements
would have to rely on their own capacities for reconciliation
and forgiveness instead of the brutalities of specially trained
gladiators. The pleasant consequences are virtually
limitless....[13]

Lawyers use incomprehensible jargon:

> [E]very time a lawyer writes something, he is not writing for posterity, he is writing so that endless others of his craft can make a living out of trying to figure out just what he said.
>
> Will Rogers[14]

> The law is bewildering and complex to those of us without law degress, but instead of giving clear and direct answers the lawyers throw around buzz words and technical jargon that only they understand.
>
> Donald P. Kelly, businessman[15]

> "Moses was a great lawgiver," said Uncle Eben. "But de way he was satisfied to keep de ten commandments short an' to de point shows he wasn't no regular lawyer."
>
> Judge Jacob M. Braude[16]

Lawyers make work for themselves:

> Attorneys are supposed to be society's peacemakers and problem solvers. Too many devote themselves to the opposite; they are troublemakers. They operate on the theory, apparently, that the more trouble they can stir up, the more law business there will be. The wise Judge Learned Hand once remarked: "I must say that as a litigant I should dread a lawsuit beyond almost anything else short of sickness and death."
>
> Jack Anderson and Les Whitten[17]

> Businessmen make decisions involving great sums of money every day, but lawyers insist on over-researching every little question before they offer an opinion. It's especially disconcerting and expensive that lawyers, like nuns, travel in pairs.
>
> Jay A. Pritzker, a businessman coming from a family of lawyers[18]

It isn't the bad lawyers who are screwing up the justice system in this country—it's the good lawyers.... If you have two competent lawyers on opposite sides, a trial that should take three days could easily last six months.

Art Buchwald[19]

A significant portion of litigation is unneeded and goes unchecked at great expense. Too often I hear lawyers themselves say a suit can't be settled, not because of unreconcilable differences, but because the other lawyer isn't interested in settling. His meter is running.

Lester Pollack, businessman[20]

Lawyers look after their own interests, not their clients':

Across the land, lawyers lurk behind the bushes waiting to pounce upon the passersby, drag them into court and drain them of their assets. Most lawsuits benefit only the lawyers, who collect fat fees and leave both parties worse off.

Jack Anderson and Les Whitten[21]

It might be to a company's best interest to take a certain position in a regulatory question, but outside counsel sometimes won't even tell a businessman about such a position. The lawyers are unwilling to take positions that would be unpopular with a government agency because they fear they might somewhat estrange themselves from the agency and hurt their dealings with it on behalf of their other clients.

Jerome R. Van Gorkam, businessman[22]

Lawyers' own interests often cloud the time to settle and the time to fight. Lawyers assume a combative posture and want to fight to the death, with the client's interests consciously or subconsciously lost sight of. They turn litigation into a personal matter, which extends the litigation and increases the cost, and afterwards they brag to their lawyer friends, "Did you hear what I did to old so-and-so in court the other day?"

Lester Pollack, businessman[23]

Lawyers are incompetent:

> Many judges in general jurisdiction trial courts have stated
> to me that fewer than 25 per cent of the lawyers appearing
> before them are genuinely qualified.
>
> Chief Justice Warren Burger[24]

> Lawyer: the only man in whom ignorance of the law is not
> punished.
>
> Elbert Hubbard[25]

Lawyers are intellectual and moral prostitutes:

> There was a society of men among us, bred up from their
> youth in the art of proving by words multiplied for the pur-
> pose, that white is black, and black is white, according as
> they are paid.
>
> Jonathan Swift[26]

> His soul moves in his fee.
> This fellow, [f]or six sols more, would plead against
> his Maker.
>
> Ben Jonson[27]

People cannot get justice:

> May you have a lawsuit in which you know you are in the
> right.
>
> Gypsy curse[28]

> [Lawyers] have been known to wrest from reluctant juries
> triumphant verdicts of acquittal for their clients, even when
> those clients, as often happens, were clearly and unmistak-
> ably innocent.
>
> Oscar Wilde[29]

> If war is too important to be left to the generals, surely justice
> is too important to be left to the lawyers.
>
> Robert McKay, former dean of
> New York University Law School[30]

Most people cannot afford to get the legal help they need:

In one *New Yorker* cartoon, a lawyer says to his client, "You have a pretty good case, Mr. Pitkin. How much justice can you afford?"

J. B. Handelsman[31]

We are over-lawyered and under-represented.
Ninety percent of our lawyers serve ten percent of our people.

President Jimmy Carter[32]

All too often, the legal decision goes to the client with the most money. He can outmaneuver and outlast his poorer opponent in the courts. The poor often cannot afford to seek redress of grievances for even the most basic injustices.

Jack Anderson and Les Whitten [33]

The laws that govern affluent clients and large institutions are numerous, intricate, and applied by highly sophisticated practitioners. In this sector of society, rules proliferate, lawsuits abound, and the cost of legal services grows much faster than the cost of living. For the bulk of the population, however, the situation is very different. Access to the courts may be open in principle. In practice, however, most people find their legal rights severely compromised by the cost of legal services, the baffling complications of existing rules and procedures, and the long, frustrating delays involved in bringing proceedings to a conclusion. From afar, therefore, the legal system looks grossly inequitable and inefficient. There is far too much law for those who can afford it and far too little for those who cannot.

Derek C. Bok[34]

In a joint study by the American Bar Association Special Committee to Survey Legal Needs and the American Bar Foundation, at least half of the public surveyed agreed with the following statements:

Lawyers are (not) prompt about getting things done

Lawyers are generally not very good at keeping their clients
informed of progress in their cases

Lawyers' fees are (not) usually fair to their clients, regard-
less of how they figured the fee

Most lawyers charge more for their services than they are
worth

There are many things that lawyers handle—for example,
tax matters or estate planning—that can be done as well
and less expensively by non-lawyers—like tax accountants

At least 30 percent of the respondents agreed that:

Lawyers will take a case...(even) if they (do not) feel sure they
know enough about that area of the law to handle the case
well

Lawyers work harder at getting clients than in serving them

Lawyers needlessly complicate clients' problems

Lawyers do not care whether their clients fully understand
what needs to be done and why[35]

Almost 40 percent of the people believe lawyers will do
unethical and illegal things to help a client in an important
case, and 42 percent believe lawyers are not concerned
about eliminating the bad apples from the legal profession.[36]

Evaluating These Criticisms

Why would a lawyer who loves and cherishes his profession repeat this stinging indictment of his profession?
First, it is my intent to lay it on the line as a basis for
helping the public develop a better understanding of how
our legal system operates. I am also interested in dispelling
unjust criticisms of lawyers. I am not an apologist for lawyers and the law profession. This book is full of criticism of
the legal profession. But many of the criticisms listed in this
chapter only apply to a small minority of lawyers, not to the
vast majority who are honest and try hard to do good work.
It is unfortunate that the profession has been painted by

the broad strokes of an unflattering few. It is also unfortunate that many of the critics speak without looking at all the facts. I have learned this from personal experience. For example, many people complain how a lawyer badly handled a relative's estate. I remember one who complained about me—the widow of a client of mine. She took a cruise around the world shortly after her husband's death. Several times I cautioned her to beware of "wolves" (men eager to take advantage of her emotionally vulnerable state). But, sure enough, she returned from her cruise and asked me to get the trustee to give her $50,000 to loan to a man she had met. The trustee refused to give her money for that purpose since doing so would have adversely affected her financial security. She was highly critical of me for writing a will "tying" up her assets, even though it was done solely to preserve her security.

Despite these criticisms, most lawyers are not cynical about their profession. They know they are not perfect, but they try to do as well as they can in the time they have. But, like it or not, lawyers serve the public and cannot ignore public criticism. It is not enough to take action only when a certain percentage of the public believes a particular criticism. Lawyers must be concerned whenever anyone criticizes them.

In evaluating these criticisms, it is important to note that many are not based on personal experience. As already mentioned, Barbara Curran's survey of legal needs found that almost two-thirds of the American people either have never consulted a lawyer or have consulted a lawyer only once in their lives. Those who *have* consulted with lawyers overwhelmingly approve of their lawyer's performance.[37] The public disapproves of lawyers as a group, not individual lawyers.

It is also important to remember that even the greatest Americans and the most revered institutions have at one time or another been held in low public esteem. Nowadays the public is critical of all institutions. People no longer believe that society is working well. And, as representatives of the institution with the most influence over their lives, lawyers have had to shoulder responsibility for all things people dislike about our society (e.g., high crime, unpopular court decisions, too many governmental regulations).

Nevertheless, much of this criticism is valid. There are incompetent lawyers, just as there are incompetent doctors, dentists, and business executives. And it is deplorable that many Americans are denied legal services because they cannot afford them. These problems are not being ignored by the legal profession. Lawyers are trying to adapt the legal profession to meet the changing needs and expectations of society. But more can be done with public help.

Lawyers have a major responsibility to improve the efficiency and quality of their performance, not just to make money or survive but to enhance their own reputations and the reputation of their profession. It is also important for their personal fulfillment. The general public cannot afford to be an unconcerned bystander to this process. The public must learn how lawyers and the legal system operate and decide how they want it to work. What lawyers and the general public are and should be doing to improve the system will be discussed throughout this book.

Chapter 4

Legal Reasoning and Analysis

> *The life of the law has not been logic: it has been experience. The felt necessities of the time, the prevalent moral and political theories, intuitions of public policy, avowed or unconscious, even the prejudices which judges share with their fellow-men, have had a good deal more to do than the syllogism in determining the rules by which men should be governed. The law embodies the story of a nation's development through many centuries, and it cannot be dealt with as if it contained only the axioms and corollaries of a book of mathematics.*
> Justice Oliver Wendell Holmes, Jr.[1]

How does a lawyer decide whether a client is right or wrong in the eyes of the law? How does a judge come to decide whether one side or the other deserves the court's imprimatur? What are these things we call laws anyway? These are things people should know but don't. The public expect lawyers to give them definite answers to their legal

questions, and they cannot understand why lawyers give
qualified opinions. The public's frustration is exemplified
by the old joke about a client looking for a one-armed lawyer
who cannot say, "On the one hand...but on the other
hand...."

It is difficult to explain what legal reasoning is. Dictionaries—even law dictionaries—do not even try. *Reasoning* is summarized by dictionaries as the mental process of
drawing logical conclusions or inferences from observa-
tions and facts, and *legal* is defined as pertaining to the law.
But the two words are not joined by a single meaning.
Looking up *reason* does not add much clarification: an
underlying fact or cause that provides logical sense for a
premise or occurrence; capacity for rational thought, infer-
ence, or discrimination; good judgment; sound sense; intelligence; with good sense and justification; to use the faculty
of reason; thinking logically.

Legal reasoning starts with a set of facts—and frequently
a conflicting set of facts. After gathering all the facts, lawyers must determine what law applies and then sort
through the facts to decide which ones are legally relevant.
For example, a warranty covering a new car is legally relevant in a controversy over who will pay to repair the car; the
color of the car is not legally relevant since it does not
matter whether the car needing repair is silver or black. The
next step is to identify what questions have to be answered
before the law can be applied.

Law schools lead students through this intellectual exercise by having them read and analyze court decisions. Students read through the facts of a case, decide what rule of
law applies, identify what questions have to be answered
before the rule of law can be applied, and then answer the
questions and apply the law. Sounds cut and dried, doesn't
it? In actual practice, it is not quite that simple.

Facts may not be quite what they seem to be. Clients
usually are convinced that they know what happened, but
so are opposing parties. Sometimes people lie, but more
often errors in reporting facts are unintentional. Some peo-

ple are not very observant. Some do not have good memories. Even if their memories are good, what people recall may be influenced by wishful thinking. Further errors can occur when people explain what the facts are since they do not always say what they mean. More errors can creep in when the trier of fact (judge or jury) has to listen to various versions of the facts and decide what the truth is. Judges and jurors are just as prone as other people to poor powers of observation, deficient memory, selective perception, and an inability to say what they mean.

Lawyers who assume that facts are what clients say they are will be in for many surprises and disappointments. Law students have the luxury of reasoning from facts they can accept as true, but practicing lawyers must become skilled investigators and analysts to make sure that the truth is uncovered so that the client can emerge victorious and/or justice can be done.

Once a lawyer knows the facts, he or she must decide which ones are important ("legally relevant") and which are not. Identifying legally relevant facts is a key step in legal reasoning since it allows courts to formulate rules. No two factual situations are the same, but many share important features (legally relevant facts), and it is the existence of these common features that makes it possible to formulate rules that can be applied to many cases. Edward Levi, former dean of the University of Chicago Law School, has called this the central problem of legal reasoning: "When will it be just to treat different cases as though they were the same?"[2]

Although the average person thinks that he or she knows what law is, legal philosophers have not been able to agree on one definition. Some define *law* in terms of results. Justice Oliver Wendell Holmes, Jr. defined laws as "prophecies of what courts will do in fact, and nothing more pretentious."[3] Others have concentrated on its source. Roscoe Pound, an eminent legal philosopher, wrote that "[l]aw is experience developed by reason and applied continually to further experience."[4] The most common definition of *law* emphasizes its function. Lon L. Fuller, while he was a professor of law at Harvard Law School, defined *law* as "the enterprise of subjecting human conduct to the governance of rules."[5] Dictionaries look at both the source and function of law by defining it as rules established by authority, society, or custom governing the affairs of humans within a community or among states.

How people view law is crucial in determining the nature of society. At varying times and places during human history, people have looked to God (or gods), natural law (laws of absolute, eternal, and universal validity), human reason, and chance experience as the source of law. Deciding the source of law is important since that decision explains how laws come into being and how they can be changed. If God (or gods) are the source of law, then laws can be enacted, repealed, or modified only through a new tablet of commandments or fresh words from the Oracle of Delphi. Belief that there is one ideal set of laws applicable throughout all time and to all societies (natural law) tends to identify law with the morality of the most powerful group in society and the most powerful society in the world. Belief that laws are the result of chance experience discourages people from trying to develop ideal laws. Only the identification of human reason as the source of law allows humans to determine their own fate.

Theories about what that fate should be have varied over time. The goals to be achieved by law have included the preservation of order, equality, security, liberty, and social justice—goals that may be mutually exclusive. Marxists, who view the economic ruling class as the source of law and believe that law will disappear in a communist society, see law as instructive, as a tool to guide society to their ideal. What function law performs for a society determines what types of activities will be regulated. As equality and social justice have eclipsed personal liberty as the goals to be achieved by American law, the number of statutes and regulations has proliferated.

The important point is that our society is governed by the

rule of law, not whim. Broadly defined, *rule of law* includes laws enacted by duly elected lawmakers (e.g., Congress and state legislatures), regulations promulgated by administrative agencies and the like, natural law (principles valid at least for American society), and stare decisis. Stare decisis, Latin for "to stand by things decided," is a principle of law requiring courts to decide cases the same way they have been decided in the past.

After lawyers gather facts, they must decide what rule of law applies to the facts. To make this decision, they must look for statutes that govern similar sets of facts and court cases that have involved similar sets of facts. Once lawyers discover statutes or court cases that seem to apply to the situation at hand, they must carefully analyze the statute or court case to see if it really does apply.

Often statutes seem quite clear in meaning until they are applied to a specific set of facts, particularly when the facts were not contemplated by legislators. For example, Title VII of the Civil Rights Act of 1964 prohibits sexual discrimination in employment. That seems clear enough, but there have been countless cases trying to decide what sexual discrimination is. Does it include sexual harassment? How about discrimination on the basis of sexual preference (e.g., firing people just because they are gay)? Or discrimination against a transsexual or transvestite? Can a job requirement be sexually discriminatory even if it only is applied to female applicants (e.g., a height requirement that excludes women from a job open only to women)?

For some time now, there have been few factual situations that have not been dealt with at least once by a court of law. The lawyer's task is to identify one or more court decisions that closely resemble the case at hand. If the legally relevant facts are identical, then the principle of stare decisis normally applies, and the results should be identical. The rationale for this principle is that justice requires equal treatment (uniformity) and that people need the security of knowing that laws will not change from one day to the next (stability).

One argument against following past decisions is that doing so really does not give people a feeling of security since they usually do not know what the rules are until they go to a lawyer. A more compelling reason not to mechanically follow the principle of stare decisis is that the earlier case may have been wrongly decided—or the result may be contrary to current views of justice. For example, if stare decisis were mechanically applied, then "separate but equal" might still be the law of the land and blacks and whites might still be separated in schools and public accommodations.

No one seriously argues that stare decisis should be mechanically applied. The real dispute is over how easy it should be to change a rule of law. Courts often pledge allegiance to the principle and then circumvent it by pointing to facts that should lead to a different result (called "distinguishing" a case) or by pretending to comply with an existing rule—often justifying their decision as within the "spirit" of the rule.

How often do courts manipulate rules of law to achieve a desired result? Frequently, according to Justice Richard Neely: "In my experience, judges work backward from the intuitive grasp of the equities of a lawsuit to a manipulation of legal rules that will achieve what they consider an equitable result."[6]

Justice Neely probably overstates the arbitrariness of legal decisions. Most rules of law are accepted as just and can be applied by judges without offending their notions of equity. Problems arise when a rule of law is being refined or needs further development or must be abrogated to meet the changing needs of society. United States Supreme Court Justice Benjamin Cardozo described this process as follows: "...the problem which confronts the judge is in reality a twofold one: he must first extract from the precedents the underlying principle, the *ratio decidendi*; he must then determine the path or direction along which the principle is to move and develop, if it is not to wither and die."[7]

Lawyers help lead courts down this path by framing issues for courts to decide. They tell courts why a statute should or should not apply to a particular factual situation (relying on such things as legislative history, the language of the statute, and the supposed intent of the statute), why a court rule should or should not apply to a particular set of facts, and what rule should be framed if there is not one already. For example, it was only recently that courts had to decide if parents could recover damages for the "wrongful birth" of a child following an unsuccessful abortion, unsuccessful sterilization operation, or inadequate genetic counseling.

Legal reasoning tends to be thought of as a form of logic instead of as a creative process. That is unfortunate because treating it as a form of logic masks the effect that laws have on people. Lost in an analysis of the applicability of a law to a certain set of facts is the effect that a decision will have on a human being.

Ideals are built into our legal system, and it is only by constantly reevaluating them that we can make sure that laws meet our needs. When ethical relativism brought the concept of natural law into disrepute, it became unfashionable to argue what laws should be. Idealism took a further beating from those who argued that the attitudes, values, and talents of judges and jurors are better predictors of a decision than a rule of law.

The danger of thinking of legal decision-making as a function of individual traits instead of human reason was summed up by Edgar Bodenheimer when he was a professor of law at the University of Utah College of Law:

> If the search for justice and reasonableness in law is abandoned by the best minds on the grounds that justice is a meaningless, chimerical, and irrational notion, then there is danger that the human race will fall back into a condition of barbarism and ignorance where unreason will prevail over rationality, and where the dark forces of prejudice may win

the battle over humanitarian ideals and the forces of good will and benevolence.[8]

No one denies that justice is shaped by the varying abilities, attitudes, and values of individuals, but it is wrong to underestimate the role of law as the construction material for justice. Laws are not set in stone. Nor are they irrelevant to the way cases are decided. Laws are made by people, both haphazardly and as a conscious act of human reason, and they can be made to serve whatever goals people want them to serve. The more laws meet the needs of people, the less likely people should be to circumvent them. Unfortunately, too often people drift into laws and let laws carry them where they will. Reason requires effort and often errs, yet, as Benjamin Cardozo once wrote, "The tide rises and falls, but the sands of error crumble."[9]

Chapter 5

The Adversary System
and Trial Advocacy

> *In short, the lawyer aims at vic-
> tory, at winning in the fight, not at
> aiding the court to discover the
> facts. He does not want the trial
> court to reach a sound educated
> guess, if it is likely to be contrary to
> his client's interests. Our present
> trial method is thus the equivalent
> of throwing pepper in the eyes of a
> surgeon when he is performing an
> operation.*
>
> Judge Jerome Frank[1]

We use an advocacy system to seek justice. In olden times,
two armored gladiators would fight to the death to test the
rightness of the cause they championed. Nowadays lawyers do not fight to the death for their clients, but they do

61

fight hard to convince juries and judges of the rightness of their clients' cause. My fifty years of active law practice have convinced me that the adversary system of resolving disputes is costly, a gross waste of time, and unduly burdensome for the participants. It clogs our courts and delays justice beyond reason. It also contributes to the poor public image of lawyers and the legal profession.

After a verdict, Monday morning quarterbacks debate the tactics used by the loser. Were the wrong jurors chosen? Should such-and-such witness have been called to testify? Was the right defense used? Were the right questions asked on cross-examination? Implicit in these questions is the notion that, had the "game" been better played, the result would have been different. Too often unmentioned is the belief that justice may have been done. Maybe the client deserved to lose.

Clarence Darrow once said, "The trouble with laws...is lawyers."[2] Well, the trouble with lawyers is an adversary system that rewards victory, not the promotion of truth and justice. Lawyers are freed from moral responsibility. So what if a client admits that he is guilty? Keep him off the stand. Don't tell a witness what to say. Just "prepare" the witness. State what the law is before interviewing a person. State it again and again if the individual does not catch on to what he or she should be saying.

Don't make available evidence undermining your client's position. Don't tell opposing counsel about a case he or she overlooked. Opposing counsel should be rewarded only for his or her own efforts. The work ethic, not the search for truth, should be encouraged. Make your arguments for a specific interpretation of the law or facts. Be relieved that your opponent does not spot the fallacies.

American poet and scholar James Gates Percival once commented: "...the custom of pleading for any client, without discrimination of right or wrong, must lessen the regard due to those important distinctions, and deaden the moral sensibility of the heart."[3] Legal scholar Felix S. Cohen recognized that "the lack of moral doubts...is so helpful to the lawyer in practice."[4] No wonder so many lawyers were involved in Watergate. Lawyers are not supposed to decide what is right or wrong. Tell them the client's goal and they will pursue it without evaluating the means or ends.

The present adversary system is great—in theory. Two sets of lawyers of equal and substantial ability represent clients zealously within the bounds of the law. Access to information is equal, and each lawyer casts the evidence in a light most favorable to his or her side.

A neutral third party is thus presented with all the available evidence and possible interpretations. Sifting through this material, the third party decides what probably happened and applies a combination of fairness predetermined by lawmakers and visceral fairness inspired by the particular facts of the case. This we call justice.

The major virtue of the adversary system is that it is supposed to be the most effective method of discovering truth. Zealous advocates are supposed to uncover all the facts and applicable law. The spirit of the contest is supposed to spur lawyers to great achievements of intellect and imagination. Deft cross-examination is supposed to root out false and misleading testimony.

Unfortunately, all lawyers are not equally competent. Which means that a case may be won or lost depending on the varying abilities of opposing counsel, not necessarily on the merits of the cause. The more competent lawyer will count his or her blessings when an opponent fails to make an effective counterargument or discover a damaging piece of evidence. An attorney builds a reputation and earnings on victories, not fair results. Facts supporting an opponent's case may never see the light of day if the opponent's lawyer does not properly prepare a client's case.

Instead of promoting the discovery of truth, the adversary system encourages lawyers to color or interpret facts in the light most favorable to their clients. Trial technique books advise lawyers how to make their witnesses look good and their opponent's witnesses look bad. Lawyers learn to use their verbal skills, usually superior to a witness', to shake a witness' testimony or discredit the witness. Skillful lawyers have been known to make rape victims with virtuous pasts look like tramps "asking" for what they got. That is why some states have had to restrict the types of questions that lawyers may ask rape victims. Questions about the reputation of witnesses have also been limited in other contexts when it was felt they were not relevant to the witness' credibility. If lawyers are unable to discredit a witness, then as a matter of strategy they try to confuse the issue to make the testimony meaningless.

The adversary system undermines the truth-seeking function of trials by putting witnesses in a stressful situation and encouraging them to be partisans. As Judge Frank has written: "They come to regard themselves, not as aids in an investigation bent on discovering the truth, not as aids to the court, but as the 'plaintiff's witnesses' or the 'defendant's witnesses.' They become soldiers in a war, cease to be neutrals."[5] The credibility of witnesses is crucial in evaluating their testimony, but judges and jurors do not have a chance to observe witnesses' normal demeanor because they are under courtroom stress. They know that opposing counsel will try to embarrass them in public. The result is, as Judge Marvin E. Frankel has written, that the "process often achieves truth only as a convenience, a by-product, or an accidental approximation."[6]

Lawyers strive to get every edge in the "battle." They dress a certain way, talk a certain way, stand in a particular spot, and react in calculated ways. Consummate trial lawyers sway jurors and judges with their "performances" as much as actors do. Trial lawyers develop good reputations not just by winning cases they should, but by also winning cases they should lose—if justice were to prevail. Some trial experts argue that jurors make up their minds after both lawyers have presented their opening statements—but before any evidence has been presented. Victory is awarded the side that is more persuasive, not necessarily the side that is right.

Not only do lawyers vary in ability, but access to evidence

is not equal. How many people have commented about "the best justice money can buy"? Lawyers hope that opponents, through oversight or lack of money, will not discover that damaging tidbit. But just in case, lawyers encourage clients to divulge the truth so that they can prepare counter-arguments.

The client orientation of lawyers looms as a more serious problem when one considers that most "justice" is dispensed by lawyers through plea bargaining in criminal cases and settlements in civil matters. There is no neutral third party to decide what is fair. Instead, interested parties—the lawyers—use predictions about the behavior of the third party as only one factor in deciding how to conclude a controversy.

Other factors include the cost and delay of litigation and lawyers' ability to bluff their opponents into thinking they have a strong case. These factors are not related to any concept of justice. A person suffering severe injuries might be forced to settle for a fraction of actual damages because money is urgently needed, while a person with a $50 claim will "settle" for $400 because it would cost more than that for the insurer to go to trial. This problem could be minimized by limiting the controversies that go to trial (e.g., by requiring no-fault insurance; not prosecuting victimless crimes), but the problem cannot be resolved until the system is changed.

The adversary system is costly for litigants and for society. Lawyers run up clients' bills by looking for each piece of evidence and interviewing every potential witness. They overprepare because they are afraid to lose. If they hear that their opponent is spending thousands of dollars on jury selection, then they have to do the same so that their opponent will not get the "edge." When lawyers are not as good as opposing counsel or cannot afford to properly prepare their client's case, then justice may not prevail.

Lack of justice is not just a problem affecting individuals. "Accidental" justice is also society's problem. Society wants to peacefully resolve conflicts but can do so only if members of society have confidence in the dispute-resolution mechanism. The adversary posture of lawyers deters peaceful resolution of conflict and leads to many costly trials. Recognizing that this is true, many have turned to arbitration and mediation as alternatives to trials. These alternatives are discussed in Chapter 7.

Lawyers have been slow to encourage such alternatives since the status quo gives them their livelihood and since they are uncomfortable with any other method of resolving disputes. Their law school training ingrains in them the attitude that they are supposed to take sides, not mediate controversies and resolve disputes short of conflict.

Society does not just want disputes to be peacefully resolved; it also wants the result to be socially beneficial. The adversary system of seeking justice assumes that society's needs will be met by resolution of individuals' needs, but that is not necessarily so. It is definitely not so if "justice" depends more on the skill of a lawyer than upon the relevant evidence and rule of law. Time and again we have witnessed criminal trials where a defendant represented by a nationally known trial lawyer has been set free even though we are fairly certain that the defendant was guilty. There even have been reports of prominent defense lawyers "bragging" that they successfully defended a guilty person. Such cases are dramatic examples of victory in court without justice. The adversary system requires an "either-or" decision; one side must win and the other side must lose. But "justice" in civil matters may lie somewhere between the opposing viewpoints.

If it is any consolation, the adversary system used to be worse at discovering truth. Common law pleading rules used to be so complicated that it took a skillful lawyer just to get a court to hear a client's case, and each side could conceal evidence. The trend in recent years has been to modify many aspects of the adversary system to promote its truth-seeking function. Pleading technicalities have been eliminated, and litigants have been given the right to "discover" pertinent evidence known by opponents. Discovery procedures make available information that otherwise might never come to light—or might come to light only at great expense. It helps both sides discover the truth and avoid surprises at trial. Unfortunately, it can be abused—and has been by attorneys who run up an opponent's expenses by demanding extensive and not always relevant information. Steps are now being taken to penalize those guilty of abusing discovery procedures.

Every system of dispute resolution should be reviewed from time to time to re-evaluate its efficiency in solving the problems it was intended to solve. Now it is time to look at an alternative to the advocacy system, even if that alternative will affect lawyers' pocketbooks.

The ultimate task is to eliminate or at least minimize contentiousness and one-sided, costly searches for facts and truth. Our system of justice has already evolved from superstition and battle between champions to a process that attempts rational decision-making. Now it is time to add expertise to the decision-making and give decision-makers the facts they need to fairly resolve conflicts.

One idea worth considering as an alternative to the present advocacy system is a panel system of judicial administration for handling civil matters. There could be panels for the various types of litigation (e.g., personal injury suits, products liability suits, antitrust matters, divorces), and each panel could be chosen from a pool of individuals knowledgeable about the subject. Panels could consist of at least three members, unless otherwise agreed by the parties. Panels would be permitted to hire a lawyer or lawyers to help them decide the matter in controversy. Initially the panels could be financed by the government, but ultimately the cost could be shifted to the litigants.

Strict rules of evidence would not be applied because what we now call juries would not be used. Instead, the panels would function as judge and jury. Panels would have the expertise that present juries lack. Experience demonstrates that arbitrators chosen for their expertise have been able to inspire confidence in disputants that conflicts will be

resolved fairly, and so should judicial panels. Disputants
could hire lawyers to help them choose panel members and
make certain that panels do not overlook or give too much
emphasis to a particular fact; or disputants could rely on
staff attorneys. Hired attorneys would be limited to an
advisory role; they would not be active participants. Staff
attorneys would be in an unfamiliar role; they would be
asked to seek a just result instead of victory.

The lawyer-client privilege would have to be eliminated
in such proceedings. Instead, all statements made to panel
members or panel staff would be recorded. There is a danger
that, out of fear of damaging themselves, disputants might
withhold information that could, in fact, help them. But if
people could be convinced that they will be treated fairly,
then they would feel free to tell all that they know. If their
goal is victory, and not fair treatment, then they should not
be helped by the judicial system to conceal damaging
information.

Because disputants would have little reason or need to
believe that an appellate court would change the result,
thousands of costly appeals could be avoided. Knowledgeable, impartial panel members are more likely to arrive at
substantial justice than conventional jurors. The elimination of the adversary system would give disputants less
reason to believe that one last "trick" or maneuver by their
lawyer could turn the tide. A panel decision could be treated
like an administrative agency decision—overturnable only
if it was arbitrary or an abuse of discretion. Costly research
into the law and facts of a matter would be reduced under
the panel system because it would only have to be done once
for all disputants.

Obviously it would be the height of folly to replace the
adversary system with panels without first testing the
panel system. Panels could be set up in a few areas, and
disputants could be given a choice of using panels or the
traditional judicial system. Enough people should be willing to try the panel system to give it a fair test since it
would be less costly and would resolve disputes more

quickly. Society would be able to compare the relative advantages of each system, improve both, and eventually choose one over the other. Logically, the legal profession, particularly the bar associations, should take the lead in exploring the possibility of a panel system, but this probably will not happen without public pressure.

Changes in law and the judicial system come very slowly. Lawyers are notoriously slow in responding to problems, and they will not be eager to adopt a system that seems likely to reduce their fees substantially. With the panel system far fewer billable hours could be chalked up than in extended litigation. If it were adopted, along with other methods of resolving disputes without litigation (and often without lawyers), then there would not be a need for as many lawyers. Judges also have a interest in maintaining the present system, and few could be expected to vigorously advocate a change.

How about the public? Certainly there are many who prefer victory to fair results. Others believe that victory is the only fair result, even if they are in the wrong, because they think what they did is not nearly as bad as what others have been and are doing. But there is general disenchantment with the legal profession, the slow delivery of justice, and the high cost of litigation both for parties and for society. Arbitration and mediation are being utilized more and more, and litigants have even hired their own judges to speed up resolution of their disputes. Perhaps the general public is now prepared to advance past superstition, champions, and "hired guns" and trust their fate to knowledgeable individuals interested in fair results.

Chapter 6

The Jury System

> *I consider [trial by jury] as the only*
> *anchor ever yet imagined by man,*
> *by which a government can be held*
> *to the principles of its constitution.*
>   Thomas Jefferson[1]

> *A jury consists of twelve persons*
> *chosen to decide who has the better*
> *lawyer.*
>   Robert Frost[2]

In recent years some people have started questioning the value of the jury system and wondering whether juries do more harm than good and should be abolished. Such an idea would have been unthinkable not too many years ago. For centuries, "trial by one's peers" was a sacred principle in Anglo-Saxon law.[3] Juries were first used in England after the Norman Conquest in 1066, but their roots have been

70

traced back to the Greeks. Socrates was condemned by a jury of hundreds.

Use of juries in England was a long step towards rational resolution of conflicts. Before the advent of juries, disputes were settled by combat (between the disputants or their champions) or by ordeal, which usually involved hot irons (reserved for nobility), hot water, or cold water. In an ordeal by hot irons, the "righteousness" of a person's cause was tested by having the person carry (in a hand sprinkled with holy water) a red-hot iron nine steps to an altar. If the person's hand healed in three days, then he or she was victorious. Victory in an ordeal by hot water meant that the accused escaped unscathed after his or her head or arm had been immersed in boiling water. Victory in an ordeal by cold water meant that the accused sank after being thrown into a lake or river.

Two other means of resolving disputes were the decision by the cross and compurgation. In a decision by the cross, a priest or youth would be asked to pick up one of two sticks laid on an altar. If the stick marked with a cross was picked up, then victory was awarded the person represented by the priest or youth. To win at compurgation, one had to have people (compurgators) swear that your cause was just. The person with the most compurgators would win (one man named Ulnothus supposedly had more than a thousand compurgators swear that certain land was his). If there were not enough compurgators (usually a minimum of twelve were required) or the compurgators were thought unworthy of belief, then it was back to the ordeal. In 1215, Pope Innocent III forbade priests from participating in ordeals, and in 1229 King Henry II banned ordeals.

The ideal juror now has no knowledge about a case, but originally people were chosen as jurors because they were familiar with the contestants and the dispute. It was not until the end of the 17th century that courts adopted the principle that a verdict must be based solely on evidence heard in the courtroom and not on any information about the dispute that the jurors know or have heard about. Until

1670 (Bushell's case) jurors could be punished for "bad" decisions (an attaint jury could require the jurors to forfeit their land and property to the king).

The jury system came to the United States with the first English colonists. One of the complaints made against King George III in the Declaration of Independence was that he was guilty of "depriving us in many cases of the benefit of Trial by Jury." Juries were revered in the Thirteen Colonies for refusing to enforce unpopular laws. The Constitution guaranteed jury trials for persons accused of crimes, and, following public clamor, the right to trial by jury was "preserved" in the Bill of Rights for "suits at common law,where the value in controversy shall exceed twenty dollars." The United States is now the home of the jury trial. Most other countries do not permit them. Even Great Britain, once the bastion for trial by one's peers, has limited the use of juries in civil suits to cases involving fraud and libel.

There are two types of juries: the grand jury and the trial (petit) jury. Grand jurors meet in secret to decide if there is probable cause that a person has committed a crime. They meet in secret so that the accused will not be tempted to flee. The accused has no right to participate in the proceedings. It only takes a majority of the grand jurors to return an indictment. If a majority of one grand jury refuse to indict a person, the government can try again with another grand jury. Because prosecutors usually dominate grand jury proceedings and get their way (there is no one to defend the accused at such proceedings), grand juries have been criticized as costly, inefficient, and time-consuming. Most states allow prosecutors to decide whether to bring a person to trial instead of requiring an indictment by a grand jury.

Trial juries decide disputes between litigants. People accused of crimes have the right to trial by jury. Those involved in civil disputes have a right to trial by jury only when they are contesting legal rights that are the same or similar to rights determined by juries in 1791, the year the Seventh Amendment was adopted. The Seventh Amendment "preserves" the right to jury trial in suits at "common law."

When the Seventh Amendment was adopted, there were competing courts—common law courts and courts of equity. Courts of equity protected rights that could not be protected at common law. For example, courts of equity had the power to issue injunctions, order restitution, quiet titles (decide who owns a particular tract of land), rescind contracts, enforce trusts, order specific performance (e.g., order sellers to transfer a house to buyers), set aside fraudulent transfers, hear a stockholders' derivative action (a suit by stockholders on behalf of a corporation), and order people to account for what they did with certain property or money. Courts of equity traditionally did not allow juries, and the Seventh Amendment did not require them to do so. Now most states do not have separate courts of equity and common law courts, but courts still have to decide whether a question is legal or equitable before they can determine whether it can be decided by a jury.

Trial juries traditionally have consisted of twelve persons (the number was fixed at twelve in 1367), perhaps because of the importance of that number in the New Testament (twelve apostles). The United States Supreme Court referred to this number in 1970 as an "accidental feature of the jury" and decided that juries could consist of fewer than twelve persons.[4] In a later case it set the minimum at six. Setting a number has been controversial since some people fear that smaller numbers make it easier to convict a defendant and more difficult to overcome the biases of jurors. The Supreme Court has said that the number of jurors should "be large enough to promote group deliberation, free from outside attempts at intimidation, and to provide a fair possibility for obtaining a representative cross-section of the community."[5] To make sure that there is a "fair cross section of the community," people may not be excluded from jury service on the basis of race, religion, or sex (women could be excluded until 1975, when the Supreme Court ruled otherwise).

Until the end of the 14th century, majority verdicts were acceptable. After that time, unanimity was required. Jurors would be locked up without food until they arrived at a verdict. Coming full circle, the United States Supreme Court decided in 1972 that verdicts do not have to be unanimous.

As mentioned earlier, individuals originally were chosen as jurors because they had the most knowledge about the dispute. Now lack of knowledge about a dispute is considered a virtue in prospective jurors. People may have knowledge about a dispute (e.g., they may have read about it in the newspapers or heard about it on TV) and a preconceived notion of who is in the right, and still be jurors—as long as they can lay aside their impressions and opinions and render a verdict based solely on the evidence presented in court. Like other aspects of the jury system, the knowledge requirement may come full circle since many people, including Chief Justice Burger, feel that more knowledgeable jurors are required for complex cases.[6]

Both critics and defenders of the jury system agree that the use of juries is inconsistent with the notion that we should be ruled by law, not individuals. Defenders see this as a virtue; critics see this as justification for abolishing the jury system. Defenders worry about the arbitrariness of law. Critics worry about the arbitrariness of jurors.

In early American history, juries were the bulwark against tyranny. The same was true in England. Winston Churchill wrote in *A History of English-Speaking Peoples* that "[t]he jury system has come to stand for all we mean by English justice, because so long as a case has to be scrutinized by twelve honest men, defendant and plaintiff alike have a safeguard from arbitrary perversion of the law."[7] William Blackstone, the leading authority on the common law, also championed juries: "a competent number of sensible and upright jurymen, chosen by lot from among those of the middle rank, will be found the best investigators of truth, and the surest guardians of public justice."[8] Writer G. K. Chesterton viewed the jury system at a more basic level:

"[I]t asks men who know no more law than I know, but who can feel the things that I felt in the jury box."[9]

"Trial by one's peers" has been considered the best assurance that people will be judged fairly. Defenders of the jury system have praised jurors for collectively reaching just results by using common sense and equity to enforce the law. Critics feel that justice should be written into the laws and not left to juries. They feel that results should be predictable and point to widely varying damage awards as evidence of jurys' unpredictability. As people lose confidence in judges and lawmakers, they see the jury system as the only defender of the individual against an oppressive government.

The existence of a jury system gives people confidence that they can obtain justice if they violate what they consider to be an unjust law. But the jury system is at odds with the rest of the legal system, which puts a premium on the rule of law. Fears that juries can be "loose cannons" have led to strict judicial controls. Judges decide what evidence a jury can hear or view, tell jurors what the law is, and set aside jury verdicts when they believe a verdict is contrary to the weight of the evidence.

Ideally jurors are supposed to decide what really happened and then apply the law to the situation, but in reality jurors decide what happened and what would be a "fair" result. Jurors face a difficult choice. The adversary system requires them to decide that one side or the other is right, but in the real world a compromise between the two positions may seem justified, and that is what jurors frequently do. They usually are told to apply the law (a few states tell jurors that they may follow their conscience), but they do not always understand what the law is. Their failure to understand the law is excusable. Think how you would feel if you were told that you had to decide whether the defendant's acts were the "proximate cause" of the plaintiff's injuries and then were read these standard jury instructions from Michigan:

When I use the words "proximate cause" I mean first, that

there must have been a connection between the conduct of
___ which plaintiff claims was negligent and the injury
complained of by the plaintiff, and second, that the occurrence which is claimed to have produced that injury was a
natural and probable result of such conduct of ___.

There may be more than one proximate cause. To be a proximate cause, the claimed negligence of the ___ need not be the
only cause nor the last cause. A cause may be proximate
although it and another cause act at the same time or in
combination to produce the occurrence.

You may decide that the conduct of neither, one or both of the
defendants was a proximate cause. If you decide that one of
the defendants was negligent and that such negligence was
a proximate cause of the occurrence, it is not a defense that
the conduct of the defendant also may have been a cause of
the occurrence. Each defendant is entitled to separate consideration as to whether his conduct was a proximate cause
of the occurrence.[10]

Proximate cause is legal cause, not actual cause. A war
may be lost for want of a nail, but the nail would not be the
legal cause of the defeat. Proximate cause is a complicated
issue, and it is not likely that a juror (even if the juror were
an attorney) could understand what the law means by listening to the instructions. Pity the poor juror who may hear
hours (even days) of such instructions and then is told to
remember what the law is and apply it to the facts at issue
(jurors usually are not given copies of the instructions to
read). As Judge Jerome Frank wrote in *Courts on Trial*:

> ...often [the jurors] cannot understand what the judge tells
> them about the legal rules. To comprehend the meaning of
> many a legal rule requires special training. It is inconceiva-
> ble that a body of twelve ordinary men, casually gathered
> together for a few days, could, merely from listening to the
> instructions of the judge, gain the knowledge to grasp the
> true import of the judge's words.[11]

Federal Judge Irving R. Kaufman has expressed concern

that jurors in defamation suits are undermining constitutional protections of the press:

> The trial judge's efforts to explain the constitutional definition of 'malice,' 'public figure,' 'actual injury,' and the like notwithstanding, I have little doubt that these elaborate instructions are lost upon even the most conscientious jury. At best, a juror can be expected to rely on common-sense notions of fairness. In the usual case, the award represents a rough monetary accommodation of the claim for compensation weighed against the media's culpability. At worst, a jury will permit its verdict to reflect its disapproval of the views espoused by the defendant or its frustration with the state of the world or national affairs reported by the media generally. In any event, the verdict is largely uninfluenced by the constitutional imperative of an unrestrained press....[12]

Suits do not just involve complicated legal issues. They can also involve complicated statistics, psychological theories, and accounting principles—all beyond the grasp of the average juror, who ends up relying more on the credibility of witnesses and lawyers than on what is actually said in court.

People with the knowledge to understand complicated disputes rarely are selected to serve on juries. Often they manage to get excused from jury service, and, if they try to serve on a jury, lawyers are likely to eliminate them with their peremptory challenges. Peremptory challenges allow lawyers to prevent a certain number of people—three in federal civil cases—from becoming jurors without having to give a reason for excusing them. Other prospective jurors can be excused "for cause" (if they indicate bias or do not meet minimum age, citizenship, residence, and education requirements).

Lawyers do not ask for juries because they believe jurors will be fairer than a judge. They ask for jury trials because they believe juries will favor their clients. According to Irving Goldstein and Fred Lane in their highly respected *Goldstein Trial Technique*, jury trials should be requested whenever the "natural sympathies of a jury will favor the client."[13] Juries are generally more susceptible to appeals to prejudice and sympathy. In fact, prejudice has sometimes been called the "thirteenth juror." Frequently large verdicts awarded in personal injury and defamation suits are motivated as much by sympathy for an injured plaintiff as by the rules for assessing damages. Notwithstanding the usual instruction by the court that the jurors should not come to any conclusions until they have heard all the evidence, jurors quickly form judgments based on the conduct and appearance of the plaintiff and defendant. The persuasiveness and charisma of a lawyer also weigh heavily on the balance of a juror's judgment.

Psychological research, which views jurors as people governed by their environment and genes, not as people able to make free choices, has caused greater consternation for critics of the jury system. Trial lawyers have always believed that the social background of people can be used to predict how they will decide a case. For example, *Goldstein Trial Technique*[14] recommends that the Irish, Jews, and Italians be chosen if a lawyer is representing a plaintiff in a personal injury case since they tend to respond favorably to emotional appeals. Blacks are also considered sympathetic to plaintiffs. Germans, the English, and Scandinavians are recommended as jurors for the defendant. So are bankers, farmers, accountants, engineers, and school teachers. I always liked to have a Jew on the jury to make certain that there was at least one person who would not be prejudiced against me and/or my client. Lawyers have also been told to look at body types.[15] Ectomorphs, lean, underweight people with fragile features, are said to favor plaintiffs. Mesomorphs, people with athletic bodies but who seem older than their age, are said to favor the side with the facts in its favor. People with small eyes are supposed to be unemotional. People with full lips are supposed to be emotional. Critics of the jury system are concerned with the new psychosocial research because they are afraid that lawyers will be able to use its research principles to choose a jury that will return a favorable verdict—even if a favorable verdict is not deserved.

Selecting juries is time consuming. In many cases it takes longer to pick a jury than to try the case itself. In one reported case, it took more than nine months to select the jury.[16] Questioning may be done by lawyers, judges, or both, depending on what the court rules provide. Questioning of jurors is usually very exhaustive. Such probing is ostensibly for the purpose of unearthing a juror's possible prejudices and competence to judge fairly and objectively. But lawyers spend much time on jury selection because many believe that the case is decided by the time the jurors are chosen.

New methods used to select juries (some lawyers even have been using psychics to help them select jurors) are dramatically increasing the cost of jury trials, already more costly than bench trials since they take longer to complete. In bench trials obviously no time is spent selecting a jury or deciding what evidence can be heard by jurors. Lawyers have started consulting experts to develop a profile of the ideal juror for the parties they represent. In one recent murder trial, consultants advised attorneys for the defendant to look for jurors who were intelligent, since the defense was complicated, and content with their station in life, since the defendant was a millionaire. In other cases, attitudes of the local community have been surveyed to see what types of jurors should be selected. This research, according to Morton Hunt, author of *The Universe Within*,

> assumes that certain juror characteristics are *likely* to yield certain kinds of juror behavior. If a survey shows that 92 percent of middle-class whites in a given town believe that the police rarely do wrong, while 89 percent of lower-class blacks believe the opposite, there is a 92 percent chance that any middle-class white juror will be pro-police and an 89 percent chance that any lower-class black juror will not.[17]

Since jurors tend to conceal or deny prejudice towards a litigant when they are questioned in court, experts have been hired to observe nonverbal communication. Experts also have been asked to assist lawyers in developing questions that will uncover bias. Hunt reported a Boston rape

trial where anti-black feelings were revealed by questions
asking prospective jurors how they felt about their neighborhood.[18] Even handwriting experts have been called in to
reveal prospective jurors' personalities.

After a jury has been selected, some lawyers have been
selecting mock juries reflecting the social characteristics of
the real jury and have used these juries to test arguments
they plan to make to the real jury. By observing mock
jurors' reactions to various arguments and evidence and by
thoroughly questioning them about what they heard and
observed, lawyers can decide what they will have to do to
persuade the real jurors that their clients should win.

Use of the foregoing techniques undermines the view of
jurors as the best dispensers of justice. Instead, a jury trial
becomes one more tool for the wealthy to subvert "justice."
These tools are not just costly to poorer litigants. They are
costly to all members of society since jury trials are expensive and time-consuming and confidence in the legal system's ability to mete out justice is already in short supply.

Defenders of jury trials point out that judges also are
biased by their upbringing and background. They note that
judges, although less susceptible than jurors to emotional
appeals, can be faulted for becoming hardened and unable
to apply the "spirit" of the law. They believe that jury
service educates citizens and promotes confidence in the
legal system, that juries are better fact-finders than judges,
and that juries shield judges from unpopular decisions.
Critics dispute the truth of these assertions and emphasize
the cost of jury trials to society and individuals—both in
money and in justice.

Many suggestions, short of abolishing juries, have been
made to improve the present system:

1. There should be greater use of blue ribbon jury panels
   (people specially qualified to hear complicated trials).
2. A three-judge panel should be substituted in complicated cases for the conventional jury.
3. Trial judges should be permitted to do more of the

questioning of prospective jurors. Trial lawyers vehemently object to this suggestion since they believe that lawyers, because they have a better knowledge of their cases than judges and know what biases might affect the jury's decision, can better uncover biased jurors.

4. Settlement of litigation and perhaps resolution by binding arbitration or mediation should be encouraged.
5. The extra costs of a jury trial should be assessed to the losing party.
6. Self-restraint by lawyers should be encouraged.

These are just some of the suggestions for eliminating problems with jury trials. My suggestion that we experiment with a panel of experts system of justice, discussed in Chapter 5, would preserve the notion of a jury but make the jurors especially qualified to decide the dispute. My experience has convinced me that the jury system is a basic guarantee of fairness and that, on the whole, jury trials result in substantial justice. Nevertheless, much can be done to limit and perhaps eliminate many of the problems with the jury system. Any change will take a long time, particularly since the right to jury trial is enshrined by the Constitution and embedded in our traditions.

Chapter 7

Arbitration and Mediation
and the Resolution of Conflict

> *To fulfill our traditional obligation
> means that we should provide
> mechanisms that can produce an
> acceptable result in the shortest
> possible time, with the least possi-
> ble expense and with a minimum of
> stress on the participants. That is
> what justice is all about.... What we
> must have, I submit, is a compre-
> hensive review of the whole subject
> of alternatives, with special em-
> phasis on arbitration.*
>
> Chief Justice Warren E. Burger[1]

ARBITRATION

As litigation has become more costly and time consuming, people have begun to take alternative paths to "justice." Two of these paths are arbitration and mediation. In arbitration, disputants agree to have a neutral third person or persons (arbitrators) resolve their dispute. The arbitrator's decision is final and can be enforced by the courts. This is in contrast to mediation, where the parties agree to have a neutral third person (mediator) help them resolve their dispute, but they do not promise to accept the mediator's recommendations. An arbitrator resolves a dispute; a mediator can only recommend a resolution.

Arbitration is not a modern development. In ancient Greece, arbitrators were used to resolve disputes.[2] Courts would not get involved in a controversy unless people refused to accept an arbitrator's decision. Medieval merchants resolved controversies through arbitration. George Washington directed in his will that "three impartial and intelligent men, known for their probity and good understanding," would resolve any disputes his heirs might have over the distribution of his property.[3] Arbitration also has been used to resolve international conflicts. During the Renaissance, the Pope often arbitrated international disputes. The Jay Treaty of 1794 established arbitral commissions to settle controversies between the United States and Great Britain left over from the American Revolution.

For centuries courts were hostile to arbitration, which they viewed as a threat to their power, and would refuse to require arbitration, even if those involved had agreed to do so. The first statute giving courts the power to enforce arbitration agreements was the English Arbitration Act of 1889. The first state to give courts that power was New York in 1920. Now if disputants have agreed to arbitration, most states provide that courts can require them to abide by their agreements. Many states even *require* parties to arbitrate certain types of disputes. For example, arbitration is often required to resolve labor disputes. Arbitration also has been required for certain other types of disputes, such as medical malpractice claims and small civil claims. Compulsory arbitration has been used to avoid strikes, clear court con-

gestion, and take controversies (such as medical malpractice claims) out of the hands of juries and give them to
people with more expertise about the controversy (who pre-
sumably will be less likely to be swayed by sympathy than
jurors and will award less money as damages).

Arbitration was a strange animal to me when I started
practicing law. I did not learn about it in law school.
Instead, I was conditioned to treat all disputes as contests
ultimately to be fought in court. As I matured as a lawyer, I
realized that litigation is costly and time consuming and
that it is better to settle as many disputes as possible. I got
involved as an arbitrator in a labor dispute and immediately realized how valuable arbitration can be for resolving disputes quickly and minimizing the hard feelings that
often result from prolonged and hard-fought litigation.

I became an arbitrator associated with the American
Arbitration Association, a nationally known nonprofit
organization heavily involved in administering all types of
arbitration. Many of the cases I have arbitrated involved
grievances by employees against employers and vice versa.
The cases involved such things as complaints about drink-
ing on the job, the use of vile language, or carelessness in
performing work. I have also acted as arbitrator in a
number of commercial arbitration cases, usually involving
the interpretation of a contract. Arbitration was a labor of
love for me. I have found the experience personally stimulating and helpful to clients, and I have often recommended
that clients make use of it instead of going to court.

Almost always, clients have been satisfied with the
procedure. Some, of course, have been disappointed at losing, but even the losers have been satisfied that their loss
did not cost as much or take as long as a judicial trial. Most
clients want a quick and fair resolution of a dispute, and
that is what arbitration gives them. Lawyers initially resisted arbitration because it deprived them of bigger fees,
but over the years more and more of them have realized how
valuable it can be, particularly in labor and commercial
matters, where quick resolution of a dispute is so important.

Disputants can agree to arbitrate an existing dispute or future disputes. I routinely have included an arbitration clause in contracts. A standard paragraph in a contract calling for the parties to arbitrate future conflicts commonly reads:

> Any controversy or claim arising out of or relating to this contract, or the breach thereof, shall be settled by arbitration in accordance with the Commercial Arbitration Rules of the American Arbitration Association, and judgment upon the award rendered by the arbitrator(s) may be entered in any court having jurisdiction thereof.[4]

When there is a controversy to arbitrate, a neutral third party has to be selected by the disputants. Any number of people can be chosen as arbitrators. Disputants may agree on one person or might each agree on one arbitrator and have those two arbitrators choose a third. The American Arbitration Association will supply a list of prospective arbitrators (usually consisting of ten names). Names that people object to are crossed off the list, and the rest are ranked in order of preference. In those few instances when no one is a satisfactory choice, the American Arbitration Association will appoint an arbitrator.

Arbitrators are often retired or practicing attorneys and judges. Key qualifications are their neutrality, ability, and expertise. The expertise of arbitrators is considered one of the plusses of that form of dispute resolution. As Judge Learned Hand once wrote, "In trade disputes one of the chief advantages of arbitration is that arbitrators can be chosen who are familiar with the practices and customs of the calling...."[5] Time and money do not need to be spent educating arbitrators about the environment in which a dispute arose (as has to be done for jurors, who are chosen for their lack of expertise), and disputants can be confident that the arbitrator understands their situations and points of view.

How arbitration is conducted depends on what the disputants want to do. Usually the parties are represented by lawyers and present evidence at a hearing, but they do not have to have a lawyer or hold a hearing. The strict rules of evidence applied in a court of law to keep certain information away from the jury are relaxed in an arbitration hearing. Arbitrators may ignore court-established rules of law and just reach a decision that they consider is "fair," based on the evidence. This "fairness" was what Aristotle viewed as the great virtue of arbitration: "an arbitrator goes by the equity of a case, a judge by the strict law, and arbitration was invented for the express purpose of securing full power for equity."[6]

Hard cases will not make bad law in an arbitration proceeding because arbitrators, unlike judges, can reach a "fair" result without worrying that they have to enunciate a rule of law that will apply to thousands of similar cases. This flexibility in reaching results is also one of the disadvantages of arbitration. Since arbitrators do not need to give reasons for their decision or publish the award or even prepare a transcript of the hearing unless the parties request them to (which they usually do not since they do not want their dispute to be public knowledge), there are no guidelines for future conduct by people in similar circumstances. Decisions are less predictable since there are not volumes of reasoned precedents covering similar situations.

Hearings may be held in the hearing rooms of the American Arbitration Association or some other place convenient to the parties, frequently where one of the parties works to make it easier to present evidence. After hearing all the evidence, the arbitrator renders a decision. The decision may be made at the end of the hearing or a short time afterwards. If the arbitrator is from the American Arbitration Association, then the decision is forwarded to that association for distribution to the parties. If the parties do not agree with the decision, they have little recourse. The decision usually may not be appealed to a court unless the arbitrator was guilty of fraud or some other misconduct. A court will not set aside an arbitrator's decision because of a mistake about a fact or the governing law.

Arbitration is designed for those who want an inexpensive, quick, private resolution of a dispute. Business executives find arbitration particularly useful because they tend to want quick, private resolution of disputes and tend to be less concerned about vindicating a principle. Vindication can be counterproductive since it can ruin a business relationship by creating hard feelings. Ending a dispute amicably and quickly can be more important than the actual result.

Many people praise arbitrators for meting out "fairer" results than courts of law. It has been my experience that arbitrators are better able to smooth out the rough edges of a law than courts, but arbitrators' dependence on those rules of law tends to be underestimated. Arbitrators need those rules of law as a guide and foundation for their decisions. If there were no courts, there would be no "reasoned precedents," just decisions by individuals, and, as those decisions became unreined by any rule of law, "justice" would become arbitrary. Praise for decisions because they were based on all the individual circumstances of a case would turn into condemnation of their "unpredictablity" and "injustice."

Arbitration works because there are courts of law painstakingly developing rules of law that arbitrators can use as guidelines for their decisions. Without those rules of law, there would be danger that justice might become arbitrary. Arbitration remedies certain deficiencies in our system of justice, but it is no substitute for that system.

MEDIATION

Mediation is quite different from arbitration. Disputing parties meet with a neutral mediator to discuss points on which they agree and disagree, with the objective of reaching a settlement acceptable to both parties. The parties do the bargaining. The mediator, unlike a judge or arbitrator, does not decide how a controversy should be resolved;

instead, the mediator tries to guide the parties to a full understanding of their dispute and a resolution short of litigation. The mediator does this by helping the parties fully consider all reasonable alternatives in an atmosphere conducive to good faith negotiation.

When mediation is successful, the parties usually have a sense of self-satisfaction because they have been able to resolve their dispute by themselves without having to have a solution imposed on them by a judge—a "solution" that might be unsatisfactory to both parties.

Mediation also can be a satisfying experience for the mediator. I was a mediator on the approved list for the United States Mediation Service (set up by the Department of Labor), and I enjoyed the experience more than my experiences as an arbitrator since I was able to take an active role in resolving disputes. As an arbitrator, I was a pseudo-judge. I had to be detached, and I had to rule one way or the other. There were some instances, however, when, during a recess in the arbitration proceedings, I was able to suggest a reasonable basis for resolving a dispute that the parties were able to accept. As a mediator I could partake in the creative process of resolving a dispute to the satisfaction of all parties, not just one—or none.

There are no formalities in mediation. The mediator sits down with the disputants in a relaxed atmosphere. A mediator does not intimidate disputants with the aura of a judge, but the threat of eventually having to turn the conflict over to a judge is ever present. Parties know that if they cannot reach an accommodation, then an accommodation will be imposed on them by a judge. In litigation only one side can be a winner; in mediation, both sides can be winners.

It has been my experience that many people pursue litigation because they want someone to listen to them and tell them that they are right; mediation gives them that opportunity. Litigation limits what people can say. Many of their grievances cannot be aired because they are not "relevant" to the issue before the court. Courts will not let spouses go into detail why they hate each other, but coming to grips with that emotion during mediation can make it easier to resolve disputes over such things as child custody, support, and visitation. In mediation, people can vent their pent-up emotions and tell the mediator how they were wronged by that "s.o.b." Giving parents the opportunity to talk out problems and vent their anger makes it less likely that children will be caught in a war between their parents. Avoiding bitter battles over children can minimize emotional damage to the children. For these reasons, several states require mediation in child custody and support cases before allowing a matter to go to court.

Mediation only can work if there is some middle ground satisfactory to both parties. If there is no middle ground, say, for instance, when environmental groups are fighting development of certain property and will not be satisfied with a compromise that will permit a project to be built but subject to certain restraints, then mediation will not succeed. That is not to say that mediation cannot be effective in environmental disputes. When environmental disputes end up in a courtroom, it is usually to resolve a narrow issue of law, such as whether all alternatives were given serious consideration by a governmental agency or whether an environmental impact statement was sufficient or whether hearings by a governmental agency were proper. A courtroom victory may give environmental groups more breathing room, but it usually does not address the groups' substantive concern, which is whether or how a dam will be built or a highway constructed. Mediation enables environmental groups to raise those issues and try to work out a mutually satisfactory resolution of a problem.

Who are mediators? They can be anyone the parties agree on, but usually they are lawyers, psychologists, social workers, marriage counselors, or others specializing in mental health problems. The American Arbitration Association has a referral service for mediators. All of these people, but lawyers in particular, face the dilemma of violating professional ethics by dealing with more than one party. For this reason, some have advocated that there be more than one mediator.

Mediators not only must be good interviewers. They also must have a good understanding of interpersonal dynamics and an ability to be nonjudgmental. They must be able to treat people fairly and with dignity. They must be sympathetic so that they can encourage trust, yet detached enough to see where compromise is possible. Legal expertise may be an important qualification, particularly when people need to know the tax consequences of any agreement they reach (particularly important in divorces). Finding a person with all these qualifications can be difficult since anyone can call himself or herself a mediator, and people can be certified as mediators with as little as a week of formal training.

It is not enough for a mediator to get the parties to agree on one way of resolving their dispute. The mediator must have a good understanding of the emotional needs of the parties and must guide the parties to a resolution that makes everyone feel like a winner. Mediators do not perform their job if they gang up with one party and bully the other party into an agreement. Nor do they perform their job if they let themselves be drawn in by the superior negotiating skills of one party (particularly a problem in divorces since women have tended to be less experienced in bargaining and less knowledgeable about financial affairs). Problems of this nature have led some to advocate separate mediators for each party.

When mediators do their job well, they satisfy the needs of the disputants, avoid the acrimony that so often accompanies a judicial resolution of a controversy, and give the parties a fighting chance of continuing a personal or business relationship. Too many lawyers, unfortunately, have managed to overlook these benefits and have resisted mediation because it lowers their fees.

To relieve crowded court calendars and reduce the amount of time it takes a case to come to trial, many court systems, especially in urban communities, have been experimenting with what is known as judicial mediation. After a suit is filed, a judge calls the disputants together and tries to get them to resolve their controversy. Judges have worried that such conferences would waste their time, but initial results have shown that judges can resolve more disputes through mediation than through trials.

For example, trials scheduled to last more than one day in the Superior Court of California, County of Riverside, used to be held about two years after a request for a trial was filed. But, in just ten months, a judge assigned to spend all of his time mediating disputes was able to eliminate the chronic backlog. During the same amount of time that he helped settle 614 cases, all the other judges held 108 trials. According to Judge Elwood M. Rich, who described his court's successful experiment, "A settlement conference judge can settle more cases in two weeks by the mediation method than a trial judge can handle by the trial method in a year."[7]

How do litigants feel about mediation? Great, according to Judge Rich:

> Litigants overwhelmingly prefer the settlement method. Trials are expensive, time consuming, uncertain in outcome, and anxiety provoking. Even after a trial, there are the possibilities of a motion for a new trial and an appeal. Settlement conferences are inexpensive, don't take much time, and enable the attorneys and parties to negotiate their own settlement with the help of a judicial mediator. They escape the agony of having a decision imposed on them by participating in the working out of their own decision by the settlement process. And there is no motion for a new trial or an appeal.[8]

Mediation is now an established alternative to litigation in small claims matters, matrimonial disputes, and many other civil cases. Increasingly, states have been funding mediation, even making it mandatory (e.g., for divorces), and, though resisting it at first, the legal profession has begun to accept mediation in lieu of hotly contested court trials. Many people and businesses have been obligating themselves in writing to first mediate any disputes before turning to an arbitrator or the courts.

Not all disputes can be successfully mediated, but those that can should be. Mediation can resolve disputes more quickly and at less expense than litigation. When people settle their own disputes, they are more likely to be pleased with the results and adhere to their agreement. Communities also can benefit. By giving people a sense of having the power to control their own conflicts, mediation can instill in people a sense of pride, cooperation, and responsibility to themselves and their community.

Courts are an imperfect mechanism for resolving disputes. They do their best to mete out "justice," but they cannot meet all the needs of the people forced to use them. People resort to litigation for many different reasons, and only they can decide what "justice" is in a particular situation. People go to court when communication breaks down and a resolution short of physical combat is desired. Mediation reopens communication and makes "justice" more human.

Chapter 8

United States Supreme Court and the Constitution

> *In no other nation on earth does a group of judges hold the sweeping political power—the privilege in practice, not just in theory, of saying the last governmental word— that is held by the nine U.S. Supreme Court Justices.*
>
> Fred Rodell[1]

Although decisions made by the United States Supreme Court can have far-reaching consequences on our lives (e.g., the decisions outlawing segregation and permitting abortions), most people have little interest in how the court makes those decisions. Occasionally there is a hullabaloo about a particular result, but most Americans do not understand how the Supreme Court operates or have any opinion about what role the Supreme Court has and should have in this society. For the past few presidential elections, Democrats and Republicans have argued that their opponent's candidate will choose Supreme Court justices who will do irreparable harm to the country by reversing good precedents established by the Supreme Court, but most people dismiss such arguments as part of the rhetorical excesses of a political campaign.

I will never forget the excitement I felt on my first trip to Washington, D.C., at age 25, especially when I visited the United States Supreme Court in session and sat on the edge of my seat listening to Benjamin Cardozo, Louis Brandeis, Charles Hughes, and the other justices sharply question counsel during their arguments. The Supreme Court I read about in U.S. history courses and whose decisions we studied in law school came alive. What a thrill it was when I got a chance to be one of those lawyers appearing in a case before the United States Supreme Court. The case involved the "earth-shaking" issue of whether a pinball machine (not a slot machine) was a gambling device subject to a $250 federal excise tax instead of a $25 tax. It was disappointing to be on the losing end of a 5 to 4 decision. But even in defeat my respect for the Supreme Court remained high. After all, four justices had thought our arguments were correct. In retrospect, it seems a shame that the Supreme Court spent any time on such an insignificant issue.

Generally speaking, the Supreme Court's function has been to make certain that the federal and state governments do not exceed the limitations imposed on them by the Constitution. Simply stated, it does this by acting as final arbiter in determining whether particular laws or actions by the Federal and state governments violate the Constitution. The court's basic challenge has been to preserve the balances between Congress and the president, the federal government and state governments, one state and another, federal and state governments and the people, and the majority and the individual. It has met this challenge by breathing life and new meaning into a constitution designed for an agrarian society that has become the most developed industrial, commercial, and military power in the world, a nation that once isolated itself from the rest of the world but which is now inextricably intertwined with countries all over the globe.

The Supreme Court has touched all phases of American life, getting involved in everything from the beginning of life to death. For example, the court has decided what rights women have to abort fetuses, how police must behave toward suspected criminals, how far government can intrude on our privacy, what restrictions may be imposed on our right to vote, how the evils of racial discrimination can be remedied, what restrictions the government can place on our right to earn a livelihood, and much more.

In the past few decades there has been much criticism of the Supreme Court, but criticism is not a recent phenomenon. In the early 1800's, Jeffersonians tried to impeach justices who bucked their policies. In 1912 the Progressive Party advocated that judicial decisions be made by popular vote.

What is new about this criticism is its source. As recently as the early 1950's, Fred Rodell criticized the Supreme Court justices because they "inevitably act as a check, a lag, on the forward momentum of government...."[2] More recently, conservatives have criticized the Supreme Court, particularly the Warren Court, for stepping ahead of Congress and the popular will, and liberals have become concerned that a conservative president will get the opportunity to appoint enough justices to reverse liberal gains over the past few decades.

During the late 19th and early 20th century, the Supreme Court blocked laws designed to regulate business and promote social change. Laws regulating child labor, setting minimum wages, and fixing maximum working hours all were declared unconstitutional. So was the first income tax law. So much New Deal legislation was struck down (e.g., the Supreme Court ruled that Congress had no power to regulate agriculture) that President Franklin Delano Roosevelt made an ill-fated attempt in 1937 to "pack" the court with appointees who would support his policies.

The Supreme Court's role as guardian of the rights of the individual was not assumed until this century. It was not until 1925 that the court even intimated that any portion of the Bill of Rights protected individuals from state action. 1931 was the first time that a state law abridging the First Amendment guarantees of freedom of speech and freedom of the press was struck down. The First Amendment's guarantee of the free exercise of religion was first applied to invalidate a state law in 1940. People were not given a right to counsel in state criminal trials until 1963.

Although the Supreme Court is now the most powerful court in the world, that was not always true. Only three of the first six justices (the Supreme Court started with six members; the number set by Congress has ranged from five to ten over the years) attended the court's first session on February 1, 1790, and the justices did not decide their first case until 1793. Their first major decision, *Chisholm v. Georgia*, was reversed by passage of the Eleventh Amendment. John Rutledge, one of the original justices, resigned in 1791 to become chief justice of the supreme court of South Carolina, which he considered to be a more prestigious position. Two men who were offered Rutledge's seat on the court declined because they preferred to remain state legislators. Chief Justice John Jay described life as a justice as "intolerable" and refused reappointment as Chief Justice (he resigned in 1795 to become governor of New York) because "I left the bench perfectly convinced that under a system so defective it would not obtain the energy, weight, and dignity which was essential to its affording due support to the national government; nor acquire the public confidence and respect which, as the last resort of the justice of the nation, it should possess."[3]

Unlike Articles I and II of the Constitution, which detail the powers of Congress and the president, Article III merely outlines the role of the federal judiciary: "The judicial Power of the United States, shall be vested in one Supreme Court, and in such inferior Courts as the Congress may from time to time ordain and establish."

At first the federal court system consisted of thirteen district courts, six circuit courts, and the Supreme Court. Supreme Court justices had to "ride the circuits" since they sat as judges on the circuit courts (it was not until 1911 that Supreme Court justices were relieved of all their circuit court duties). Riding the circuits was burdensome. One justice had to travel more than 10,000 miles in 1838—before planes or cars.[4]

John Marshall, Chief Justice of the Supreme Court from 1801 to 1835, was instrumental in making the court the power it is today. As Alexander Bickel wrote in *The Least Dangerous Branch*:

> Congress was created very nearly full blown by the Constitution itself. The vast possibilities of the presidency were relatively easy to perceive and soon, inevitably, materialized. But the institution of the judiciary needed to be summoned up out of the constitutional vapors, shaped and maintained; and the Great Chief Justice, John Marshall—not singlehanded, but first and foremost—was there to do it and did.[5]

So persuasive were his opinions (he started the practice of having one opinion for the court instead of separate opinions by each justice) that even one detractor had to admit, "All wrong, all wrong, but no man in the United States can tell why or wherein."[6] Fittingly, legend has it that the Liberty Bell cracked while tolling in mourning of John Marshall's death.

The Marshall Court's key contribution to the growth of judicial power was its assertion of the Supreme Court's right to nullify acts of Congress and the states. Nowhere in the Constitution is the Supreme Court specifically given that power. But the court's power to do so was inferred from Article VI of the Constitution, which makes the Constitution the "supreme Law of the Land." As Marshall wrote in *Marbury v. Madison*, decided in 1803:

> The judicial power of the United States is extended to all

cases arising under the constitution. Could it be the intention of those who gave this power, to say, that in using it, the
constitution should not be looked into? That a case arising
under the constitution should be decided without examining
the instrument under which it arises? This is too extrava-
gant to be maintained.[7]

In 1816 the Marshall Court ruled that the Supreme Court
has the power to review and overrule state court decisions.

Alexander Hamilton justified this notion of judicial
review as necessary to keep the rest of our federal system in
check. Starting with the premise that the Constitution
reflects the will of the people, Hamilton argued in *The Federalist Papers* that "the courts were designed to be an
intermediate body between the people and the legislature,
in order, among other things, to keep the latter within the
limits assigned to their authority."[8] Hamilton did not feel
that this power made the Supreme Court superior to Congress. On the contrary: "It only supposes that the power of
the people is superior to both...."[9] Most scholars of constitutional history agree that the framers of the Constitution
intended the Supreme Court to have the power to nullify
acts of Congress and state law. State courts had already
been voiding state laws that violated state constitutions, so
the concept of judicial review was well-recognized. Besides,
the Founding Fathers' fear of the tyranny of the majority
made it important to have an independent judiciary to protect the rights of the minority. Independence has been
assured by giving justices their jobs for life.

The power this gives the Supreme Court should not be
underestimated. As Thomas Jefferson complained: "The
Constitution, on this hypothesis, is a mere thing of wax in
the hands of the judiciary, which they may twist and shape
into any form they please."[10] Justice Harlan F. Stone recognized the power of having the last word when he said "the
only check on our own exercise of power is our own sense of
self-restraint."[11]

Most people believe—and are encouraged in that belief by
the courts—that law is carved in stone and only needs to be

read to be understood. Most people have confidence in the Supreme Court's ability to "correctly" read the Constitution because members of the court are "above politics."

In reality, the Constitution merely outlines the power of the federal government and is filled with words like *commerce, due process, liberty,* and *equal protection* that can be twisted to rationalize any result the court wants to reach. Nowhere in the Constitution are *Miranda* warnings spelled out. Nor does the Constitution say anything about "one person, one vote." Conservative judges can find one meaning in the Constitution, and liberal judges can find something completely different. That is why presidents and Congress are so concerned about who is appointed to the Supreme Court. They want justices who will agree with their interpretation of the Constitution. As Chief Justice William H. Rehnquist has said, "Presidents who have been sensible of the broad powers which they have possessed, and been willing to exercise those powers, have all but invariably tried to have some influence on the philosophy of the Court as a result of their appointments to that body."[12]

Sometimes they are successful, and sometimes they are not. Teddy Roosevelt's feelings about one of his appointees, Oliver Wendell Holmes, Jr., were that someone "could carve out a banana a Judge with more backbone than that!"[13] When Dwight D. Eisenhower was asked if he had made any mistakes while he was president, he replied, "Yes, two, and they are both sitting on the Supreme Court."[14] He was referring to Earl Warren and William J. Brennan, Jr., two of the ablest justices to serve on the Supreme Court.

The Brethren, by Bob Woodward and Scott Armstrong, provides many examples of justices who decided what a result should be and then looked at the Constitution to decide how to justify that result. Their description of the deliberations over *Roe v. Wade*, which legalized abortions during the first two trimesters of pregnancy, pictures justices "openly brokering their decision like a group of legislators."[15] When the court nullified all existing death penalty statutes in 1972 because it felt that judges and juries had been given too much discretion, justices argued about whether or not there *should* be a death penalty, not whether the Constitution had been violated (interestingly, at least two members of the court mistakenly believed that they had ended death penalties in this country).[16] *The Brethren* demonstrates how the upbringing and personal attitudes of justices have a great influence on their decisions.

In recent years, many have praised the way justices have exercised their discretion to rewrite the meaning of the Constitution. Erwin N. Griswold, a former Solicitor General, has praised the court as the "conscience of the country."[17] Others, even when they have agreed with the results of a decision, have expressed concern with the Supreme Court's willingness to give a meaning to the Constitution that the Founding Fathers never imagined, let alone intended. As Raoul Berger, when he was a professor of law at Harvard Law School, commented:

> What the "national conscience" is at any given moment depends on shifting personnel and the nature of the appointees. The replacement of one or two justices may result in a complete reversal of the prevailing conscience.... How can we put our trust in a conscience that changes color with every judicial succession, itself subject to shifting political winds?[18]

How true Berger's comment is can be seen from statements by liberals who fear a conservative turn by the court. Those who applauded a "liberal" conscience now fear what a "conservative" conscience will do to the country.

Critics of an "activist" Supreme Court would prefer that it limit itself to "policing" the other branches of the federal government and state governments (where "policing" stops and "policy-making" begins is not clear). Those critics usually do not object to "liberal" court interpretations, such as of the Commerce Clause, that have greatly expanded the power of Congress and the president well beyond the role envisioned by the Founding Fathers. There is little objection to those changes in the Constitution because theoretically Congress and the president are controlled by popular will. Those institutions theoretically reflect the will of the people and have the resources to make intelligent decisions about public policy—resources that courts lack. What these critics (not to be confused with "strict constructionists," who often want an "activist" Supreme Court, but with different results), find most objectionable are decisions that expand the rights of individuals (e.g., requiring police to inform people they have arrested of certain constitutional rights; recognizing a right to privacy), the types of rights that tend to be protected only by the Supreme Court.

As with many other aspects of life, a balance must be drawn between a court that acts like a legislature and a court locked into past decisions. By now liberals and conservatives should know that it is best for courts in general to avoid policy-making since liberal policy-making can suddenly become conservative policy-making and vice versa. But that does not mean that the court should never make policy, only that it should intervene when decisions cannot be made by the other branches of government. Certain changes in our society, particularly those securing the rights of the minority against the tyranny of the majority, probably can only be made by the Supreme Court. Legislators could not be expected to redraw the boundaries of their districts to make sure each person has one vote—not if that would risk the loss of the legislators' seats. And who can realistically expect public clamor for laws banning censorship of communists, guaranteeing counsel for alleged criminals, or calling for desegregation? The tremendous growth of the federal government has made it necessary for some institution to look out for the rights of the individual, and the Supreme Court has filled the bill in the 20th century.

Few would argue that the Supreme Court has made some bad policy decisions (e.g., the *Dred Scott* decision, where the court decided that Congress had no power to halt the spread of slavery; *Plessy v. Ferguson*, where the court okayed "separate but equal" facilities for blacks), but so have the other two branches of the federal government. That is why we have a system of checks and balances. The court's willingness to reverse itself—more than 100 times so far—shows that it is not locked into mistakes.

The real fear of those opposing an "activist" court is that there are no effective checks on the court. True, only one justice has ever been impeached (and he was not convicted), and it is very difficult to pass a constitutional amendment to overrule a Supreme Court decision (it has been done only four times so far, most notably to reverse the *Dred Scott* decision and to make income taxes constitutional), but both steps could be taken if the Supreme Court convinced the public that it had abused its power.

Though its effect is denied by many, public opinion is an important check on the court. The court's doctrine of judicial self-restraint, which limits the types of decisions the court will make, helps the court conserve its "credits" with the public. Cynics have criticized the court for following the election returns, but it should be comforting to know that the court is leery of straying too far afield from public sentiment. Change is necessary, but there must be groundwork for that change. The Supreme Court survived the controversy over its school desegregation cases because the racial attitudes of the country in the 1950's were more tolerant than they were in the 1890's. During Roosevelt's administration, when it became clear that the public wanted New Deal legislation, the court did a sudden about-face and approved it. Throughout the court's history, there have been attempts to limit its power (e.g., there have been bills to require an extraordinary majority before a law could be invalidated as unconstitutional, and there has been legislation to take away the court's power to make decisions in certain types of cases), but public outcry has never involved enough citizens to carry the day.

Ironically, at the same time people have been concerned with the court's power to make final decisions, there also has been concern that there are so many cases on the court's docket that it cannot make enough final decisions. In 1850, the court had to consider 253 cases. That number increased to 723 in 1900 and 1,321 in 1950, and then exploded past 4,000 in recent years. Some have advocated the creation of a national appellate court (sometimes called an "Intercircuit Tribunal") to relieve the Supreme Court of some of its burdens and give it a chance to hear important cases it now has to ignore because of lack of time. One proposal would have the national appellate court resolve conflicting decisions among the courts of appeals. Twenty to thirty percent of the cases that the Supreme Court hears involve such conflicts. Such a new court has been opposed by many court-of-appeals judges, who do not want another court to tell them they are wrong and do not want their prestige reduced.

Many have blamed the Supreme Court for mishandling its workload. Former Justice Arthur Goldberg has attributed the workload crisis to the justices' poor choices in selecting which cases to decide.[19] He feels that the court has been deciding too many unimportant cases. He also has argued that the court is writing too many and too lengthy opinions: "It's time to call a halt to the proliferation of legal writing. The only ones who benefit from all the opinions are the legal publishers."[20] Justice Goldberg fears that a new appellate court might actually compound the work of the Supreme Court since the justices would have to first decide whether to refer a case to the national appellate court and then would have to decide whether the national appellate court's decision should be reviewed by the Supreme Court.[21] Another solution that has been proposed to reduce the court's workload is to give the court more discretion over what cases it decides. The court now has to hear about twenty percent of the cases on its calendar. Reducing the number of cases that the court is required to hear, many of which do not warrant the court's time, would give the court time to hear more significant cases and resolve more important issues than it does now.

Unlike elected officials, who can vigorously respond to and frequently flay their critics, most justices of the Supreme

Court have chosen throughout the history of the court to remain silent and "above" the political scene. That is as it should be, since it is essential that the Supreme Court justices, as final arbiters of what our Constitution means, be held in high esteem.

As an observer of the American political scene for many years, I am satisfied that the Supreme Court has served the purposes intended for it by the framers of the Constitution. Moreover, by its intelligent and courageous expansion of the meaning of the First, Fourth, Fifth, and Fourteenth Amendments, the Supreme Court has defused potential social and political conflicts among Americans during more than two centuries of sometimes overwhelming changes. The Supreme Court has made an 18th century Constitution fit a 20th century society. Short of a serious erosion of our democracy, I am confident that it can continue to make the Constitution meaningful in the 21st and later centuries.

Chapter 9

Divorce Merry-go-round

One of the shames of law and the legal profession is the way divorces and child custody have been handled over the years. Instead of helping families make the difficult transition from married to divorced life, lawyers and the adversary system of justice have tended to aggravate the emotional and financial hurts. Not surprising, divorce law and divorce attorneys have been highly instrumental in giving lawyers a bad image. Many people speak derisively of the "divorce racket."

Lawyers may not turn love into incompatibility, but too many have helped turn anger, hurt, and depression into vindictiveness. Even caring lawyers, though, have been bloodied by their involvement with the adversary system. When there are spouses fighting over every cent and potholder, vicious mudslinging battles for custody of children, husbands thrown into jail for failing to pay alimony or child support, divorced heads of household making up a new class of poor, states having to look for fathers who have fled to avoid support obligations, prosecutions of parents for childnapping, hotly contested trials to prove who was at "fault" for the breakup of a marriage or who is unfit to rear children, reams of perjured testimony—how can any participant's image not be tarnished?

We like to congratulate ourselves for having "modern" and "liberal" attitudes towards love, marriage, and divorce, but easy divorce did not start in America in the 1970's. As Voltaire once said, "Divorce is an institution only a few weeks later in origin than marriage."[1] What we consider a new liberalism in reality is only a return to the law that existed up until Christianity became dominant in Europe.[2] The Romans treated marriage like any other contract and allowed it to be ended by mutual consent of the parties or unilaterally if certain conditions were met (e.g., the husband was guilty of murder or introduced immoral women into his home or the wife dined with men or went to the theater despite her husband's objection).

The rise of Christianity changed the European attitude toward divorce by transforming the concept of marriage from a civil union into an indissoluble spiritual union. Just as there could be only one God and one Church, there also could be only one marriage during a lifetime. Ironically, the first secular ruler to declare divorce a crime was Charlemagne, who was married nine times, had several mistresses, had liasons with his daughter, and who, despite all that, eventually was canonized.

Declaring marriage a sacrament, however, did not end dissolution of marriages. Instead, it merely tested the ingenuity of lawyers. Obtaining annulments and separations for adultery, impotence, cruelty, infidelity, becoming a nun —or monk, or consanguinity became a good business for both lawyers and the Church. Consanguinity was a favored reason for annulment since blood ties as remote as the seventh degree qualified. The ties did not even have to be blood. Marriage into the family of a godparent or priest officiating at one's christening could qualify as a "spiritual" tie justifying an annulment.

Divorce became more difficult to obtain after the Reformation, except, of course, for the wealthy and well-connected, but social realities soon expanded the grounds for divorce. Intolerance for divorce became associated with political repression. One of the first changes made following both the French and Russian revolutions was to make it easier to obtain a divorce.

When I started practicing law, obtaining a divorce was more a social than a legal problem. Sure, people had to go before a judge and prove that one spouse was "guilty" of adultery, desertion, physical or mental cruelty, nonsupport, a crime, habitual drunkenness, drug addiction, or insanity, but if both spouses wanted a divorce the law was not going to stop them. Judges, spouses, and lawyers all knew that testimony was perjured, but all looked the other way since forcing people to remain married seemed the greater sin.

There were few conflicts over child custody since it was assumed that the mother was the "fitter" parent. Up until the beginning of this century, fathers routinely were granted custody of their children since both wives and children were considered the husband-father's property. The pendulum swung over to the mother after courts recognized that changing family economics had taken fathers out of the home into the factories and away from their children.

For a mother to be denied custody, she had to be an unfit parent. Unfortunately, that legacy still affects child custody decisions. Even though both parents usually work and both spouses can be fit parents, most courts still give the benefit of the doubt to mothers, and mothers tend to treat adverse decisions as slandering their reputations. This legacy also has worked against the promising development of shared custody. With shared custody, both parents share legal and physical custody. That means that they not only divide the children's time between them but that they also cooperate in making decisions affecting the children's welfare. No one pretends that it is an easy relationship to maintain—some have called it an unrealistic ideal—but it has worked when courts and spouses have been willing to give it a try.

The real impediment to divorces when I started practicing law was its social stigma. Social attitudes towards divorce have been so different since the 1970's that it is difficult for people to believe that not so long ago it was considered better to remain in a bad marriage than to become "branded" by a divorce. I remember how divorces impeded the political careers of Adlai Stevenson in the 1950's and Nelson Rockefeller in the 1960's. Both men were hurt politically by their divorces. Yet only a few years later when Ronald Reagan became our first divorced president, his divorce was irrelevant to his political fortunes, even among those calling themselves the "Moral Majority."

One consequence of the so-called "sexual revolution" of the 1960's was a removal of "guilt" from divorce. In 1970, California became the first state to have a "no fault" divorce law. State after state fell in line and made it possible for people to obtain a divorce without having to "legally" and publicly blame someone for the breakup. By 1985, all states permitted "no fault" divorces.

As the name implies, "no fault" laws allow couples to end a bad marriage without having to have a court publicly decide which spouse was to blame for the failure of their marriage. The whole notion of "fault" defies the reality of married life. The typical marriage breaks up because the spouses have grown apart, not because one spouse committed adultery or became insane or did anything bringing him or her within one of the former preconditions for a divorce.

Before "no fault" divorces, it was not unusual for spouses to lie that one had committed adultery or had been guilty of mental or physical cruelty or some other "ground" for divorce. Those few who could not agree to lie would resort to the sordid practice of hiring a private detective to dig up enough dirt to justify a divorce. "No fault" laws reflect the modern attitude that no one person is responsible for the breakup of a marriage, and they may reduce the spouses' bitterness towards each other by discouraging the public airing of their dirty laundry.

Contrary to popular belief, the addition of "no fault"

grounds for divorce, such as incompatibility, did not make divorce easier for most people to obtain. Most people already could obtain a divorce by fabricating a "legal" reason for ending their marriage. Those who contested a divorce did not do so because they truly believed their marriage could be saved. Instead, divorces were contested because one spouse wanted more money than the other was willing to pay or because the spouses just hated each other.

Imposing obstacles to divorce has been justified as necessary to preserve the "sanctity" of marriage. But they have only been obstacles to those with such a poor relationship that they could not amicably agree on how to settle their differences. Most couples were able to come to terms, and then they would have to go through the charade of satisfying the state that there were good (often fabricated) reasons for untying their marital knot. Instead of preserving the "sanctity" of marriage, the obstacles to divorce succeeded in creating disrespect for the law.

The farce was exposed daily during "proveups," where in assembly-line fashion spouses in mostly arranged, uncontested cases would slander their soon-to-be ex for thirty seconds to a minute before a judge would gavel an end to their marriage. It made me sad to see lawyers line up several women, lead each through a few questions, and then signal them to hurry off the stand so someone else could quickly go through the same motions. Judges wasted their time listening day after day to lies that had no place in a court of law, and the emotional well-being of the spouses could not have been enhanced by trivializing a traumatic event in their lives.

Rewriting divorce laws to include "no fault" reasons for divorce was more helpful to lawyers and the judicial system than to the average person since legalizing "consensual" divorces helped restore some integrity to the judicial system. No longer do lawyers and clients have to conspire and violate the law to come up with a reason the state will accept for dissolving a marriage. No longer is it necessary for lawyers to coach clients what to say in front of a judge to qualify for a divorce. And no longer do judges have to look the other way when the charade is played out.

A big disadvantage of "no fault" divorce is that it hurts the economically disadvantaged spouse—usually the wife. Lenore J. Weitzman, on the basis of a ten-year study of California divorces, found that "divorced men experience an average 42 percent rise in their standard of living in the first year after the divorce, while divorced women (and their children) experience a 73 percent decline."[3] According to Weitzman, this unintended result of divorce reform has resulted because "[w]hen the legal system treats men and women 'equally' at divorce, it ignores the very real economic inequalities between men and women in the larger society."[4]

Before "no fault" divorces, the threat of a contested divorce could be used to coerce spouses into more advantageous financial settlements. For example, if a husband was anxious for a divorce, his wife could refuse to cooperate and hold out for more money from her soon-to-be ex. Threatening to fight a divorce was no idle threat since before "no fault" it was almost impossible to "win" a contested divorce, and any victory was sure to be costly and bitter. The same testimony accepted during proveups of uncontested divorces would not be accepted by judges during a contested trial. Even if the testimony was sufficient to establish "guilt," it could easily be contradicted in open court.

If one spouse was "guilty" of one of the grounds for divorce, it usually was the spouse anxious for a divorce, which left it up to the "guiltless" spouse to sue. That gave the "guiltless" spouse bargaining leverage since he or she could refuse to sue unless certain financial conditions were met. Even when the spouse anxious for a divorce was suing someone "guilty" of one of the grounds for divorce, it was still almost impossible to win a contested divorce since the "guilty" spouse could argue that his or her improper actions were condoned or provoked by the other spouse. The most ridiculous situation was when both parties proved the other was at "fault." When that was true, then neither spouse was entitled to a divorce. The result was that those spouses most in need of separation were told to continue to live in marital "bliss."

Involving lawyers, courts, and the adversary system in marital problems has exacerbated the pain of breaking up. Many lawyers have neither the skill nor the temperament to help people through the emotional trauma of divorce. A few unscrupulous lawyers have even been known to take advantage of their client's trauma for their own sexual gratification.

The sad fact is that too many lawyers cannot get excited about the legal fees generated by an average person's divorce, and therefore they do not devote the personal attention necessary to help the family adjust to a new lifestyle. Instead, the emphasis is on pushing both parties into a quick settlement. It is sad to see lawyers hovering over people in courtrooms or courtroom corridors trying to come up with a last minute settlement agreement. Often the spouses are in no mental state to agree or disagree about the terms of their divorce but feel pressured by the circumstances to settle.

In some states, attorneys' fees are made part of the divorce decree. That is great for the lawyers because it encourages the practice, seldom mentioned publicly by lawyers, of matrimonial lawyers giving each other more money than they could expect to receive if the fees were agreed to independently by the lawyer and client.

I still remember the time that a well-known divorce lawyer representing the wife of my client asked me how much I planned to charge my client. I told him I did not plan to charge my client anything since I regularly handled his business affairs. He then told me that he was planning to charge $50,000 for what he expected would be 14 hours worth of work. I was shocked first by his greed and then by his suggestion that I charge the same so that he could justify his fee. I refused to go along with him. Fortunately my client's wife was also unwilling to have my client pay such an exorbitant sum and discharged her lawyer.

It did not take me long to realize that marital problems cannot and should not be solved by the adversary system. People tend to lose their good sense during the emotional upheaval of a divorce, and lawyers tend to aggravate the situation instead of helping to restore their client's good judgment.

Divorce is an emotional problem that cannot be remedied by a legal "solution." The adversary system is geared to winners and losers, but marital problems cannot be solved by declaring a winner and a loser. Litigation consumes funds that families could better use to help them make the transition from marriage to separate households. It also asks judges to make difficult decisions, often on the basis of unreliable testimony. Custody usually is awarded based on the "best interests" of the child, but what are the child's best interests? A parent who is firm but loving? Or a parent who is loving but more indulgent? A parent who can spend much time with the child? Or a parent who will spend "quality" time with the child? As our notions of proper parenting have changed, it has become difficult for judges to make "just" decisions. Lawyers tend to measure their own success by the amount of money they are able to obtain for their client, not by whether the "solution" can be accepted by both parties. Lawyers act that way because that is their role in the adversary system. They are doing exactly what they are taught to do.

Some lawyers have become notorious for their ability to swing the best possible deal for a spouse. Often such lawyers are as flamboyant, publicity-seeking, and scandal-seeking (plus a host of other unflattering adjectives) as the non-client spouses say they are. Some lawyers press—some would say harrass—the parties to encourage settlement. They might enjoin the spouse from using or selling his or her property. They might start talking with business associates. They might threaten a custody battle. They might keep hauling the spouse into court—anything to pressure the other spouse into a quick, unfavorable settlement.

Their clients may be momentarily happy to exact retribution from their former spouses, but the ill will engendered cannot make future relations amicable. Keeping relations amicable is particularly important if the two have children and still plan to have dealings with each other. Pitting spouses as adversaries makes the situation more stressful for spouses and children and cannot but encourage shameful situations where "losers" evade their legal and moral support obligations, one or both parents try to poison their children's feelings toward the other parent, or "losers" kidnap their own children.

"No fault" laws have not eliminated the adversarial "get-all-you-can" approach to matrimonial matters. There are still battles over property settlements and support payments, with lawyers encouraged to get all they can for their client and rake the other client over the coals. Worse are the fights over custody and visitation of children. There fathers and mothers battle to prove which is the better parent. Children, traumatized by divorce, need the support of both parents, but the result of custody battles too often is that one parent is driven out of their lives. After all the name-calling, humiliation, and ill will, cooperation, even if it is in the children's best interest, becomes very difficult, if not impossible. One parent becomes entirely responsible for child rearing, and the other parent is encouraged to abandon all interest in his or her offspring.

The federal and state governments have finally been taking steps to curb childnapping and force recalcitrants to pay their support obligations to former spouses and children. But perhaps the most constructive development in resolving matrimonial problems has been the increasing use of mediation and arbitration to more amicably end marriages. In 1975 lawyers did not mediate divorces; now thousands specialize in divorce mediation.[5]

Mediation and arbitration can lead to fairer results since they rely more on the equities of the situation than on the negotiating skills of lawyers and the vindictiveness of clients. Mediators often are able to give couples the support they need to get through a trying time—something most lawyers are not trained to do. The resulting settlement agreements tend to be more satisfactory to both spouses, and, since neither feels "taken" or humiliated by the other, each has more incentive to comply with the terms of the agreement and not try to "get even" by evading agreed to responsibilities. As Robert Coulson, President of the American Arbitration Association, has written: "Mediation encourages families to fight fair. It enables them to control their own disputes. It also provides a powerful learning experience. With the help of a mediator, they learn who they are and what they truly want."[6]

In recent years when people have come to me seeking advice about a divorce, I have recommended that they try mediation. It is less costly than an agreement negotiated by lawyers, much less costly than a contested divorce, and usually is more satisfactory to the husband and wife since they have control and final say over all the details of the agreement and do not feel intimidated by the presence of a lawyer to agree to something that they have a gut feeling is wrong.

Too often people feel compelled to sign a lawyer-negotiated agreement just because their lawyer approves it. What they have to realize is that they are the ones who have to live with any agreement, and they are the ones who have to be satisfied with it. Husbands and wives usually can be confident that the mediated agreement is fair to both sides since good mediators agree up front not to approve any settlement that favors one spouse over the other.

Another advantage of mediation is that nothing said during discussions has to be publicly disclosed so long as the parties agree in advance not to repeat anything said in court. This makes the parties freer to bring everything out into the open without fear that some tidbit will later be turned against them in open court.

It usually takes four to nine hours to resolve custody

matters and eight to fifteen hours to resolve custody, property, and support issues. Some mediators work with both
spouses in the same room. Others prefer to keep the spouses
separated, at least when the sessions begin. Usually there is
only one mediator, but sometimes there is a mediator for
each spouse. If a mediator requires the special knowledge of
someone else, say a tax adviser, then the spouses will be
referred to that person.

The largest hurdle usually is to vent the spouses' hatred
towards each other so that a constructive solution to their
problem can be reached. This venting of anger is an advantage of mediation over the adversary system since the
adversary system discourages parties from expressing
their feelings. Instead, those bottled up feelings are chan-
neled through destructive haggling over family finances,
child custody, and often petty details, such as who will get
to keep the coffee pot. Mediation helps people heal their
hurts; the adversary system too often intensifies the pain.

Judges now frequently use mediation to settle disputes
over the division of property, child custody and support,
maintenance (once called alimony), and related issues.
Mediation is used not only during the divorce but also
afterwards to help resolve later disputes. Use of mediation
and arbitration is probably the most promising development in our judicial system for minimizing the negative
effects of the adversarial system and should be encouraged
by lawyers to minimize the time, stress, and financial
burdens of resolving marital disputes. Mediation also has
the advantage of saving taxpayers money by resolving
marital disputes outside the courtroom. But will lawyers be
willing to sacrifice the money they can make from divorces?
And if they will not, will the public clamor for a better way
to resolve marital disputes? That remains to be seen.

Chapter 10

Estate Planning—A Growth Business

> There is only one way you can beat
> a lawyer in a death case. That is to
> die with nothing. Then you can't
> get a lawyer within ten miles of
> your house.
>
> Will Rogers[1]

> If Al Capone could return to Chi-
> cago, he wouldn't bother with the
> beer business—he'd be a specialist
> in probate practice.
>
> Norman Dacey[2]

Estate planning and administration, which involve such
matters as wills, trusts, and that particularly hated word,
probate, comprise another area of law that has given the
legal profession a black eye. Since this is an area of law that
I have practiced extensively and written and lectured about
during my years as a lawyer, I am particularly troubled by
its occasionally poor public image.

116

When people talk of estate planning, what they mean is planning to accumulate, manage, and dispose of assets to maximize their benefit to the owner and any loved ones. Estate planning is the arrangement of a person's assets to minimize income taxes and estate taxes and to assure that assets will be available for the estate owner and anyone else that the estate owner wants to provide for after his or her death. Estate planning has become a growth industry for lawyers, accountants, life underwriters, trust companies, financial planners, stockbrokers, tax shelter experts, and others, with each trying to profit from "assisting" the estate owner, and each taking a bite out of the estate while the owner is alive and sometimes after the owner's death.

There have been horror stories about attorneys who loot people's estates or drain off assets by making extra work for themselves, relatives, or friends. There have been some instances where probate judges have appointed relatives, friends or political hacks to collect unnecessary fees as administrators, executors, guardians or appraisers, and these relatives, friends, and political hacks have in turn hired their cronies to "send some business their way"—all at the expense of the estate owner's loved ones.

My experience has been that very few lawyers illegally deplete a client's estate by putting client's money into their own pocket or "legally" deplete a client's estate by charging excessive fees or making more work for themselves than necessary. But far too many lawyers and judges have pretended not to see those who do. Some years ago, one probate judge told me how lawyers who had been caught taking money out of an estate would beg him for time to replace the funds—and how he would give many that opportunity. Far too many lawyers and judges have been lax in recommending reforms to streamline the probate process and make it less costly. Unfortunately, it took muckraking lay people to make abuses a national issue and finally prod lawyers to take a serious look at the probate system and initiate needed reforms.

Overemphasis on the few horror stories about lawyers

has masked a more serious problem. The public has focused too much on the very few outright thiefs and not enough on the real problem, which is that too many people drawing up wills and trusts and otherwise dispensing advice about estate planning are clearly incompetent to do so.

I am not limiting my criticism to lawyers. Accountants, life underwriters, banks, trust companies, financial planners, stockbrokers, and tax shelter experts all have leaped into the estate planning business. Unfortunately, too many of those specialists are not competent to give sound and complete advice in estate planning. Even those who are competent to give advice may have an incentive to give some wrong advice. For example, life underwriters have a financial incentive to sell people more insurance than they really need, banks have a financial incentive to encourage people to use the banks' services, and stockbrokers earn their living by selling stock, bonds, and tax shelters. Many of these people have adopted the dignified title "Financial Planner," but that title should not obscure their special interest apart from planning an estate.

When I started practicing law, estate planning was not the growth industry it has become today. During the 1930's, lawyers did not talk much about estate planning. Wealthy Americans like the Rockefellers, Whitneys, Fords, and Harrimans set up revocable, irrevocable, long-term, lifetime, and testamentary trusts for their children, grandchildren, and favored charities, carefully planned their gifts and investments, and did everything else they could to minimize the taxes that would have to be paid at their death.

But the average American had no need for anything more complicated than a simple will and maybe a modest life insurance policy to cover funeral expenses and provide modestly for his or her family. Even a last will might be unnecessary if all property was held jointly with another person (joint tenancy with right of survivorship has long been known as the "poor person's will") or if the individual was content to let the state decide who should get his or her property after death. We were in the midst of the Great

Depression, and few people had enough assets to live on during their own lives, let alone enough to support their children and grandchildren during their lifetimes. Even people fortunate enough to own a modest home and a small life insurance policy did not have enough assets to worry about death taxes, and federal income taxes were low.

About all the estate planning that lawyers did was to write a simple will for the husband and wife leaving everything to the other spouse and then to their children. As the country emerged from the Depression and money became more plentiful, people began to accumulate more assets, and the state and federal governments became greedier about the size of their share of a person's estate.

Greed was not the only motivation for the increased estate tax rate. When the first estate tax was enacted by the United States in 1797, it was designed to raise revenue to repay the government's debt from the Revolutionary War and actually was repealed in 1802 once the extra money was no longer needed. Estate taxes were also temporarily imposed in 1862 and 1898 to help pay respectively for the Civil War and Spanish-American War. The German War Tax was passed in 1916, and that was the first estate tax that did not go away once it was no longer needed to help repay a war debt.

The amount of money raised from the estate tax has never been substantial, but it became popular for its hoped-for social impact. Some proponents felt that inherited wealth was tainted and that people should only be able to reap the benefits of their own labor, not the labor of their ancestors. The maximum estate tax rate, which was 10% in 1916, gradually rose to 70%. Then came the 1980's when the attitude towards inherited wealth changed and legislation was passed to gradually lower the maximum rate to 50% and allow an unlimited amount of money to be transferred to a spouse tax-free. By raising the amount of money exempt from estate taxes, Congress assured most people that they would not have to pay any death taxes.

We take it for granted that we can transfer property to

whomever we please, subject to taxes. In fact, we regard this right as one of our fundamental freedoms. But we have not always had that right.[3] In primitive societies, land passed back to kin, and personal effects were either destroyed or buried with the dead. Under the English feudal system, all land was owned by the king, and only personal property could be passed by a last will. Land automatically passed to the oldest male heir (this was called primogeniture). The purpose of primogeniture was to keep large estates intact and their owners strong.

There has been a long history of people making money off property transfers at death. If we want to blame anyone for estate taxes, maybe it should be Caesar Augustus, who has been credited as its inventor.[4] He imposed a 5 percent estate tax to help support his armies. In England, there was a power struggle between the king and Church over who would have the right to administer estates—and collect fees for that "service." The Church eventually won that struggle and was able to make even more money by encouraging deathbed bequests to itself.

Not surprising, at the same time that people were prohibited from making certain property transfers that would take effect following their death and were taxed on those transfers that they did make, there were lawyers helping them evade the restrictions and save taxes. The law of trusts developed in England to help people circumvent the prohibition against land transfers. Since people could not transfer land following their death, they began transferring land during their lifetime to a third person, who would promise to hold it for someone else's benefit, usually the original owner and whomever he wanted to have the land after his death. The result was that a father could transfer land to a third person but continue to use it until his death and then be assured that it could be used by his children.

Out of this history came the notion that government should get involved in wrapping up a person's affairs following death. Probate, which now has a negative public image, was envisioned as an orderly process to make certain that a person's last will was valid, that all debts and taxes would be paid, and that the people who were meant to benefit from a decedent's estate would in fact benefit. The government was supposed to make certain that all these things would happen.

Unfortunately, probate also carried with it the history of people unrelated to the decedent trying to benefit from that person's death. Also carried over was the history of people avoiding the costs of death administration. Evasion is possible because property that passes to a joint tenant or that is distributed to a trust beneficiary is not subject to probate and probate expenses. (Taxes, however, are not avoided.) For some time, gifts of property were able to escape taxation, but Congress closed that loophole in the estate tax law by enacting a gift tax in 1926.

Once more and more people began to accumulate assets and become concerned that taxes and probate expenses would reduce the amount of money that they could leave to their loved ones, there was an opportunity for lawyers and various financial counsellors to make money. Lawyers began to draft more last wills, living and testamentary trusts, and short term trusts to deflect income to others, usually family members, so that the family's overall income tax burden would be minimized. Life underwriters recognized the growing importance of life insurance as an instant estate, and sales of life insurance skyrocketed. Trustees were needed to administer the growing number of trusts and pension plans for employees, and banks and trust companies took advantage of the opportunity to make themselves some money. Choice of investments took on a growing importance to minimize taxes and maximize the growth of a person's estate, and some stockbrokers started characterizing themselves as estate planners.

Today estate planning is one of the most popular areas of law practice. The main reason for its popularity is that it is a good way for lawyers to obtain other legal business. Lawyers often will give a cut-rate fee on drafting a last will so that they later can get work administering the person's estate. When I started practicing law, we were encouraged to charge lower rates on last wills because the opportunity to later handle the legal affairs for the estate was considered a good source of future income. Since estate planning frequently gets a lawyer involved in most aspects of a person's personal and business affairs, the estate planner may be able to get work representing the client in business, real estate, and various personal dealings. There is also the promise of future fees when an estate is probated and administered.

Estate planning is much more than merely taking a trust or will form and filling in the blanks. Before an attorney can give competent advice about planning estates, he or she must know such things as what assets a client owns, what funds a client and any loved ones need to live on, and what the client would like to do with any funds remaining after his or her death.

An attorney practicing estate planning ideally should have not only a reasonably thorough knowledge of investments, insurance, accounting, and financial management (particularly the income, gift, and estate tax consequences of various types of ownership, sales, and exchanges) but also must know the law of wills, trusts, real and personal property, and business sales and exchanges.

Estate planners also must have a good understanding of people's needs and motivations and be able to make clients feel free to confide personal information to them. I have come across many people who are reluctant to disclose how much they are worth, reveal that there are any conflicts among family members, or admit that a family member needs professional help to manage his or her financial affairs. Without such information, an estate planner cannot do a thorough job of planning a person's estate. I remember one estate plan that I prepared for a friend and his wife. I assumed that their marriage was congenial, but a few months later the wife sued her husband for divorce and tied up all his assets. It took some doing to straighten everything out.

Good estate planning also requires a lawyer to educate a client about the various estate planning tools. Through books and advertising, people learn about and become intrigued, sometimes even obsessed, with certain estate planning tools, such as the marital deduction, trusts, transfers of life insurance policies to a spouse, and gifts. For example, some people are so enamored with the idea of setting up a trust that they want one even if it would cost them more money to administer than it is worth.

Unfortunately, some lawyers are clearly incompetent to practice estate planning. Some still believe that drafting a simple will is all that is required for estate planning. Even that task is treated too lightly. Instead of taking time to understand a client's needs and desires, they tend to use a standard form. Occasionally lawyers have been so careless that they have allowed spouses to sign each other's will instead of their own.

Many lawyers dwell too much on the tax aspects of estate planning. They think that their main task is to minimize taxes. But doing so ignores non-legal and non-tax aspects of estate planning that often are more important to the client than just saving taxes. For example, what good is it to take full advantage of the marital deduction if the client really does not want that much money going to his or her spouse and would prefer that it go to someone else, perhaps children from a previous marriage. There also may be unwise gifts to minors who lack the skill to manage such funds. Worse, I have seen people who are so eager to minimize death taxes that they deplete their own estates with excessive gifts and are forced to rely on the children who have received the gifts to support them during their retirement years.

Business considerations often are overlooked. Family members may be unable to operate a family business without the founder's help, but too many lawyers fail to consider whether the business should be sold or whether competent successor management is available. Some people might want to retain a family business to provide jobs for not-too-competent relatives, but if that will hurt the business it may be better to maximize the security for the family by selling the business.

Because lawyers have an interest in earning legal fees when a client dies, too many fail to minimize probate expenses for their clients by utilizing living trusts (trusts set up during a person's lifetime). Probate expenses can take a significant chunk out of an estate, particularly if the estate is small. Tying up an estate in probate also may delay the time when beneficiaries can begin to make use of the assets. There are also privacy considerations. Probate assets are a matter of public record. In many situations, a living trust may be appropriate to avoid probate.

Some lawyers do not clearly draft wills and trusts and do not clearly explain to their clients what those instruments mean. Unfortunately, too many lawyers are poor writers and tend to use archaic expressions handed down over the centuries instead of modern language that is just as legal and can be understood by a non-lawyer reader. As a result, clients may have no idea, at least from reading a last will or trust, what their will or trust says. This means that it may very well not entirely reflect their desires.

Some lawyers also fail to draft last wills and trusts that are flexible enough to accommodate changing circumstances, particularly changing needs of family members. As children grow up and start their own families, some may need more financial help than others. The same is true for the estate owners. Their economic circumstances change over the years, and an estate plan developed for a struggling business person may no longer be adequate for a successful entrepreneur. Changes in the health of various family members also may call for changes in the estate plan.

Some of this inflexibility is encouraged to minimize death taxes. For example, giving the creator of an irrevocable trust too much power to make changes in the trust can negate the trust's tax savings value. Some of it, though, is the result of lawyers' indifference, which is also reflected in their failure to develop follow-up procedures to notify clients when they should make changes in their estate plans. This is a problem because too many people think that once they have written a last will they are through with estate planning for the rest of their lives. Unfortunately, that is not true. In recent years Congress has given estate planners extra business by frequently changing the tax laws. Some of these changes have been referred to as "Lawyers' Relief Acts." Changes in family resources and needs also may require changes in estate plans.

Inadequate attention is paid to the naming of executors and trustees. It is very important to choose people or institutions that have the skill and interest to perform such duties, particularly if discretion is required, since that requires intimate knowledge of the beneficiaries' needs. Unfortunately, sometimes a bank or trust company will be chosen, not because the bank or trust company is best able to handle the job, but because the bank (thankful for the business) will reciprocate and hire the lawyer to handle the estate's legal affairs. This practice is particularly objectionable if the lawyer does not tell a client that the bank or trust company probably will employ the lawyer to represent it during estate administration.

Lawyers also tend to overlook possible conflicts of interest resulting from naming themselves as executor or trustee or co-executor or co-trustee. Usually a client wants the lawyer to act as executor or trustee, but the lawyer too often does not make it clear that the client can name someone else. Worse are situations where the attorney acts as trustee or executor and continues to also act as lawyer for the beneficiaries or family business, which may put the lawyer in the position of representing conflicting interests since what may be best for the estate may not be best for the beneficiaries or family business or vice versa.

For example, a lawyer representing a family business has an incentive to favor those managing the business. Often those people may want to keep cash in the business, but other beneficiaries of the estate may need dividends to live on. Moreover, when someone offers to buy the family business, who will the lawyer support? The beneficiaries who could use the security of cash realized from the sale? Or the people who want the security of their high-paying jobs? I have been involved in such situations and have avoided problems by explaining the situation and telling everyone that they should feel free to consult another lawyer for independent advice.

Attorneys also can get into a conflict of interest by drafting estate planning instruments for more than one member of a family. For example, if both spouses can agree how they want their assets distributed, then there is no problem. But there are many times when they do not really agree but pretend to agree in a lawyer's presence to avoid a marital squabble. It is usually best for spouses each to have their own lawyer if they each have property or there are children from a previous marriage. Many lawyers will advise spouses of the possible conflict of interest, will recommend that they each consider consulting his or her own lawyer, and will repeat that advice in writing.

Often one spouse does not even know what the other's last will says—until that spouse is beyond the reach of earthly wrath. There was one married client who asked me over several years to add codicils leaving $500,000 to Girlfriend A, $250,000 to Girlfriend B, and $1,000,000 to Girlfriend C and her son. Some years later my client died, and his wife and all three girlfriends showed up for his funeral. I had the unhappy task of telling them that their friend had died owing millions of dollars in federal taxes—a debt that was to take all that was left of his wealth.

Over the years I have had to correct many people's errors in estate planning—including lawyers'. For example, I have had a few cases where lawyers prepared trusts and last wills without carefully examining how property was owned. As a result, the trust or last will was meaningless. Because trusts are ineffective unless property is properly transferred to the trust and because last wills do not cover certain types of property, such as property held in joint tenancy with right of survivorship, it is important to examine how property is owned.

What should people do about planning their estates? Probably most important, they must realize that estate planning is not just for the wealthy. It is the person who does not have hundreds of thousands of dollars who must worry most about coping with serious illness or death in the family and about distributing an estate.

Once people realize that they need to plan their estates, they should consult a lawyer recommended by friends and should check to make sure that the lawyer is experienced in estate planning. A competent estate planner should show an interest in all aspects of a person's financial and personal affairs, and a prudent client should be willing to divulge all information requested, even if it is embarrassing. A competent estate planner may recommend consultation with accountants, life underwriters, bankers, trust officers, and other financial planners.

A client has to learn to trust gut feelings about lawyers. He or she must question the lawyer and make certain that the lawyer understands his or her wishes and will carry them out. In the final analysis, people have to demand proper service from lawyers and anyone else involved in helping them plan their estate. They also must demand that legislators reform the probate system to make it work for the individual and not for those who grease its wheels.

Chapter 11

Morality and Professional Responsibility for the Lawyer

> *You're an attorney. It's your duty to lie, conceal and distort everything, and slander everybody.*
> Josephine in
> *The Madwoman of Chaillot*[1]

Lawyers have been maligned throughout history ("if there were no bad people, there would be no good lawyers"—Charles Dickens[2]) by all types of cultures (" 'Virtue in the middle,' said the Devil, as he sat down between two lawyers"—Dutch proverb[3]) and even by fellow attorneys ("Lawyers and judges, if they think of ethics at all...are likely to conceive of ethics as dealing chiefly with the problem of sex"—Felix S. Cohen[4]).

Like individuals in all walks of life, there are lawyers who cannot be trusted. When I started practicing law, I thought, naively, that lawyers were paragons of propriety, morality,

128

and honesty and that they were devoted to the public interest. But the more lawyers I met, the more lawyers I found
who were willing to indulge in delaying tactics during litigation just to raise the cost to opponents, who were guilty
of connivance just short of criminality, who would file base-
less cases just to make a fee, who would charge legal fees
unwarranted by time and service devoted to the client, who
would threaten to smear prospective litigants to discourage
them from filing suits, who would hold clients' funds longer
than necessary, and who would double-deal clients.

But my fifty years experience has convinced me without
any doubt whatsoever that, by and large, the standard of
conduct of lawyers is above that of any profession or business. I have met and worked with hundreds of lawyers as
adversaries in litigation and in business transactions of all
kinds. I have taught in law school. I have associated with
lawyers in public and charitable causes. I have met lawyers
who were stubborn and irascible. But seldom have I met a
dishonest lawyer. There were some who skirted the canons
of ethics, but I have found that even these were more likely
to change their ways than people in business, who try to get
every edge they can in a business transaction. I do not mean
to suggest that lawyers are angels or that lawyers are all
moral and principled—although, in fact, there are such
lawyers. But I do not know of any group of professional or
business people who say more often than lawyers, "No, I
won't do this because it is immoral or unethical or just plain
wrong."

The public remembers the lawyers involved in the Watergate scandal but not the lawyers who brought the guilty to
justice. The public remembers the lawyers who get criminals off on a technicality but not the lawyers who remedy
injustice by freeing the wrongly accused or the lawyers who
risk their livelihood defending unpopular individuals and
causes from the tyranny of the majority.

Lawyers were the midwives of the American Revolution
and have nurtured individual rights for more than two
hundred years. They have contributed their talents to all

levels of government and have helped make American society a better place to live by getting courts to bar segregation, defend the environment, look out for consumer safety, and make certain that each person has one vote—no more, no less.

The average lawyer guides clients between the Scylla and Charybdis of our laws, making sure that clients actually will own the house they are buying and that estates are distributed the way the deceased wanted his or her estate to be distributed. The average lawyer does his or her work skillfully and honestly.

If I am right in saying that individual lawyers are no less ethical than people in other walks of life and that the standard of conduct expected of lawyers is more stringent than that of any other profession or business, why is it that the public's perception of lawyers is so unflattering? One of the reasons is that society gives lawyers conflicting duties, thus creating a no-win situation. A lawyer can "ethically" carry out one duty but be perceived as "unethical" because his or her actions failed to fulfill one of the lawyer's other duties.

Doctors basically have one role to fulfill—they are supposed to help people be healthy—certainly a popular function. They have been criticized for making it too costly for people to stay healthy, but their ultimate goal is clear.

So, too, is the goal for business people. They are supposed to make money. There are "fair" and "unfair" ways of making money, and business people must be aware of that, but their ultimate goal is clear.

Not so for the lawyer. As the Preamble to the American Bar Association's Model Rules of Professional Conduct states: "A lawyer is an officer of the legal system, a representative of clients and a public citizen having special responsibility for the quality of justice." A lawyer has not one but three roles—and three allegiances—all of which may conflict in a given situation.

A client has every reason to expect "zealous" representation by a lawyer. The client pays the bill and wants victory, not necessarily "justice." Suppose that opposing counsel fails to discover a crucial piece of evidence that could doom your client's case. As an officer of the legal system, you want all evidence to be presented so that justice can prevail (remembering that "justice" does not pay your family's bills). Should you tell opposing counsel that he or she is about to blow the case? Should you "hint" that not all evidence has been discovered? What if your client will seriously pollute your home town if it "wins"? How do you react to that as a "public citizen having special responsibility for the quality of justice"?

What if you can run rings around your opponent? Your client certainly would be happy. But as an officer of the legal system, you should feel upset that both sides of the issue are not being given an adequate hearing. And, as a public citizen with a special interest in justice, you should be upset if your client wins when he or she should not have—but did because you were so competent and clever.

Suppose that a lawyer handling a divorce discovers $100,0000 never reported to the client's spouse—or the Internal Revenue Service. Allegiance to the client requires the lawyer to say nothing. But as an officer of the court the lawyer wants all assets disclosed so that a fair settlement can be reached. And as a public citizen the lawyer wants the client to pay taxes like everyone else.

When I have told close friends, who were active in business, accounting, engineering, medicine, and consulting, that lawyers are confronted with many more ethical and moral dilemmas than people in their professions, they have usually scoffed and said, "not any more than in my work."

What they do not consider is the nature of a lawyer's work. Every day lawyers must deal with laws that regulate what people may and may not do and what the consequences of any action will be. Laws prescribe and encourage a certain standard of conduct, but that standard may be different than the standard of the community and individual consciences. We may feel that people have a *moral* obligation to rescue a person in distress, but they usually do not have any *legal* duty to do so. Many people believe that abortions and divorce are immoral, but laws now leave those decisions to the individual's conscience.

Moral standards enforced by law may differ from state to state and from city to city. Gambling and prostitution are legal in certain areas of the country but not others. New moral questions (e.g., which has precedence—the belief that life should never be taken or the belief in "death with dignity"?) force lawyers to help set new moral standards for the community.

Often dilemmas arise from a conflict between moral values. That often happens in criminal matters, where the belief that people should be punished when they do something wrong may conflict with the belief that certain standards should be followed before anyone can be convicted of a crime. For example, when police violate the law to seize evidence that a person was peddling drugs, the lawyer is forced to overlook the illegal actions of either the police or the client. Lawyers, like the general public, are concerned with results, and it can be difficult to defend someone who clearly is a "bad" person but who did not commit the specific crime he or she was charged with.

As the moral values of a community change (as they have towards abortion and divorce), laws reflecting an old moral consensus begin to seem immoral. But since there is no abrupt shift in moral attitudes (people do not get up one morning and all decide that abortions are moral), changes in the law do not automatically eliminate moral dilemmas for individual lawyers, who may oppose the result they are asked to achieve. In fact, as long as the moral values codified into law are different than the moral values of individuals and the community, there will be moral dilemmas for lawyers. Following one's conscience can put one at odds with legal and community morality. But blindly following legal or community morality can put one at odds with oneself.

I have never permitted myself to be harassed by ethical problems. I have resolved them according to the law, the

ethics of the legal profession, and, most important, according to my own conscience. It is not enough to say, "Well, I'll
act according to the canons of ethics and that's that." I
have had to satisfy my own conscience. I have never
wanted to have to live with doubts about my standards of
ethics and morality. That is not to say that I have never
made a mistake or later questioned a decision. I have. But I
have never felt guilty for the decisions I have made. I have
done the best I could.

Riding home from Springfield, Illinois, where I received
my license to practice law from the Supreme Court of Illinois, I resolved that under no circumstances would I ever
use my skills and knowledge as a lawyer to assist a client in
any wrongdoing. By wrongdoing I meant any action that
involved a violation of law, the legal canons of ethics, my
religious principles, or my conscience. I suppose it would be
expecting too much to have every reader believe that I have
kept that resolution, but that is the fact. I have had many
opportunities to make money by representing the "wrong
guys," but I have let those opportunities pass me by without
a second thought.

My conscience would bother me if I helped a client "put
one over" someone else, so I have never knowingly represented anyone in a transaction involving fraud or misrep-
resentation or any unconscionable conduct, even if it was
not illegal. For example, at times I have seen lawyers omit
contractual provisions beneficial to their clients. When that
has happened, I have given those lawyers a chance to correct their mistakes. My clients might have enjoyed me telling them how we had slipped something past the other
party, but I believe it is important that everyone be treated
fairly. Sometimes I have had to persuade clients not to lie.
For example, there have been times when I would represent
a seller in the sale of a business and know that the financial
statements I was supposed to show the buyer were not
accurate. I also remember one business owner who did not
want potential buyers to know that his company's product
was becoming obsolete. Ironically, when I persuaded him to

admit the business was in trouble and hire a consultant to see what could be done with it, we were able to use the consultant's recommendations to our advantage and sell the company for $750,000—instead of the $500,000 he had hoped to get.

Canons of ethics and codes of professional responsibility, which vary from state to state, regulate everything from which cases a lawyer may handle and what lawyers can and must say about and to a client to what fees may be charged. Legal canons of ethics and codes of professional responsibility go far beyond the strictures of the law regulating morality—and the punishment for disobedience is more severe. A lawyer not only may be subject to civil or criminal penalties but may also lose his or her livelihood by being disbarred.

Public officials may accept substantial campaign contributions and vote in favor of the special interests of their contributors with hardly a slap on the wrist. Woe to the lawyer who acts despite a conflict of interest. People in business can use certain confidential information about competitors to their financial advantage. Not so with lawyers, who may not use confidential information they gather from their clients for their personal benefit.

Business people do not have to tell suppliers that they plan to resell parts at a higher price. In contrast, lawyers have to disclose all conflicts of interest. No business person will be disciplined for trying to do something beyond his or her competence. Not so lawyers, who will be disciplined, perhaps even disbarred, for undertaking matters beyond their expertise. Businesses may charge what the market will bear; legal fees must be "reasonable."

It is quite common for people to condemn lawyers who defend criminals. But when is a person a criminal? When the press reports an arrest? When there is sufficient evidence of guilt? What is sufficient evidence? When can evidence be believed? Do you need one, two, or three witnesses? What if they disagree? Whom do you believe? How good are their memories? Are they lying? Exaggerating? In the

Soviet Union, the defendant is judged by what is best for the state, but here in the United States we go out of our way to protect the rights of the individual.

Are lawyers who regularly defend the "mob" or "criminal syndicate" immoral? Even if they do not participate in mob activities? Aren't members of the mob or syndicate entitled to a defense? Aren't they innocent until proven guilty? What about Clarence Darrow, who defended Richard Loeb and Nathan Leopold in the notorious and brutal Bobby Franks murder back in the 1920's? I remember well the attacks on Darrow for defending them. No one denied their guilt. Darrow argued for clemency and nothing more. He even conceded that the sentence could restrict them from ever getting parole. The families of Loeb and Leopold simply wanted to save their sons from the hangman's noose. Did pleading for the two murderers make Darrow a party to their immoral conduct?

Suppose a lawyer for someone accused of committing a crime finds a crucial piece of evidence that proves beyond a reasonable doubt that the defendant is guilty. Or the defendant admits guilt. Should the lawyer continue to defend the accused? Should the evidence be disclosed to the judge or prosecutor? What should the lawyer do with the evidence?

Lawyers have defended the Rosenbergs, Sacco and Vanzetti, Eugene Debs (alleged communists, anarchists, and a socialist) and well-known Hollywood figures who refused to tell Joe McCarthy which people they thought were communists. Were these lawyers immoral because they defended unpopular causes? Certainly not! The lawyer defending someone accused of an immoral or illegal act should not be characterized as immoral for using his or her skills to prove that the accused did not violate the law. People should be convicted for violating the law, not for offending community morality.

Criminal cases are not the only situations that can pose moral dilemmas for lawyers. What should we think about the ethics of a lawyer who prosecutes or defends a civil suit but does not believe in the merits of the client's cause? Should a lawyer judge the merits of a suit? Should a lawyer take a case just because liberal fees can be earned?

Think of the dilemma lawyers face—every day: Lawyers make their living by working for people who want "victory," not necessarily "justice," but their ethical reputations are judged by a public concerned with "justice." Only by selectively accepting clients could an attorney ever hope to meet the public's demand for justice. But would that careful choice put bread on the family table? Should lawyers suffer calumny because they do not have the will of a Thomas More? Should a whole profession be maligned because all are not saints?

What if a corporate counsel tells the board of directors that their dumping of hazardous wastes is illegal and the board says thanks for your opinion but the dumping will continue? Should that corporate counsel report the company to the federal government and effectively end his or her career with the company?

Lawyers have always had trouble deciding when to be a "whistle-blower." For years they have been free to squeal about a client if necessary to prevent imminent death or substantial bodily harm. But financial fraud has been a different matter. Should the possibility of financial fraud justify breach of the attorney-client relationship? If lawyers do not blow the whistle, then are they not helping clients commit a criminal act? Ethics may require lawyer-citizens to prevent crimes, but ethics also require lawyer-representatives to give clients their best advice and an effective legal defense.

Attorneys do not escape hard ethical choices by working for the government. Should lawyers keep mum if they know their boss (e.g., a United States Senator) is withholding unfavorable information about a pet bill? Disclosure certainly would be in the public interest, but will the public rally to their cause when they are trying to get work with another senator? Who does the lawyer work for? The public? Or the government? Who deserves the lawyer's allegiance?

One lawyer getting rich by defending drug smugglers has argued that he is helping the cause of justice. He believes that everybody is entitled to a good defense, that interpretations of laws may differ, and that his client is entitled to his best effort to have the law interpreted in his client's favor. Few defendants would quarrel with that argument, yet the public often does—especially if a lawyer's best effort gets a miscreant off on a technicality. But do individuals want to hire lawyers who will "win" their case for them, or would they be willing to be represented by lawyers who want to make sure that all facts and arguments are fairly presented so that there can be a "just" result? If individuals are not willing to hire the "ethical" lawyers they clamor for as the "public," then is it fair for them to malign lawyers for being as "unethical" as clients want them to be?

This does not mean that lawyers should stoop to any level to "win" cases for their clients. For centuries, lawyers have been struggling to define the limits of proper representation, and they will continue to do so, adjusting their notions of accountability to the imperatives and attitudes of their generation. As the notion of the "public good" has grown in importance, so has the lawyer's obligation to the public—at the client's expense. Which means that now and in the future lawyers will be as "ethical" as the public wants them to be.

Chapter 12

Lawyers' Competence (or Incompetence?)

Like other professions and businesses, law has competent and incompetent practitioners. Chief Justice Burger started a storm of controversy in 1973 when he estimated that up to half the lawyers appearing in federal courts were incompetent to try a case.[1] Some have said that he underestimated the true figure; others that he blew the problem out of proportion. No one denies that there are some incompetent attorneys. Nor does anyone argue that some incompetence should be tolerated. The debate has been over what can be done to reduce the number of incompetent lawyers. For lay persons needing legal services, the basic question is how they can tell the difference between a competent and incompetent lawyer.

Much of the literature on the subject discusses the lawyer's "ethical" duty to be competent, but analyzing the subject on that level is pretentious. In many respects it is no different than a shoemaker or tailor representing that he or she can repair shoes or tailor a suit of clothes in accordance

138

with his or her advertised or oral representation of competence. It is simply living up to the representation of being competent to perform a particular task.

Incompetence is hard enough to define let alone evaluate. The American Law Institute-American Bar Association Committee on Continuing Professional Education has said that:

> Legal competence is measured by the extent to which an attorney (1) is specifically knowledgeable about the fields of law in which he or she practices; (2) performs the techniques of such practice with skill; (3) manages such practice efficiently; (4) identifies issues beyond his or her competence, relevant to the matter undertaken, bringing these to the client's attention; (5) properly prepares and carries through the matter undertaken; and (6) is intellectually, emotionally, and physically capable. Legal incompetence is measured by the extent to which an attorney fails to maintain these qualities.[2]

The American Bar Association's Model Rules of Professional Conduct requires lawyers to be competent but does not provide a clear definition of what is expected: "Competent representation requires the legal knowledge, skill, thoroughness and preparation reasonably necessary for the representation."[3] In Dorothy Maddi's study, judges listed 6,244 factors they believed most important in determining competence.[4] Unfortunately, even this unwieldly list is not helpful in defining incompetence since it is difficult to decide what is a passing grade for each factor. A study by Anthony Partridge and Gordon Bermant[5] illustrates how "incompetence" may be in the eye of the beholder. Judges and lawyers asked to rate videotaped performances could not agree on what was competent or incompetent performance. Ratings varied all the way from "first rate" to "very poor" for the same videotaped presentation. Bar examinations eliminate some incompetents (and some potentially competent lawyers), but they are no real test of a lawyer's competence.

Generally speaking, lawyers are incompetent if they lack adequate knowledge of the applicable law, if they do an inadequate job of uncovering all relevant facts, or if they do not have the persuasive ability to adequately represent clients before judges, juries, or opposing counsel. Other faults of lawyers, such as inattention to clients, suggest irresponsibility but not necessarily incompetence.

Unfortunately, competence or incompetence rarely can be determined without examining all the facts of a particular situation. Only in an extreme case, such as when a lawyer handles a case even though he or she has no knowledge of that particular branch of law and no intention of acquiring necessary knowledge, is there a clear case of incompetence. Some people may think that a lawyer must have special training or experience handling a client's problem, but that is not necessarily so. As the comment to Rule 1.1 of the ABA's Model Rules of Professional Conduct says:

> A lawyer need not necessarily have special training or prior experience to handle legal problems of a type with which the lawyer is unfamiliar. A newly admitted lawyer can be as competent as a practitioner with long experience. Some important legal skills, such as the analysis of precedent, the evaluation of evidence and legal drafting, are required in all legal problems. Perhaps the most fundamental legal skill consists of determining what kind of legal problems a situation may involve, a skill that necessarily transcends any particular specialized knowledge. A lawyer can provide adequate representation in a wholly novel field through necessary study. Competent representation can also be provided through the association of a lawyer of established competence in the field in question.

As I write this, I am reminded of a time some years ago when I represented a father and his four sons in their purchase of a multimillion dollar business and then was asked to sit in on the renegotiation of a union contract covering some 500 employees. I explained to the client that although

I had handled some labor matters I was not an expert in labor law and felt that he should hire a lawyer who specialized in that field. He said that he liked the way I negotiated the purchase of the business and insisted that I head up the company's labor negotiating team. My son, working in my office after having graduated recently from the University of Chicago Law School, said, "But, Dad, you're not experienced in the field. You said you are not an expert." I agreed, but told my son that I would be a near-expert before the negotiations started.

I spent a few days in conference with my clients identifying the problems that were likely to arise during the negotiations. I then ordered the *Prentice-Hall Labor Relations Guide.* I made note of all portions of the set of books dealing with the problems we anticipated. Every night for two weeks I took home a volume of the set and studied it until the wee hours of the morning.

In three weeks the negotiations were successfully concluded. At a dinner party celebrating the purchase of the business and the success of the labor negotiations, my client said, "And I thought Ben said he was not an expert! That's the kind of lawyer I want, someone who readily acknowledges what he does not know and gets down to business learning whatever there is to know about the law and how to resolve the problem."

Frequently clients will label their lawyer incompetent because their expectations were not met, either because they lost a case or did not feel that the lawyer made the best possible deal in settling a case. It is understandable that such a client would be unhappy, but that does not mean that the client's lawyer was incompetent. The client may have lost because he or she deserved to lose. Maybe the facts did not support the client's position or the client exaggerated the facts or the judge or jury just did not believe the client's testimony. While it is true that some lawyers are more capable than others and that the difference in skills may mean the difference between losing and winning, the lawyer with less skill may not necessarily be incompetent. The point is

that one must be skeptical about using clients' complaints
to generalize that lawyers are incompetent.

In the last 100 years or so, but particularly during my
years in the profession, law practice has become very complex. Not only are there many more fields of law now than
when I first started my career (before computers, complex
tax laws, great environmental concern, and most civil
rights laws), but the amount of information a lawyer has to
be aware of has become staggering, far beyond the ability of
most lawyers to master in a busy daily practice. Legal
problems no longer can be analyzed with reference to one
field of law. For example, business law now requires expertise not only in what was traditionally business law (e.g.,
corporations, partnerships, and sole proprietorships), but
also many other fields, such as labor law, environmental
law, property law, taxation, bankruptcy, sometimes even
divorce law. Specialization has resulted from necessity, and
it has become increasingly important for lawyers to be able
to tap sources of specialized knowledge. Group practice
(e.g., partnerships, legal corporations) may give lawyers
access to that knowledge.

The need for specialized knowledge has put a premium on
a lawyer's ability to work effectively with others. Increasing specialization also has created the need for lawyers who
can gather and synthesize advice from other disciplines.
Just as medicine has required doctors to know whom to
send patients to for advice, so must there be lawyers who
can direct clients to the right practitioners. Coordinating
specialized advice is particularly difficult in law since there
is so much overlap of specialties. It is rare for a problem to
involve only expertise in one field of law.

If lawyers lack the ability to effectively communicate
with colleagues, then the quality of their work will suffer.
Compatibility decreases the chances that something may
be overlooked. Compatibility also speeds the training of
lawyers newly admitted to practice. Many people believe
that it is more important to look at compatibility than competence when hiring attorneys since competence can be

developed with time but incompatibility will cause things to go wrong, even if all attorneys involved are highly competent individuals. I have had the privilege of meeting and working with many great lawyers. What sets them apart from average lawyers is their drive to be and do the best. But this goal is not pursued at the sacrifice of individual relationships with other attorneys. Great lawyers know that they have to rely on others' skills to improve their own.

Chief Justice Burger has been critical of the lack of training lawyers receive for trial work and of the bar's failure to adequately monitor the quality of trial practice. The Chief Justice's comments at the ABA's national convention in 1978 are typical of his comments over the past decade:

> Perhaps one of the most serious problems facing our profession today is the professional competence of those lawyers who come into the courts. I emphasize not the competence of lawyers generally but those who seek to use the courts, which are provided at great expense by the public.[6]

It should be noted about the Chief Justice's criticism that the adverse consequences he has been most concerned about are the increased costs of litigation and waste of time resulting from incompetent performance. What he calls "incompetent" performance is not the incompetence that changes the result of a trial. It is important to keep this in mind when evaluating his estimate that as many as half the attorneys appearing in court are incompetent to try a case. He feels that many lawyers are wasting the time of both courts and litigants and are costing litigants and taxpayers extra money, but he has not argued that justice is being denied on a large scale because of poor performance.

It should also be noted that the Chief Justice's criticism is limited to trial practice and does not extend to other aspects of legal practice. This is important to remember since many lawyers never set foot in a courtroom during their professional careers and most lawyers spend very little of their time arguing cases before the courts. I suspect that there is

as much incompetence among these lawyers as among
those appearing in court, but unfortunately too little attention has been paid to this aspect of incompetence.

The changing economics of the law profession has made
it more difficult to become and remain competent to practice
law. It used to be that a newly admitted attorney would be
taken under the wings of a mentor and shown the ropes of
practicing law. I was fortunate enough to have several
lawyers willing to watch over me as I tested my wings. But
pressure to hold down costs and pressure to keep up with all
the changes in the law have placed a premium on mentors'
time and discouraged old-style apprenticeships. At the
same time, the tremendous increase in the number of newly
admitted attorneys has flooded the profession with people
who need seasoning.

This is not to suggest that newly licensed lawyers are
incompetent, at least to the extent that the term implies lack
of ability. But it does mean that they usually cannot practice as efficiently as experienced lawyers and that they
require additional training before they can competently
perform many tasks.

Most newly licensed attorneys recognize that their practical skills are limited, and they seek employment with law
firms and experienced practitioners who can give them the
needed training. Unfortunately, the general public cannot
assume that association with a law firm is a guarantee of
proper supervision. Some attorneys take their responsibility seriously and do a good job. But others are either preoccupied with their own work or lack the skill or interest
necessary to properly supervise another's work.

Mounting legal malpractice claims have had the beneficial effect of forcing law firms to at least reevaluate their
training programs, not only for newly licensed lawyers but
also for established lawyers who may not have kept up with
all the changes in the law or may never have had the skills
necessary to practice.

One possible solution to the problem of inadequate supervision would be for state Supreme Courts or other organizations to certify especially competent practitioners as preceptors for new lawyers who want the opportunity to serve an apprenticeship. In time, states might want to require an apprenticeship with a preceptor as a condition for full licensing.

The organized bar has been concerned about legal incompetence. Malpractice claims against lawyers are on the rise, and there has been increasing public disenchantment with lawyers' performance. Analogizing the courtroom to an operating room, Chief Justice Burger has pressed for specialized training in trial advocacy.[7] He has proposed that lawyers interested in practicing before federal courts be required to pass an examination dealing with federal law and practice and handle a certain number of state cases before they can try a case in federal court. The emphasis on improving trial advocacy in federal courts has been criticized by those who are interested in improving advocacy in all courts and are fearful that state courts might get the reputation as the refuge for incompetent lawyers.

Chief Justice Burger's proposals for alleviating the problem of incompetence in federal trial advocacy are sound, but putting them into effect would tend to create an elite of federal court practitioners—without providing complete assurance of competent federal advocacy. Another disadvantage of such prerequisites is that they can add years to the time required for women and minorities to enter the mainstream of the profession.

The proposals smack of the barrister-solicitor division in Great Britain (barristers and solicitors are lawyers, but only barristers may try cases in certain courts). Most lawyers who go to court spend most of their time practicing before state and local courts. Some extend their practice to federal courts. Chief Justice Burger's criticisms are equally applicable to state and local trial practice. There is certainly plenty to learn about state and local court practice.

But should lawyers have to take special courses of study and examinations and submit to peer review before being able to practice before each type of court?

Suppose a lawyer also practices before administrative agencies. Is he or she also supposed to take special courses and exams in the specialized matters coming before each of those agencies and submit to peer review before being allowed to handle a case before any of those agencies? And who and where will we get all the peers to review the lawyers practicing before each of those courts? What are the qualifications for peer reviewers? And who will select them?

I agree that lawyers' competency to try cases should be improved, but I am not convinced that any improvement gained by requiring special courses or examinations or peer review will be worth the added expense of those requirements. I am concerned that there will be an overemphasis on *pre*requisites for admission to trial practice and not enough attention to assuring continuing competency.

What really is needed is for judges to step forward and identify those lawyers they think need additional training. If inadequacy is found, then such lawyers should be required to obtain the necessary training before being permitted to again practice before the court. Such a threat should encourage lawyers to attain necessary skills by taking advantage of the many courses teaching trial advocacy sponsored by various bar associations.

As I mentioned earlier, assuring competency in trial advocacy only would solve one aspect of the problem of assuring competency in the practice of law. In fact, competency in trial advocacy is easier to assure than competency in other aspects of legal practice because it is more visible. Judges and other lawyers can observe the competency of a lawyer to try a case. But many other legal tasks, such as the preparation of wills, divorce settlements, and real-estate closings are witnessed by non-lawyers, who usually cannot recognize incompetent performance, and by opposing counsel, who unfortunately do not want to point out deficient performance. Suggestions for improving the competency of lawyers to perform tasks other than trial advocacy have included:

—more extensive practice courses in law school
—mandatory attendance at continuing legal education courses and prescribed prelaw courses
—state certification of lawyers as specialists
—recertification in specific disciplines at regular intervals
—peer review
—more effective enforcement of discipline
—a requirement that lawyers publicly list, in an official directory, information about their number of years of practice, fields of practice, years of experience in each field of practice, and any significant details about their experience, including suits for malpractice and grievance complaints filed against them.

Norman Krivosha, Chief Justice of the Supreme Court of Nebraska, has argued (as chairman of a committee of the Conference of Chief Justices dealing with lawyer competence) that prescribed prelaw education and increased clinical training will not eliminate incompetent lawyers.[8] He has pointed out that most criteria of competence cannot be measured prior to actual practice; nor can competence be assured by even extensive clinical training:

It is almost an insult to those who perform competently to suggest, for instance, that one may learn to be a trial lawyer by handling four matters in a court of limited jurisdiction or to suggest that one may learn the art and skill of negotiating and settling by visiting with a practitioner for a week in a classroom setting. Skills of the accomplished lawyer are a result of a number of years of hard work and effort in a concentrated, intense manner. It is foolish to suggest, for example, that the task performed by the lawyer is of so little demand that, like microwave cooking, it can be taught in a semester of group action.[9]

Chief Justice Krivosha is right not to minimize the level of skill required to competently practice law, but his criticism should not obscure the value of clinical training in improving a lawyer's skill. Clinical training may not by itself make lawyers competent, but at least it can improve a lawyer's basic skills and encourage lawyers to remedy any deficiencies.

Requiring certain prelaw courses, on the other hand, does not strike me as a good way to improve lawyers' competence. As Chief Justice Krivosha noted, prescribing prelaw courses might discourage the lifeblood the profession needs (Roscoe Pound, the great legal philosopher and graduate botanist, might have been discouraged from attending law school if he had had to go back and take prescribed courses): "What we need to concern ourselves with is that law school candidates be intelligent, informed persons with inquiring minds. Let us not concern ourselves about how they gain that knowledge and intelligence, as long as it is there."[10]

Mandatory continuing legal education has been advocated to reach lawyers who do not know what they are missing and to stave off government regulation of lawyers by assuring the public that the profession is trying to eliminate incompetence. Opponents have argued that mandating certain course work would waste the time of people who do not need it and probably not motivate those who do need it to become competent. Unfortunately, opponents may be right. It is rare for a lawyer to graduate from law school and pass the bar examination and yet not be capable of competently practicing law. Lack of ability is not usually the problem; lack of desire to become competent is. A special task force of the American Bar Association Section of Education and Admissions to the Bar agrees:

A lawyer's actual performance may fall short of the appropriate standard for any number of reasons unrelated to competence: inattention, lazinesss, the press of other work, economic factors, or mistake. Indeed, available evidence suggests that reasons such as these, not a lack of capacity to do a proper job (incompetence in the narrow sense), are the cause of most instances of lawyer failure.[11]

That necessary desire is not likely to be instilled in people by mandating continuing legal education.

Although as a practical necessity lawyers must confine their practice to a few fields of law, formalizing this practice by certifying lawyers as specialists would raise many practical problems. Deciding what specialties there are is a difficult problem. So is the matter of deciding what qualifies an individual as a "specialist" and agreeing on who should make that decision. If only a few lawyers become certified as specialists, then those lawyers will be given the privilege of charging more money, and the overall competence of lawyers in general probably would not be improved since the "specialists" would probably be lawyers already competent to practice their specialty. Even if all lawyers were required to become specialists (assuming it ever became possible to neatly compartmentalize all the fields of law), it is not clear whether the public would benefit from increased competence or would only incur increased charges. Much would depend on the requirements for certification and whether there would be peer review to assure continuing competence following certification.

One adverse effect of requiring specialization (particularly if a certain number of years of practice were required before a lawyer could be certified as a specialist) would be that it would place one more obstacle in the way of women and minorities attaining their rightful place in the profession. Even if specialization could increase the overall competence of attorneys, there would be a danger that it would create an anticompetitive elite. What good is enhanced competence if artificially increased costs deny legal services to a greater number of people?

Statewide peer review programs have run across two major obstacles: (1) should peer review be linked with discipline or be merely therapeutic and (2) who should be able to trigger peer review. Keeping it therapeutic (i.e., not putting a person's career in jeopardy) encourages people to voluntarily take advantage of the program (particularly important when counseling is needed to overcome drug dependence or alcoholism) and encourages others to refer people to the program. This attempt to avoid the *taint* of discipline creates the risk that it might become a means of *avoiding* discipline (a sort of plea bargaining). But if the result is a more competent lawyer, does it really matter that the lawyer is not publicly tainted with past misdeeds? Many think that peer review should be triggered only by complaints from judges and lawyers, but others, skeptical that judges or lawyers will report problems of their brethren, think there should also be client involvement. Since clients have been permitted to trigger disciplinary action against attorneys, it seems reasonable to let them trigger proceedings that have less severe consequences for an attorney.

Most people concerned with the problem of lawyer incompetency agree that disciplinary commissions have been unable to deal with the problem of incompetent attorneys. Unfortunately, it is not just their limited resources but also the nature of the problem that makes it difficult for disciplinary commissions to be effective. Lawyers are disciplined for clear violations of their duties as lawyers, but, as I pointed out at the beginning of this chapter, incompetence is impossible to define precisely without reference to a particular factual situation, and most incompetent acts are unintentional, exactly the type of conduct disciplinary commissions are not equipped to deal with.

It is quite clear that the organized bar has dragged its collective feet too long in easing and solving a problem that has been with us for many years, yet law is no different than other professions, which have had equally leaden feet. While waiting for lawyers and bar associations to solve the problem of lawyer incompetence, the public must be especially vigilant in selecting a lawyer for a specific task. The lay person seeking legal services should ask friends and business acquaintances to recommend lawyers who have handled similar matters. Non-lawyers also should check local bar associations for the qualifications and specialties of recommended lawyers. Prospective lawyers should be visited and asked for a recital of qualifications and a list of references. Prospective lawyers also should be asked about fee arrangements, probable out-of-pocket expenses, the lawyer's practice about keeping clients informed about what is going on, and any other aspect of the prospective relationship that concerns the lay person. From there on, unfortunately, clients take their chances.

Chapter 13

Client-Lawyer Relationships

> Who taught me first to litigate,
> My neighbor and my brother hate,
> And my own rights overrate?
> It was my lawyer.
> Who lied to me about his case,
> And said we'd have an easy race,
> And did it all with solemn face?
> It was my client.
> Judge Jacob M. Braude[1]

Ill will between lawyers and clients usually develops from a client's misunderstanding of what a lawyer can and cannot do, from a lawyer's exaggerated promises, or from a lawyer's failure to dispel the unreasonable expectations of a client and consider a client's needs.

A client's notion of "justice" is "victory." When clients are convinced of the rightness of their cause, they expect lawyers to vindicate them. When clients know that they are in the wrong (e.g., traffic tickets), they expect lawyers to exculpate them. Rare is the client who can objectively look

152

at his or her situation. Most clients will not tolerate any doubts raised about the rightness of their cause. Any doubts articulated by a lawyer raise doubts in a client's mind about the lawyer's competence.

Emotions are running high by the time people decide to use the courts to resolve their differences. Clients who win think that their lawyer is great; clients who lose think that their lawyer is incompetent. I have yet to meet a client who lost a case but said, "Well, you did your best. It was a tough case. Maybe I should have lost it."

Clients frequently become so obsessed with the justice of their cause that they fail to recognize that there are two sides to every case, sometimes even three—the client's side, the opponent's side, and the right side. It is for the judge or jury to decide which party is either in the right or at least closer to the right side. Lawyers simply do the best they can to present their client's case. They do not make the law; they do not create the facts. Lawyers must work with the law and facts as they are; yet lawyers are blamed for their clients' mistakes. Rarely will clients concede that they got themselves into a legal mess. And if a lawyer recognizes the weakness of a client's case and urges the client to settle, the lawyer will be charged with "giving in to the other side."

The most effective way of changing a client's mind about settling a case and avoiding a lawsuit is to say, as I have said many times with success, "You know, Bill, if we go to court on this and you lose, as I expect you will, the only one who will make any money on the deal is your lawyer. That's me. I don't want to make that kind of a fee when I am fairly certain that you are going to lose the case. You will be the loser, not me. So let's settle it for what we can and go on with the task of running your business." Nine times out of ten the client will listen and act on the advice. The one out of ten, however, will want "satisfaction." And so the lawyer goes ahead with the suit, and the client's resentment of the lawyer becomes exacerbated as the bills for legal fees and court costs mount.

As advocates, lawyers have a duty to "zealously" represent their clients. This should not make them, however, "hired guns" doing the bidding of a client. Unfortunately, there are lawyers who will take any kind of a case to make a fee. Lawyers are also officers of the legal system, and, as such, they should not help clients commit crimes or fraud. Nor should they abuse the legal system by filing frivolous lawsuits or by making frivolous arguments or objections. A lawyer's agreement to represent a client is not an endorsement of a client's political, social, economic, or moral views or activities or a client's business ethics. It is merely a continuation of the age-old tradition that all people are entitled to a lawyer, no matter how controversial or unpopular they are.

Clients do not contact lawyers merely to resolve legal problems; many want sympathy, understanding, respect, and satisfaction. Many also want reassurance that all will be well. They have heard horror stories about the law and lawyers and the legal system, and naturally they are afraid that a legal matter will be their undoing.

In the final analysis, lawyers must abide by their clients' decisions, but as counsellors they must exercise independent judgment based not only on the law but also on political, economic, social, and moral factors. Advice should be candid and understandable, not couched in jargon or sugar-coated to make it palatable to a client. If a lawyer feels that the client should consult with an expert in another field, such as psychology, chemistry, engineering, or accounting, then the lawyer should make that recommendation.

When people first come to lawyers, they are often understandably angry and complaining. That is why some lawyers say, half-jokingly, "Practicing law would be great if we didn't have to deal with people." Occasionally lawyers would prefer to be given a case but not the client. I still remember one client who always had to have everything done exactly her way and expected me to be available at any hour of the day. She got a hold of my home telephone number and would call in the wee hours of the night. Fortunately my wife never was the suspicious type.

Acting as legal counsellor requires thorough knowledge of human nature and society, as well as law. Lawyers must learn what clients really want (e.g., are they more interested in vindication, compromise, or revenge) before they can recommend a strategy to satisfy a client's needs. Clients must get in touch with their own needs so that they can tell lawyers what they would like to accomplish. I cannot over-emphasize this point. If clients do not know what they will accept as a satisfactory resolution of a conflict, then they risk getting both more and less than they really want.

Clients sometimes feel that their lawyer is not working on their case when days or weeks pass and there is no resolution of their problem. Sometimes lawyers do put a matter on the back burner. But more often lawyers are doing the work but neglect to explain what has to be done. Unless lawyers explain what they are required to do, clients cannot be expected to know why resolution of their conflict is taking so long.

I never had a law school course on how to deal with clients, but I soon learned the importance of keeping clients informed about what was happening in their cases. Either by telephone or letter I would tell clients where matters stood and would send them copies of correspondence, investigative reports, witness statements, and anything else I thought would be of interest to them. If a client could not understand something that I had written, then I would rewrite the document. Such attention was always appreciated by my clients.

Unfortunately, most clients do not understand what a lawyer is required to do, and lawyers fail to take time and explain their work to clients. Clients do not see their lawyer pursue investigations, gather all the facts, study all the documents, identify legal problems, research applicable law, plan strategy, and carry it out. Lawyers need to antici-pate everything that reasonably—and even unreason-ably—can occur, not just in litigation but also in any trans-action. Whether it is the purchase of a home or a complicated corporate acquisition, lawyers have to anticipate every

possible contingency so that they can protect their client
and make sure that the transaction complies with the law.

The same people who criticize the complexity of the law
will complain that "my lawyer made a complicated deal out
of a simple transaction." Sometimes it is the law that is
complicated. But often it is not the law that is complicated;
it is life. Anything can happen. A shipment of goods can be
diverted by war or destroyed by lightning; a partner can die
or become incapacitated; property bequeathed in a will can
be sold before the testator dies; a buyer may change his or
her mind and renege on a deal. If a lawyer does not explain
the consequences of such occurrences, then a court will—at
great expense to the client.

Clients have the right to expect loyalty from their lawyer.
Disloyalty calls into question the value of a lawyer's advice.
Disloyalty also threatens a client's confidences. Certainly
clients would not take too kindly to a lawyer asking their
adversary for a job or for money to pay off a loan. I would
never handle legal work for two business competitors. As
their lawyer, I would be exposed to important information
about their businesses—their sales, their profits, their customers, perhaps even some trade secrets—and each of them
could not help but wonder, "Is Ben disclosing any of this
information to my competitor?"

Conflicts of interest have to be avoided. Lawyers must
not represent opposing parties. They also must not represent a client in one case and then oppose him or her in a
related matter. Nor should lawyers take cases they cannot
handle competently for a reasonable fee just because they
are desperately short of cash.

All transactions between lawyers and their clients must
be fair. A lawyer who spots an autographed first edition of
"Macbeth" or the *Bible* cannot take advantage of a client's
ignorance of the item's value to get a "steal." When there is
a transaction between a lawyer and a client, it is usually
best to have it reviewed by an independent counsel. Clients'
money should be kept in a separate account, and securities
and other valuables should be kept in a special safe deposit

box and may not be commingled with securities or valuables belonging to someone else.

Sometimes clients will become upset when a lawyer speaks out on a public issue and does not agree with the client's views. But a lawyer's duty to avoid conflicts of interest with a client does not bar him or her from speaking out on matters of public concern. Lawyers may urge reforms in the law and the legal system even if a change may adversely affect a client's interests (e.g., a lawyer for a chemical manufacturer may urge stricter controls on hazardous wastes even if such controls would cost the manufacturer extra money).

As a member of the Chicago City Council I urged that the city consider taking over the Commonwealth Edison power plant and operating it as a public utility. A valued client read about my suggestion and requested an urgent appointment. He thought it was unfair and thoughtless on my part to make such a suggestion when I knew he was a stockholder of the Commonwealth Edison Company. Some clients resented my participation in local politics and were particularly unhappy that I was outspoken on civil liberties issues.

If there is a conflict of interest that is not likely to prevent a lawyer from giving independent advice, then a client can consent to having the lawyer represent him or her despite the conflict. This rule has posed problems for me over the years. I have had clients (e.g., divorcing spouses or the seller and purchaser of a business) willing to consent to me representing both sides. They would become angry at the thought that I would force them to pay fees to two attorneys to avoid a conflict that they refused to accept as a problem.

Conversations between lawyers and clients are privileged and generally may not be repeated without the client's consent. This rule of ethics, which bars a lawyer from repeating a client's admission of wrongdoing, has long been controversial. Jeremy Bentham, arguing against the attorney-client privilege, felt that if it were abolished then "a guilty person [would] not in general be able to derive so much assistance from his law adviser, in the way of concerting a false defence, as he may do at present."[2]

It is clear that the rule of confidentiality may suppress damaging information. But proponents argue that concern for the individual should take precedence over the search for the truth. As the *Los Angeles Times* said in an editorial defending the privilege, "Lawyers should be lawyers....[I]f they represent a client, they should represent only that client and not be cast in the double role of lawyer and watchman. Police and prosecutors are assigned to that duty."[3]

The purpose of the rule, according to the United States Supreme Court

> is to encourage full and frank communication between attorneys and their clients and thereby promote broader public interests in the observance of law and administration of justice. The privilege recognizes that sound legal advice or advocacy depends upon the lawyer being fully informed by the client.[4]

Although critics focus on truth that is suppressed by the privilege, defenders worry that the truth might not be disclosed if the privilege were abolished. Without assurances that what they say will not be repeated, clients, it is argued, would avoid legal assistance and would make the legal help they do seek less valuable because they would be inclined to conceal information that is embarrassing or that they think is legally damaging. Defenders point out that most people want to comply with the law and will follow a lawyer's advice—advice that would not be as valuable if the lawyer did not know all the facts. They feel that, by encouraging people to seek lawyers' advice and freely communicate with lawyers, the rule lets lawyers prevent wrongdoing.

Defenders also believe that abolition of the privilege would not promote truth; instead, clients would not reveal any guilty secrets. As the *Los Angeles Times* editorial noted:

It would be an unsophisticated client indeed who, in confiding to his lawyer, would not understand that he also might be confiding in a prosecuting attorney. Such rules would erode, if not destroy, the lawyer-client relationship.[5]

Critics worry that the rule impugns lawyers' honor by associating them with wrongdoing. Critics have also said that lawyers only want to discover the truth so that they can prepare counterarguments. Defenders say that their honor would be stained if they had to "snitch" on their clients.

According to the American Bar Association's Model Rules of Professional Conduct, lawyers can reveal clients' secrets without their consent only to prevent a client "from committing a criminal act that the lawyer believes is likely to result in imminent death or substantial bodily harm" or to defend themselves.[6] This rule has been particularly controversial since it says that lawyers *may*, but do not have to, reveal secrets to prevent a client from killing or seriously injuring someone. It is assumed that, unless a client says otherwise, lawyers may reveal a client's confidences while negotiating a settlement or plea bargain or when talking to another lawyer in the same firm.

Although the American Bar Association's Model Rules of Professional Conduct generally prohibits lawyers from revealing their client's confidences, it also prohibits lawyers from helping clients conceal or commit criminal acts and prohibits lawyers from presenting false evidence to a court.[7] Lawyers may try to persuade clients not to lie or convince them to admit that they have lied. What other steps lawyers may take to prevent courts from hearing false evidence has been the subject of much debate.

The attorney-client privilege applies to lawyers who represent the government. Such lawyers are not supposed to reveal their "client's" secrets even if they disagree with the government's policies. But one would think that the lawyer's client is the public, not the government, and that the real client is entitled to information bearing on the wisdom of a governmental policy.

The first meeting between a potential client and lawyer should be the time when both parties consciously decide whether they can work together. Clients should never feel "stuck" with a lawyer. Unfortunately some do, even when they have had several bad experiences with a particular attorney. It should not matter whether a lawyer has been recommended by a dozen friends and relatives, is often mentioned in the newspapers and magazines, or is only a name in the yellow pages or on a referral list. Lawyers' competence and personalities differ, and it is up to people seeking legal advice to find lawyers who mesh with their needs and personalities.

I never agreed to undertake a matter unless I was fairly certain that the potential client and I had a clear understanding of what was to be done and could be frank with each other. Without mutual trust and candor, I knew that our relationship could become turbulent and counterproductive for both of us.

Those seeking legal advice should not hesitate to ask lawyers about their experience and expertise, what their chances are of winning, and how much any legal action will cost. If the lawyer is merely a name to the potential client, it is also appropriate to ask for references. People seeking a lawyer have a right to expect their money's worth. They are the ones with rights that need protection. They are the ones most affected by any legal action. They are the ones who have to be satisfied that they are getting the services they bargained for.

Potential clients and lawyers must decide not only whether their personalities mesh but also whether the client has a problem that can be solved by a lawyer and whether the lawyer consulted has the skills necessary to help the client. People too often think that the law will rectify all wrongs. It will not. For example, it may be morally offensive to know that people stood by idly while a child was raped or drowned, but those people may not be prosecuted or sued for doing so because the law usually says they do not have to try to help someone in trouble. A football referee's call may be dead wrong—and may have cost your team a victory—but the courts will not intervene and reverse the result.

When potential clients call to arrange a first meeting, they should give the lawyer a general idea of their problems. That way, lawyers can immediately tell whether the matter is outside their expertise and, if it is something they can handle, bone up on the types of questions they will have to ask the potential client. The more information a person can give a lawyer, not only during their first meeting but also throughout their relationship, the more time and legal fees the client will be able to save.

Like any first meeting between people, there is usually some uneasiness. Clients should not expect to have immediate rapport with their lawyer. They should be prepared to fully explain their situation and why they think they need a lawyer. Lawyers should be prepared to listen and encourage potential clients to talk. Because it is difficult to take notes and listen carefully to someone, many lawyers will tape the conversation instead of taking notes.

Lawyers have to be careful not to put words in people's mouths, and clients should be careful not to let them. Potential clients usually do not know what information is important. Facts that they think are unimportant often have legal significance. Therefore, clients should feel free to tell lawyers everything, no matter how insignificant it may seem. Clients should expect lawyers to devote all their attention to them and not keep interrupting a conversation to answer a telephone call or talk to someone else in the office.

It is difficult to get people to talk freely and not say what they think the lawyer wants to hear. Lawyers do not want people to "remember" things that did not occur, but they also do not want people to omit important details. That means that lawyers should encourage people to elaborate and clarify certain statements and prod for additional information, yet do so without suggesting that a certain

answer is desired. Lawyers should try not to ask too many
questions until the client has gone through his or her story
at least once since the way questions are phrased can influence a person's memory of an incident. In a study by Elizabeth Loftus,[8] people's estimates of how fast an automobile
was going before an accident varied depending on the verb
used to describe the impact. When the verb *smashed* was
used, people estimated the car's speed as 40.8 miles per
hour; *contacted* was only good for 31.8 miles per hour. *Col-
lided* (39.3 miles per hour), *bumped* (38.1 miles per hour),
and *hit* (34.0 miles per hour) all elicited different estimates
of the car's speed.

It should go without saying that lawyers should not put
words in anyone's mouth and generally should not inter-
rupt someone speaking. Nor should lawyers discourage
potential clients from expressing their feelings. Not only
does it show respect for clients to let them express their
feelings, but doing so also helps lawyers understand why
clients are pursuing a matter and helps lawyers make sure
that their clients' expectations are realistic. Legal advice
should not be given until the lawyer is clear what the facts
are; otherwise a client may be encouraged to "steer" statements in a particular direction. Never should a lawyer con-
descend to a potential client.

If a lawyer sounds skeptical, clients should realize that
they have to be. The client may be telling the truth, but
experienced lawyers usually can name many others who
either deliberately lied or misperceived what was happening to them. People naturally try to put themselves in a good
light when they describe past events, and they tend to suppress unfavorable facts. I remember one client who seemed
to have a very good case—until I learned during a recess in
the trial that the opposing counsel was prepared to attack
my client's credibility by questioning him about his conviction and jail term for making certain false statements.
When I asked my client why he had not told me about his
conviction, he told me he did not think it was relevant. It

was. We had to settle the case for substantially less than we had expected.

Lawyers will ask clients to repeat portions of a story—particularly out of sequence—to test a story. If the same expressions are used to describe a situation, then the story may have been rehearsed. Lawyers will point out gaps in a client's story (e.g., something said may be physically impossible, such as a car travelling 60 miles per hour yet stopping in five feet) to try to discover what really happened. Lawyers will directly but politely confront a person about his or her truthfulness if they suspect that someone is deliberately lying to them.

Clients may expect their lawyer to unquestioningly believe everything they say, but, if their lawyer has doubts, you can be sure that opposing counsel will have even more questions. It is better to clear up what really happened before matters proceed too far than it is to risk great embarrassment and adverse consequences in a court of law. Often after first meeting a client I would ask him or her to write up a summary of the relevant facts just to have a record of our conversation. Written summaries are important because invariably they differ from what a client will tell a lawyer in person.

Once lawyers are convinced that they have a good idea of what help a client needs, then they explain to the client whether those needs can be met. Risks, possible benefits, and chances for success should be detailed if litigation is contemplated. If I thought we might lose, I would prepare clients for that possibility.If I knew we should win, I would tell clients that we should win and that we would appeal if we lost.

Clients should expect lawyers to be honest about what they can and cannot do. Lawyers should explain what can be done and should solicit the potential client's reaction to and opinion of the options. Potential clients should not let themselves be intimidated by a lawyer's advice. Lawyers try to recommend strategy that they think will meet an individual's needs, but only the individual knows for sure what those needs are and how best they can be satisfied. I have seen too many people go with a lawyer's advice despite gut feelings that they do not like the way things are proceeding, and the inevitable result is that the client is needlessly dissatisfied with the lawyer's performance. I say needlessly because the lawyer may have pursued a more satisfactory course of action if he or she had been told about the client's qualms. Clients who are not assertive about their feelings do both themselves and their lawyers a disservice by not resolving differences when they still can be resolved.

If both parties agree that the lawyer's legal services are called for and the client is comfortable with the lawyer, then they should confirm their relationship, preferably in writing to avoid any misunderstandings. It is particularly important to come to an agreement about fees so that the bill does not come as an unwelcome surprise.

Many times during my years as a lawyer, I have found that clients do not know how to effectively deal with and utilize the services of their lawyer. I feel that the following tips will help clients develop a good client-lawyer relationship:

What clients should do to help develop
a satisfactory client-lawyer relationship:

1. Check a lawyer's credentials to make sure he or she has the experience and skill to competently handle your legal problem.

2. Decide what result you expect—and communicate that information to your lawyer. You both should have the same goal.

3. Find out what your lawyer plans to do to reach your goal.

4. Do not withhold information from your lawyer, even if it is embarrassing or seems insignificant. You are paying your lawyer to tell you what the law deems significant.

5. Ask your lawyer to explain what you do not understand. You are the only one who knows what you do and do not understand.

6. Be assertive. If you do not like the way your lawyer is handling things, make your feelings clear. Give your lawyer a chance to explain what is being done and correct things that displease you. Remember that you are the one affected by what a lawyer does or does not do and that you have to live with the final outcome. If you feel uncomfortable with what is happening, do not let it continue. Lawyers are paid for advice, not to take control of your life. If you do not agree with what a lawyer is doing and a lawyer fails to either shift directions or give you a satisfactory explanation why he or she cannot do what you want, then get another lawyer.

7. Agree in advance what the fee will be and feel free to ask your lawyer to explain any charges that you do not think are proper—or that you have any questions about.

What clients should expect from their lawyers:

1. Clients should feel confident about their lawyer's abilities. Lawyers should have the necessary skills to do the work. If they do not, then they should not hesitate to recommend someone who does.

2. Clients should be given the opportunity to approve (or at least acquiesce to) all important decisions. All settlement terms should be fully explained and documented.

3. Work should be done without undue delay. Any delays should be explained to a client.

4. Clients should be kept regularly informed about what is happening. Generally, a copy of all correspondence and pleadings should be sent to a client.

5. Fees should be reasonable. Fees should be explained, and detailed records of the time a lawyer has spent on a case should be available for inspection.

6. Lawyers should show respect for their clients. They

should listen to what a client has to say and not talk down to a client.

7. Lawyers should never exaggerate what they can do or guarantee a result.

8. Lawyers should not hesitate to tell a client that they do not know an answer but will find out.

9. Lawyers should not limit themselves to the legal aspects of a problem. Lawyers should also explain how a client's business and personal life can be affected by a problem.

10. Lawyers should defend their judgment and principles, not just cave in to a client's whims.

11. Lawyers should avoid getting involved in business deals with clients. Doing so immediately creates a conflict of interest (e.g., as an investor in your client's corporation, you may want dividends but the client may want to use the money for future expansion).

Interestingly, surveys have shown that clients are more interested in the quality of their relationship with a lawyer than with the results achieved.[9] Most of the complaints about lawyers relate to how a lawyer treated a client, not what the outcome of a legal matter was.

Like marriages, both parties have to work to make a good lawyer-client relationship. Clients must make it clear not only what their needs are but also when they are not being fulfilled, and lawyers must treat clients with the dignity all humans deserve.

Chapter 14

Legal Fees—Too High?

> We trust...our fortune and some-
> times our life and reputation to the
> lawyer and attorney. Such confi-
> dence could not safely be reposed in
> people of a very mean or low condi-
> tion. Their reward must be such,
> therefore, as may give them that
> rank in the society which so impor-
> tant a trust requires.
>
> Adam Smith[1]

> A lawyer is a learned gentleman
> who rescues your estate from your
> enemies and keeps it himself.
>
> Lord Brougham[2]

Although non-lawyers complain about high legal fees and "greedy" lawyers, they generally do not patronize law-yers who practice in squalid conditions, who have difficulty paying rent, who cannot feed their children—who do not at least appear to be "successful." Lawyers so financially insecure that they cannot risk losing a fee or a client are not likely to give clients the independent advice they need (e.g. when to hire a lawyer).

Contrary to popular myth, law is not a "get rich quick" profession. The average earnings of lawyers are neither the highest nor the lowest among all professionals. Unlike business entrepreneurs, most lawyers earn their income from their own labor, not the labor of others. Most lawyers, other than partners in large law firms, only earn money when their "meter is running"—they only earn money for hours they actually work for a client. Lawyers do not pay people a dollar for widgets that can be resold for ten dollars. Nor do most lawyers have people making profits for them while they are asleep or on vacation. Considering the time that it takes to become a lawyer (four years of college undergraduate work and three years of law school) and the additional time that must be spent keeping abreast of changes in the law and building a clientele, many lawyers might be able to make more money in business than in law.

This does not mean, however, that all legal fees are reasonable or that people in need of legal services should not bother comparing the fees of lawyers who can provide competent services. Prospective clients should do as much comparison shopping for legal services as they would for other types of services.

There are four basic methods that lawyers use to decide how much to charge for their work: 1) by the task, 2) by the hour, 3) retainer, and 4) contingent fee. It is important for people using legal services to understand what these fees are and when a particular method is appropriate so that they can be informed consumers and get the most services for their dollar.

Many times lawyers will charge a set fee for a particular job. For less complicated tasks, such as writing a simple will, closing a house sale, or obtaining an uncontested divorce, lawyers have a good idea how much time they will have to work and can set a fee in advance.

Other times, lawyers do not know how much work will be required. For example, if litigation is contemplated, a lawyer will not know in advance how much research will have to be done, how many hours will have to be spent in court, or how much time will have to be spent conferring with witnesses and opposing counsel. In such situations, lawyers may charge by the hour.

Retainers are paid to secure a lawyer's services for a specific period of time or particular task. Business clients frequently will pay lawyers a retainer to handle all their legal needs for a specific period of time. Such an arrangement enables businesses to budget their legal expenses and assures them that the lawyer or law firm that they have confidence in will be available to handle their legal problems—and will not be on the opposite side in a legal controversy. Because their relationship is ongoing, lawyers on retainer generally keep their clients informed of any changes in the law affecting them—when the change occurs, not when the client comes in with a problem—so that the client can avoid trouble. The advantage to a lawyer of steady income is obvious. Retainers to secure a lawyer's services for a period of time or particular job can be kept by lawyers even if no work has to be done. Retainers cement the client's relationship to the lawyer. The amount of the retainer may be adjusted each year to reflect the number of hours that lawyers are expected to work for their clients.

A retainer may be required for a particular job as a downpayment for legal services. A downpayment may be necessary as security for payment, particularly when there is a chance that a client will not pay, either because of credit problems or because of dissatisfaction with the results. For example, a lawyer representing someone charged with a crime is usually careful to get full payment in advance. Retainers are also important for an attorney's cash flow when substantial work is contemplated before any payments otherwise would be due. Retainers used as advance payments are not earned until a lawyer actually does equivalent work for a client.

Contingent fees, the most controversial of the four types of legal fees, are collected only if a client wins; nothing (except perhaps court costs and the lawyer's out-of-pocket expenses) is owed if the client loses. If a client wins, then the lawyer usually collects between 20 percent and a third (sometimes as high as 50 or 60 percent) of any money the client obtains. Contingent fees are controversial because they give lawyers a financial stake in the outcome of a suit, a stake that can run counter to the client's, and public's, best interests. For example, lawyers needing money in a hurry may be tempted to urge a client to settle quickly so that they can get their percentage now instead of having to wait several years for the court to award a potentially much larger sum of money. These fees are unpopular with the public because the ones reported in the press (running hundreds of thousands, even millions, of dollars) seem out of proportion to the amount of work performed by the lawyers.

Contingent fees are illegal in most countries. The main justification for contingent fees is that they encourage lawyers to represent clients too poor to pay lawyers by the hour. Unfortunately, many clients who can afford to pay lawyers by the hour are not given that choice. Contingent fees running hundreds of thousands or millions of dollars are defended as making up for uncompensated work on lost causes. But it is more likely that large awards overcompensate lawyers for time spent on contingent fee cases since lawyers usually do not accept contingent fee cases that they are likely to lose. Most lawyers racing to Bhopal, India to sign up victims of the Union Carbide poison gas leak to contingent fee agreements probably were not concerned about whether victims would be able to afford legal services. More likely, they were there to personally share in the recovery. Contingent fees also are defended as encouraging lawyers to zealously represent their clients—something they should do without additional financial incentive.

The American Bar Association's Model Rules of Professional Conduct permits contingent fees except for two instances when they would be against the public interest: lawyers may not make their fees contingent upon obtaining a divorce or certain amount of alimony or support for a client; nor may their fees be contingent upon successfully defending a client charged with a crime.[3] The comment to this rule says that lawyers should give clients a choice of fee arrangements "[w]hen there is doubt whether a contingent fee is consistent with the client's best interest" and should explain the implications of the alternative fee arrangements.

For lower and middle class clients, this is Hobson's choice. They cannot afford to pay out money for a benefit that may come only after years in the courts—or, worse, may never come. Then, when they do receive money to compensate them for their injuries, a third or more will be taken off the top to compensate their lawyers. Contingent fee arrangements have to be available to give all people access to our legal system, but caps placed on the total amount of the fee could assure that the fee is "reasonable."

One other type of fee that sometimes comes up is the referral fee, a fee charged by one lawyer to another (or by a lay person to a lawyer) for referring a client to the lawyer. Such fees are charged but are not approved by most states. The American Bar Association's Model Rules of Professional Conduct permits lawyers from different firms to divide fees only if 1) the division is in proportion to the services actually rendered by each lawyer or a written agreement with the client makes the lawyers jointly responsible for handling the case, 2) the client knows about and does not object to the lawyers' participation, and 3) the total fee is reasonable.[4] Proponents of referral fees have argued that they may as well be approved since they are widely used (they are usually a third of the total fee), that use of them encourages lawyers to direct clients to the best lawyer for the client, and that clients are not hurt by referral fees because the overall fee remains the same. Opponents have been appalled by the notion that lawyers have to be paid to tell clients that they cannot handle the client's problem and believe it is unseemly to have lawyers make money for work not performed. Opponents agree that fee-splitting occurs but believe that it is wrong and should be policed. They question whether the fee a client pays would really be the same if there were no referral fees. They believe that there is a serious question whether clients would be directed to the best lawyers or only to the lawyers paying the highest referral fees.

Fees may be set by courts, by law (fees for representing clients before federal agencies may be limited by statute or administrative regulation), and by lawyers themselves. Usually fees must be "reasonable." The American Bar Association's Model Rules of Professional Conduct lists many factors that must be considered to determine whether a fee is reasonable:[5]

1. time and labor required
2. novelty and difficulty of the legal questions at issue
3. skill required to properly perform the legal services
4. likelihood, if apparent to the client, that working for the client will prevent the lawyer from accepting other clients (e.g., a conflict of interest might result)
5. fee customarily charged in the area for similar services
6. amount involved
7. results
8. time limits imposed by the client or by the circumstances
9. nature and length of the professional relationship the lawyer has with the client
10. experience, reputation, and ability of the lawyer
11. whether fee is fixed or contingent

Note that a client's ability to pay does not justify lawyers in charging them more than the services were worth. Lawyers may not charge wealthy clients extra to compensate for pro bono work.

Until 1975, it was easy for lawyers to decide what fees to charge since they could look at minimum fee schedules developed by local bar associations. Such schedules have been ruled illegal by the United States Supreme Court, which decided in 1975 that they violated the antitrust laws.

Clients become outraged when they are charged hundreds

of dollars for the answer to what they consider to be a simple question. Unfortunately, clients rarely see their lawyers at work. They think that after passing the bar examination an attorney knows all the law; they do not realize how much research may have to be done before a lawyer can answer a client's "simple" yes-or-no-question. Thousands of court and administrative decisions, new laws, and new regulations are published each year, and lawyers may have to put in many hours of research before they can be confident that they have the correct answer to a client's legal question.

When the public hear that a lawyer makes $100 an hour, they do some quick calculations ($100 multiplied by 40 hours/week multiplied by 52 weeks/year) and decide that the lawyer is making more than $200,000 a year. What they do not understand is that the hourly fee is for a "billable" hour, not necessarily each hour in the office, and that lawyers have to pay all their office expenses from the hourly fees.

Lawyers do not spend each hour of their day working on matters for their clients. In an eight-hour day, they are fortunate to be able to bill clients for five or six hours of work. The other hours are spent handling general administrative functions and drumming up business. Additional hours may be spent keeping up with current developments in the law—time not charged to any client. Lawyers cannot charge anyone for time they are ill or on vacation. Nor do they generally charge for hours spent lying awake at night thinking about a client's case.

Without working overtime, lawyers can expect to bill clients for approximately 1300 hours of work a year. Associates in large law firms may be expected to bill clients for more than 2000 hours a year, which means they end up working 80-100 hours a week. So when you hear that an associate is making $40,000 a year, remember that he or she may be making $8-10 per hour of actual work (assuming two weeks of vacation)—less than he or she could make in many other jobs.

Lawyers set their hourly rate by estimating how much

lawyers with comparable skills and experience make per year and then calculating how many hours they expect to bill clients per year and how much their overhead (expenses such as rent, secretarial services, gas, electricity, telephone calls, supplies) will be. Overhead averages 40 percent but can be as high as 50 to 60 percent of a lawyer's gross receipts. How much lawyers with comparable skills and experience make is estimated by talking with other lawyers and looking at surveys conducted by bar associations and private entrepreneurs.

Many client complaints about fees result from lack of communication between lawyers and their clients. The American Bar Association's Model Rules of Professional Conduct imposes an ethical obligation on lawyers to tell new clients how they will be charged (e.g., by the hour or a flat fee), preferably in writing, either before or within a reasonable time after a person becomes a client.[6] Contingent fee agreements must be in writing and must explain what percentage of any recovery must be paid to the lawyer, what expenses will have to be paid by the client, and whether expenses are or are not to be deducted from the client's recovery before a lawyer's percentage is calculated. Advance payments may be required, but any unearned portion must be returned. Lawyers can accept property as payment as long as the property is not involved in a client's suit.

People seeking legal advice not only have a right but also a duty to themselves to find out how much they will be charged—and when. Lawyers usually cannot quote a specific sum, but they should be able to estimate within a range how much their services will cost. For minor disputes involving small sums of money, it will not pay to hire a lawyer, and lawyers should be quick to point that out to prospective clients and steer them to alternative methods of resolving their disputes, such as small claims courts. Although the public sometimes thinks that lawyers are obsessed with fees, many actually do not pay enough attention to them. They look on fees as a necessary evil and are so absorbed with solving a client's problem that they fail to analyze whether it is worth it to the client to use a lawyer. It is to a lawyer's advantage to explain clearly in writing how much a client will be charged; otherwise a potentially good client may be lost, work may end up being done for nothing, and charges may be filed with an attorney disciplinary commission. Once a legal matter is resolved—either for or against a client—the lawyer's value drops considerably, and setting fees is almost certain to arouse animosity. Suits by lawyers to collect fees from clients may be counterproductive since they sometimes result in counterclaims for malpractice and adverse publicity and cost lawyers time that could be devoted to paying clients.

Matters that should be discussed in a fee agreement include:

1. client's goal
2. services to be performed by the lawyer, including an estimate of how much the services will cost, or a statement of hourly rates and examples of time charges; estimate of how long services will take (both the number of hours and the period of time it will take to finish services for the client)
3. amount of any retainer (or deposit) plus an explanation of how the money will be used (e.g., to pay costs and/or fees)
4. frequency of billing and, if permitted in the state, a delinquency charge for late payments
5. name(s) of lawyers(s) who will handle the matter
6. client's obligation to pay costs (costs may include such things as the fees of clerks, marshalls, court reporters, and witnesses, printing and copying expenses, docket fees, compensation of court-appointed experts and interpreters) and an estimate of the costs
7. explanation of what happens if court-awarded attorney fees are more or less than fees received from the client

ON TRIAL!

8. resolution of fee disputes (e.g., by arbitration)
9. promissory note as security for payment of fees
10. explanation that lawyer cannot guarantee a decision
    in client's favor; explanation of any risks involved in
    what client is doing
11. possible conflicts of interest (particularly when multi-
    ple clients in the same matter are represented by one
    lawyer)

The fee agreement may be drafted as a letter or as a contract. A letter is friendlier and more personal; a contract emphasizes the importance of the step the client is about to take. Ambiguous language will be construed in a client's favor. Clients must make certain that they understand that all time will be counted, even telephone calls, letters, and consultations between members of the same firm. By knowing this, clients can reduce their bills.

In England, litigation is discouraged by requiring losers to pay the attorney fees of the winner, but in the United States each party must pay his or her own legal fees. Some statutes, such as the Civil Rights Attorney's Fees Awards Act, allow the prevailing party to collect attorney fees from the loser, but, in the absence of a statute, all parties, even those suing to safeguard the public interest, must pay their own legal fees.

When services are to be performed over a period of time, clients should insist that they be billed on a regular basis. That way, any disputes about the fee can be resolved at an early date. Interim billing lets clients monitor legal costs and adjust their goals if it looks as if their case will cost more or less than they expected. Interim billing also helps a lawyer's cash flow and makes it more likely that a client will pay since a client is more likely to pay a series of small bills than one large bill.

Bills should itemize the services performed and the charge for each service. Such bills should be sent to clients so that they will know that their attorney is doing what should be done.

As might be expected, taxes must be considered when clients are billed. Allocation of fees to various legal services has tax ramifications since legal expenses that produce taxable income usually are deductible. For example, legal expenses incurred to draft a will are not deductible, but fees paid for documents relating to income-producing property covered by the will may be. Fees paid to help a client recover damages for personal injuries are not deductible, but fees that help a client recover lost profits are. Clients must make certain that fees are properly allocated so that they do not lose any valid tax deductions.

Many lawyers will allow clients to use a major credit card to pay their bills. Others may ask for a promissory note. Clients should not sign a note until they are certain that they understand what their obligations will be.

Some clients will complain no matter what the charge is. I had one client for 20 years, from the time he started a business with about $5,000 until the time he sold it for more than three million dollars. My fees were nominal at first, then increased somewhat as his business grew and more legal problems arose. When it came time to sell the business, I sat in on the negotiations and discouraged him from selling it to two potential buyers in exchange for stock, which would be worthless now since both potential buyers went out of business. I then helped him sell his business for more than $3,050,000, all cash. My fees were paid by the buyer. No money came out of my client's pocket, but he complained that the bill was too high. He said it was a "hold-up." To this day every time I see him he complains about this or that lawyer. But he is typical of some business people, who believe that they are the only ones entitled to earn a reasonable return for their efforts. They resent paying for anything that does not represent a profit to them. They complain about a lawyer's "greed" while they ask help to work out a business deal that will net them millions of dollars. They do not consider the many hours that their lawyer has to devote to their interests.

Another client I had was sued for $100,000 for defaming

an employment agency. He was absolutely in the wrong
and was sure to lose the suit, but he refused my recommendation to settle for $2,000 plus court costs. Sure enough, we
tried the case, and the judgment against him was for
$15,000. He squawked when I billed him $3,500, which was
about half what it should have been based on time spent but
much more than it would have been if he had followed my
advice and settled the suit.

Over my years of active practice, I had few complaints
about fees. I never asked a client for a retainer as downpayment for a particular task. Most lawyers would think
this unbusinesslike. Many clients thought I was too trust-
ing, and some wanted to pay me money up front, but I would
tell them, "I haven't done any work for you yet. Why don't
we see what it takes." To reassure clients that their bill
would not be unexpectedly high, I would add, "When you
get a bill, if you think it's too much, you tell me what is fair
and I'll take what you think is fair. But if I don't think it's
fair, you'll never come through these doors again." I never
lost a client because of a fee dispute. One client actually
paid me twice as much as I asked because he felt I had
undercharged him.

Some lawyers charge more than their services are worth,
which is wrong, but policing them cannot be left to the
various bar associations. The most effective means of controlling legal fees is for the public to do some shopping
around and come to an understanding with the lawyer
about fees at the start. Businesses have already begun
doing so, and this trend has had an effect on what prices
lawyers will charge. Gone are the days when lawyers could
just add up their expenses, add an amount they felt was an
appropriate salary, and then charge accordingly. Now
management consultants make a fortune advising lawyers
how to control their costs so that they can make money and
yet hold the line on fees.

The public hears about the salaries of lawyers at the top
of the profession and mistakenly assumes that other lawyers receive comparable amounts. Of course this does not

mean that the average lawyer's salary is bordering on the poverty level. Many lawyers may not earn as much money as other professionals, but they earn a decent living, enough to take care of their families.

When people complain about the money lawyers make, they should also remember the important role lawyers play in our society in protecting people's rights. Lawyers come cheap in the Soviet Union (they earn about half as much as many teachers and factory workers[7]), but that is also the value placed on individual rights by the Soviet government.

Chapter 15

Legal Education

Legal education sounds like a topic of no interest to the general public. Certainly it is a subject that most members of the public have been content to let lawyers deal with. But they are wrong to avoid thinking about it. Legal education not only is important for students and professors but also for the entire society. How lawyers are educated should be of concern because the training lawyers receive helps determine how well they can serve the public interest.

Dramatic presentations such as the TV show *Paper Chase* portray law school as a place for long hours of hard work, intellectual challenge, and intimidating professors. At some time or another during the first year of law school probably every law student is told: "Look at the person on your right. Now look at the person to your left. Three years from now one of you will not be graduating from this law school." Second and third year students comfort their new classmates with the adage: "The first year they scare you to death, the second year they work you to death, and the third year they bore you to death."

Thomas Jefferson has been credited with introducing systematic legal instruction into the United States.[1] In 1779, William and Mary appointed George Wythe, one of the signers of the Declaration of Independence, as the first American law professor (he taught "Law and Police").[2] Other colleges followed William and Mary 's lead but were unable to attract many students. Harvard Law School opened in 1817 with six students and had 19 students in 1820; but by 1829, when Harvard's first attempt at operating a law school ended, it was down to one student.[3]

Before this century, most lawyers did not go to law school. Instead, they apprenticed themselves to practicing attorneys and "read law." As late as 1900, about 85 percent of American lawyers were not college-trained, and it was not until 1928 that any state required lawyers to go to law school.[4] West Virginia was the first state to make law school compulsory.[5] It was not until around 1950 that the number of lawyers with some college education finally exceeded the number who had never been to college.[6]

The modern American law school was invented in the 1870's by Christopher Columbus Langdell, dean of Harvard Law School. Langdell, who had little experience practicing law, helped popularize what is known as the case method of studying law, which involves the study of written court decisions. To Langdell, the library was the center of legal education.[7]

Until Langdell, and for many years after his tenure as dean of Harvard Law School, law schools and legal education were given little academic respect. Law schools, many of which were not associated with any universities, generally were considered trade schools, and even legal training offered by universities was accorded second class academic status. Colleges generally treated law as an undergraduate program, and admission standards for law were lower than for liberal arts studies. Because of these lower standards, it was possible to find a disproportionate number of athletes enrolled in law school.[8] Hugo Black, one of the great United States Supreme Court justices, was denied admission to the University of Alabama's College of Arts and Sciences in 1904 but had no trouble being accepted by Alabama's law school.[9]

Langdell helped make legal education academically respectable by divorcing it from the technical skills needed to practice law, such as the ability to counsel clients, draft documents, and negotiate settlements and other types of agreements. Before Langdell, people were chosen as law professors because of their long experience as lawyers, but Langdell wanted professors unsullied by practical experience. As he put it: "What qualifies a person...to teach law, is not experience in the work of a lawyer's office, not experience in dealing with men, not experience in the trial or argument of cases, not experience, in short, in using law, but experience in learning law."[10] Harvard's appointment in 1873 of James Barr Ames as an assistant professor of law was controversial because Ames had little experience as a practicing attorney.[11]

For many years there has been controversy over the proper function of a legal education. Apprenticeship originally was the preferred form of legal education because it seemed most important to give lawyers the technical skills necessary to practice law. Langdell believed that students could actually learn all substantive law by studying court opinions, but later advocates of the case method of legal education have recognized that all substantive law cannot be learned in law school. Instead they have emphasized that legal education should give students the analytical skills necessary to become lawyers. Judge Jerome Frank criticized the emphasis on analytical skills to the exclusion of skills training because he believed it gives students an unreal picture of law and law practice:

The law students are like future horticulturists studying solely cut flowers; or like future architects studying merely pictures of buildings. They resemble prospective dog-breeders who never see anything but stuffed dogs.[12]

When I studied law at DePaul University College of Law in the early 1930's, I did not learn the practical aspects of practicing law. For example, I learned what a last will is but not how to plan an estate. I learned all about fee simple titles, the Rule in Shelley's case, life estates, and residuary estates, but I did not learn how to close a real estate purchase and sale. I learned all the substantive law about corporations but not how to organize a corporation. I learned all about matrimonial law but nothing about how to actually prosecute a divorce.

A short course on legal ethics taught me not to solicit legal business. I did not learn how to handle clients or build a law practice. I should at least have had a lecture or two on how to handle the first client who comes in. Do you wait for the client to tell you all the facts? Do you try to show the client how smart you are and ask a lot of questions? Do you cross-examine the client? How intimate should you become with clients? How do you handle the matter of fees? Under what circumstances do you take a contingent fee matter? How do you build up a client's confidence in you? Do you try to make your client a close friend? Do you invite clients and their spouses to dinner? Do you take advantage of an opportunity to invest in your client's business? Can you become your client's business partner? If you feel that your client's business judgment is not so good, do you try to discourage him or her from going into a new business? After all, if you do you may lose an opportunity to earn some money. How do you go about building a law practice? Do you sit and wait for the first client to come in? I knew no one, not even a relative, who could give me some business. I could not advertise. How could I get people to know that I was practicing law?

My classmates and I were supposed to be able to advise clients, but we learned little if anything about how to deal with the psychological needs of clients in order to smooth the resolution of their legal problems. We proudly placed our names over the entranceway door of our new law offices. We had business cards printed. But we knew nothing about the economics of practicing law. We had to learn about it from other lawyers or on a hit or miss basis, sometimes at the expense of clients. Much of my practice was spent negotiating matters, but I never had a course telling me how it should be done.

Beginning in the late 1960's, law schools increasingly were criticized for not training students how to practice law. Chief Justice Burger was in the forefront of those advocating that law schools provide more skills training. A special task force of the American Bar Association Section of Legal Education and Admissions to the Bar studied this problem and concluded in 1979: "Law schools should provide instruction in those fundamental skills critical to lawyer competence. In addition to being able to analyze legal problems and do legal research, a competent lawyer must be able effectively to write, communicate orally, gather facts, interview, counsel, and negotiate."[13] The special task force rejected the traditional argument against skills training by law schools, that such skills could be picked up after law school: "The notion that young lawyers should gain an acceptable level of competence in the practice, in effect learning at the expense of their first clients, is today not an acceptable one."[14] In 1981, the American Bar Association amended its standards for accrediting law schools to require that they "offer instruction in professional skills."[15]

Some law professors argued that they had their hands full teaching analytical skills and substantive law and did not have time for anything else. Nevertheless, law schools responded to the criticism by adding courses discussing the more practical aspects of practicing law (e.g., trial advocacy, legal drafting, client counseling, and negotiating). Clinical education programs have given students a chance to get hands-on training supervised by experienced attorneys. Although clinical education is costly, it has the advantage of being able to mix theory and practice. For example, a student can be steeped in the theory of divorce law and can gain insight into the trauma of a breakup and battle over custody and property.

Such courses can help prepare students for a career in law, but they can only be a start, not an end, to a person's legal education. Continual study and refinement of skills is necessary if lawyers are to remain competent to practice law. When I started my law practice, and even in later years, I found it helpful to use checklists to guide me through basic transactions, such as closing a real estate sale or selling a business. I would prepare a checklist before handling a transaction and would refine the checklist after completing the transaction. A representative from a legal publisher happened to see one of my checklists and encouraged me to turn them into what have become two successful books for practitioners.

The case method is only one of several methods of legal instruction. Others include lecturing, problem solving, and clinical education. Under the case method of studying law, students are directed to read court decisions, pick out the facts and rules of law relied on by the court, state the issues and the court's decision, and then explain how that decision was reached. During classroom discussions, students are closely questioned about what they have read and analyzed. Students' understanding of a principle of law is tested by varying the facts. A whole class session might be spent studying a single principle of law, sometimes a principle of law that has long since been overruled.

No other method of teaching law has proven as effective in developing students' analytical skills—in teaching students how to "think like a lawyer." But a disadvantage of the case method is that students learn less substantive law than they would through lectures. Law students realize how little substantive law they have learned during their three years of law school when it comes time to start studying for the bar exam and they have to start plowing through study guides filled with rules of law they never studied during law school.

No one disputes the notion that students have to develop skill in legal analysis, but many have questioned what percentage of a student's legal education should be devoted to learning that skill and how much time should be devoted to learning substantive law and practical skills. In 1978 Chief Justice Burger proposed that the third year of legal education be replaced by a year of clinical education.[16] Herbert L. Packer and Thomas Ehrlich, in their report prepared for the Carnegie Commission on Higher Education, agreed that two years is sufficient to teach students how to think like a lawyer.[17]

Many legal educators have tended to minimize the importance of learning the actual rules of law during law school by noting how quickly laws change and by arguing that students can pick up the substantive law they need after law school. That may have been true when I first hung out my shingle, before courts and government started to regulate almost every aspect of our lives, but it is not true now. Without a general background in a subject, the newly licensed lawyer may not even know what further study is required. This is particularly true for tax law. I learned tax law as it developed, but now it is so complex that a lawyer coming out of law school without a good background in the subject could not competently handle a business or real estate transaction without the help of someone familiar with tax law. It is not the type of material that can be picked up quickly during breaks in daily practice. It takes many hours to develop an expertise in tax law—hours that the beginning lawyer does not have.

Realizing this problem, law schools increasingly have relied on lecturing and less on questions and answers to cover subjects in second and third year courses. Lecturing allows professors to convey more information during a class than the Socratic question-and-answer method.

A fundamental question that has been raised about legal education is whether the public should want people to "think like lawyers." The case method of study in particular has been criticized for making logical consistency, not justice, the ideal, for discouraging creative solutions to problems, for teaching law students to put distance between themselves and their clients, and for perpetuating the status quo. Thomas L. Shaffer, now a professor of law at Washington and Lee University School of Law, and attorney Robert S. Redmount, in their book *Lawyers, Law Students and People*, have criticized legal education for its lack of humanism and for encouraging "the view that law is a technical enterprise."[18] They criticize lawyers trained by these schools for preferring

> an impersonal coolness. They avoid sticky human encounter. They seize, in law school and after law school, opportunities to put distance between themselves and people who need them.... Problems are seen as opportunities for investigation, defense, abstract persuasion, and argument, rather than as opportunities for involvement.... They tend to deal with human feelings by ignoring them when possible, and battering them away when they will not be ignored. They prefer faith in words to faith in people.[19]

Part of this problem has been attributed to many law professors' lack of practical experience. As Judge Charles W. Joiner has written: "The problem is that not enough of these excellent teachers have spent sufficient time with other lawyers in the profession to acquire a first-hand knowledge of how it works. They know how to deal with the law but not how to make decisions about the law as it affects people and their institutions. They do not have the capacity to fit the technical aspects of lawyering to the social aspects of lawyering."[20]

Others have criticized legal education for emphasizing litigation instead of peaceful resolutions of conflict. As Jon W. Bruce, a professor of law at Vanderbilt University School of Law, has written: "Our present system of legal education is so overwhelmingly geared toward producing litigators, that socially valuable attitudes (such as empathy and compassion) and skills (such as counseling and negotiation) are often neglected if not disdained."[21] Derek Bok has agreed: "...law schools train their students more for conflict than for the gentler arts of reconciliation and accommodation."[22] This is not a new criticism. In 1891 the American Bar Association Committee on Legal Education criticized the case method for encouraging lawyers to be too willing to litigate.[23] More recently, Chief Justice Burger has said that: "Legal education should include substantial instruction in arbitration, negotiation, client counseling and interviewing. Prospective lawyers must learn that they do not have to structure all the needs of their clients in adversarial terms, and that it is in no one's best interest to litigate every dispute."[24] In response to these criticisms, some law schools have begun to teach students how to resolve disputes without resorting to litigation and how to use preventive law to reduce the possibility of disputes arising.

Students reading about conflicts between individuals can easily lose sight of the social, political and economic consequences resulting from a court's decision. For example, when I started practicing law, there was a rule that someone injured because of a defective product could not recover damages from the product's manufacturer unless there was proof that the manufacturer was negligent in manufacturing the particular product. As you might imagine, it was very difficult to prove that a defect was the result of a manufacturer's negligence and not the result of something that happened after the product left the manufacturer's plant. The result was that the economic cost of injuries had to be borne by consumers.

Students reading about such cases may develop a restrictive view of the problem. When we heard that someone was injured because a tire exploded or some piece of equipment malfunctioned, we started wondering whether the defect could be attributed to the negligence of a particular company instead of taking a larger view of the problem and asking whether the cost of such injuries should be borne by innocent consumers or by manufacturers profiting from sales of the product. Eventually, people began to ask the right question, and the rule now is that manufacturers are strictly liable for injuries caused by defective products. This rule makes the economic cost of injuries part of the price of the product and not a cost that an injured person has to pay.

Legal education also has been criticized for conditioning students to accept existing rules and not to ask whether the rule really meets the needs of society. Legal education has tended to perpetuate a legal philosophy known as Legal Positivism,which defines law as a set of rules and which assumes that answers can be logically deduced from these rules. Legal education has been criticized for separating what "is" from what "ought to be," thus tending to legitim- ize the status quo. Legal Positivists look at what the rules are, not at the social, political, economic, moral, and psy- chological factors that produced the rules and someday may change them.

For years people objected to the rule barring an injured person from recovering damages if he or she was guilty of any negligence (contributory negligence). They objected to the rule because it led to egregious results. For example, a pedestrian straying from a crosswalk might not be able to recover damages for injuries caused when he was hit by a speeding, drunken driver because both might be considered negligent. It did not matter how slight an injured person's negligence was. Few liked the rule, but, instead of changing it, lawyers conditioned to expect slow changes in the law looked for loopholes. For example, some courts developed a rule called the "last clear chance doctrine," which disre- garded an injured person's negligence if, despite that negli- gence, the defendant still had a "last chance" to avoid an accident. In recent years almost all states have abandoned this rule and replaced it with the doctrine of comparative negligence, which in its "pure" form allows an injured per- son to recover damages even if he or she was also slightly negligent. The amount of damages is reduced by the injured person's negligence.

Some people point to these new rules as proof that the system can change, and they feel that the slowness of the change is a virtue. Because changes are made only after many people have come to agree that change is necessary, it is more likely that changes will be good when they are finally made. But critics have pointed to all those years when the results were inequitable, people agreed that the results were inequitable, but change was not forthcoming. They also have expressed concern that many law students will never learn to think constructively and creatively about society's complex problems. There are always some people who will be able to look beyond the facts of a controversy between individuals and analyze the social impact of any particular result. But the intellectual talents of many others may never be applied to these problems because they are too used to accepting the law as it is.

The main criticism of legal education has been that it emphasizes the head at the expense of the heart. Success is measured by intellect, not compassion. "Thinking like a lawyer" may be interpreted by inadequate professors as emotionally sterile analysis. Expressing emotions may be frowned on as unprofessional and a hindrance to legal reasoning. Law students may learn to value logical consistency and continuity with the past, even if a past decision was wrong or right for its time but not for ours. The legal system may become an end in itself, not a means to resolve conflicts among feeling human beings. Clients may become legal problems to be solved instead of individuals deserving respect and help in resolving conflicts often rooted in social problems. Students told to check their morality and social conscience outside the classroom may become less sensitive to the needs of others, less tolerant of human frailties, and less concerned about social problems.

Legal educators have the responsibility to give lawyers the head and heart necessary to fulfill their public responsibilities. Lawyers have the skills and power to improve this country, but first they must care about their fellow human beings. Law without intellect is fiat; law without compassion is a set of rules irrelevant to people's needs. If lawyers are to make sure that laws meet people's needs, they must learn to think critically of laws and legal institutions. The public should expect no less.

Chapter 16

Legal Profession as a Way of Life

What is it like to be a lawyer? I have been asked that question many times during my years of practice, usually by young people who are interested in law as a career. But there are also people who are tired of the way they have been earning a living and want to try doing something different. Once when I was teaching a course in legal drafting at DePaul University College of Law, my best student was a man who had been an executive for a major U.S. company but who had always wanted to be a lawyer. Now he was fulfilling his lifelong ambition—at age seventy-two.

I learned quickly that practicing law is not as dramatic as it was then portrayed on radio and later on television. TV does not show lawyers spending long hours on research or waiting several years for a case to come to trial. TV does not show lawyers dealing with average people with average problems.

That does not mean that law practice is dull. There are always new clients, new adversaries, new factual situations, and new legal problems to resolve. Law practice involves getting to know people, figuring out what makes them tick, their motivations, their ambitions, and their problems. I have found it challenging and satisfying to help people resolve disputes.

When I was sixteen and smitten with success as a high school debater, I began working for a court reporter. I delivered transcripts during the Richard Loeb-Nathan Leopold-Bobby Franks murder case. What a thrill it was to hear and watch Clarence Darrow question witnesses, argue motions, and make his appeal to the court that Leopold and Loeb should be sentenced to life imprisonment instead of death. I will never forget the day Darrow turned around to me and said "thank you" for delivering a transcript to him on time.

Most studies show that people are attracted to the law because they have a greater than average desire for certainty in life and think of themselves as knights on white chargers who will set things right. Unfortunately for them, they soon discover that little in law is certain and that it is easy to be unhorsed.

A recent survey indicated that more than 40 percent of young lawyers (47 percent of young female attorneys) are unhappy with the reality of practicing law and would reconsider going into law if they were to start all over again.[1] People disappointed with their career choice complain that they have to deal with unhappy clients, incompetent attorneys, and aloof superiors. Too many people going into law think that a law degree is a winning lottery ticket. Sure, most lawyers make a good living, and competent lawyers have no difficulty making better than a good living, but few get rich just by practicing law. Lawyers only make money when their time meter is running. Particularly when they are young, they have to work long hours to earn a living.

People who think of law as a winning lottery ticket do not realize how stressful it can be to juggle many cases and problems while trying to find time to do a good job for each client. Nor do they realize how much routine work a lawyer does. Few lawyers get great burning legal questions to argue all the way up to the United States Supreme Court. Few lawyers even get cases that they can argue all the way up to a state supreme court.

I am not saying this to denigrate the practice of law. Law is a great profession—for the right person. No day is the same as another. There are always new people to meet and new challenges to face. Lawyers can have the satisfaction of resolving disputes between individuals, between people and organizations, between businesses, and within families. As Justice Oliver Wendell Holmes, Jr., once said:

> Every calling is great when greatly pursued. But what other gives such scope to realize the spontaneous energy of one's soul? In what other does one plunge so deep in the stream of life—so share its passions, its battles, its despair, its triumphs, both as witness and actor?[2]

If every person lived alone on an island, there would be no need for lawyers. But whenever people congregate, there is conflict and a need for laws and lawyers to resolve that conflict in a way that will keep society from splintering into anarchy.

For lawyers involved in commercial and corporate practice, there is satisfaction in nurturing new businesses and in guiding existing businesses through the shoals of our business and tax laws. For lawyers involved in public causes, there is the satisfaction of helping to ameliorate or solve major social, economic, and political problems. For lawyers involved in criminal law, there is satisfaction in protecting society from incorrigibles and in defending wrongfully accused Davids from the Goliath we call government.

I have found it gratifying to participate in the creation of new enterprises for clients, whether a profit corporation, charitable foundation, or partnership. I have been midwife and counsellor to the birth, growth, and emancipation of at least a hundred different businesses. I have enjoyed serving as counsel and trustee of a number of foundations funded by clients for scholarships.

I am particularly gratified that I conceived and organized a foundation that funded scholarships for Polish youths studying the American way of life and American youths of Polish descent studying the history of their predecessors. Shortly before the turn of the century, William Zelosky, then twelve, came to the United States from Poland. He worked hard and long hours as a youngster and by the middle of the 1920's was one of Chicago's leading land subdividers and house builders. During the Depression, when thousands of Chicagoans were losing their homes in mortgage foreclosures, Bill Zelosky would cancel and forgive part of the principal and defer interest payments in order to let the homeowner save his or her property. During the Depression Bill did not foreclose on a single home.

Throughout his youth and during his adult years, Bill was a voracious reader of American history. He loved his adopted country. One day after his nephew, Edward Warden, and I moved into one of his offices to start practicing law (we agreed to give him legal services in lieu of rental payments), he wanted to know how he could leave part of his estate to educate Polish youngsters in the American way of life.

We worked out a charitable remainder trust under his will whereby, after the death of his wife and sister, the remaining estate would be used for scholarships for Polish youngsters coming to the United States to study the American way of life and for American youngsters of Polish descent travelling to Poland to study Polish traditions. When Mrs. Zelosky died, there was a trust valued at more than a million dollars, and the trust is still in effect. We had to work our way through considerable Polish red tape in order to get the government's permission to allow students to come to the United States and study the American way of life. We had to defend the will in a will contest instituted by a relative who claimed it was against American public policy since it permitted communists to come to the United States and propagandize our youth. We won, and over five hundred Polish students (undergraduate and graduate) have come to the United States to study our nation. As a trustee, I have spoken with a good number of them before they returned to Poland. I can testify to the goodwill and respect that this project has generated for the United States.

A career in law can bring out the best of a person's analytical abilities. As Justice Holmes said in a ringing endorsement of law as a career:

> The law is the calling of thinkers. But to those who believe with me that not the least godlike of man's activities is the large survey of causes, that to know is not less than to feel, I say—and I say no longer with any doubt—that a man may live greatly in the law as well as elsewhere; that there as well as elsewhere his thought may find its unity in an infinite perspective; that there as well as elsewhere he may wreak himself upon life, may drink the bitter cup of heroism, may wear his heart out after the unattainable.[3]

Studying law stretches the limits of one's thinking powers. The observational powers of a Sherlock Holmes may be necessary to ferret out all relevant facts. Rigorous logic is required to distinguish between facts and mere assumptions or inferences. Great imagination may be required to prepare for everything that might happen. Sound judgment is called for to navigate a true course through facts, law, and the random occurrences that make life so interesting—and infuriating.

After getting my law license it gave me a feeling of importance suddenly to be expected to express my opinion on all types of subjects, even matters not involving law, simply because I was a lawyer. Being a lawyer was my ticket to respect, not only among my friends but also in my community. As a lawyer I was viewed as a leader of the community. As years went by, I became disappointed at the number of lawyers who were not as aware as I thought they should be of economic, social, and political problems, both in this country and internationally.

Practicing law is a lifetime intellectual challenge. Successful lawyers do not have to have superior intelligence, but they must be willing and able to expand their knowledge and combine such knowledge with logic and persuasive ability to accomplish their tasks. People interested in becoming lawyers should enjoy and hunger for continuing and unlimited knowledge of many disciplines. Some lawyers carve out a limited area of law for practice, but most find themselves participating in a perpetual quest for all types of knowledge necessary to do their job right. During my years of practice I have had cases that required me to learn about such subjects as chemistry, accounting, physiology, gerontology, finance, business management, and metallurgy.

Good lawyering requires great sensitivity to the feelings of others. To resolve problems, lawyers must learn to understand what makes people tick—what their motivations and objectives are and how they act. Law is not just an intellectual game, though some lawyers try to treat it that way. Laws affect individuals, groups, even society itself, and lawyers must always be sensitive to the very real consequences of their actions. Sterile logic cannot provide the creative solutions necessary for society to continue to evolve and not stultify and die.

Luck is less a factor in the success of a lawyer than it is in other endeavors. Some breaks may be helpful, such as marrying the child of a senior partner in a prosperous law firm or having a client walk in with a large-fee case. But lawyers still need talent to succeed. Businesses may be able to find a place where the incompetent child of the president can do no harm, but law firms cannot afford to carry incompetent lawyers, even if they are children of a senior partner.

Having said that, I have to admit that I got my taste of big firm law practice by chance. I was practicing law with someone I had gone to law school with when I received a letter from Irving Florsheim asking if he could count on me again for a $10,000 contribution to the Chicago Jewish Federation. Since I was earning less than $5,000 a year, I knew he had made a mistake. He had—the letter was addressed to Benjamin *V.* Becker instead of Benjamin *M.* Becker.

I did not think much about the error until a year later when I got an identical letter from Irving Florsheim. This time I decided to meet Benjamin V. Becker, who turned out to be a little man in stature with an especially large chair matching his importance as senior partner in a big firm with an illustrious history. The firm had partners who had gone on to become judges and United States Senators. After we talked for awhile, he asked me to come work for him—an opportunity to practice "on Broadway"—and I took him up on it. I was afraid that I could not meet their standards, but I worked late into the night and really learned the law. It was important to me when B.V. (I was B.M.) would slap me on the back and say "good work."

It is difficult to generalize about what it is like to be a lawyer since there are so many different ways to use a law degree. A person may be self-employed, work with a few or many other lawyers, work for a corporation or the government, specialize in any number of areas of law, teach law, manage a law firm, do public interest work, or write about the law. Some people never intend to practice law but just want a legal background, which can be particularly helpful in business and law enforcement agencies.

I have practiced on my own, as a partner with one and two other persons, and in the 1940's with what was then considered a large firm. When I first started practicing law, solo practice was the ideal. Most law students looked forward to passing the bar exam and hanging out their shingles. There was no certainty of success, but we had confidence that we could succeed on our own initiative. Now solo practice carries the stigma of not being good enough for "big time" law practice. People who pass the bar exam and hang out their shingle are thought to do so because they could not get a job with a big law firm.

Why this dramatic change? Partly it is because of the growing complexity of the law. Most law school graduates do not feel adequately prepared to open their own offices and competently handle all the types of cases that can come in. Even if a graduate feels confident that he or she can handle whatever problem a client brings in, there may not be enough clients who feel the same way.

Another reason why there are fewer solo practitioners is that growing competition has required lawyers to practice law as a business, requiring skill and capital not possessed by most law school graduates. Opening a law office is costly. An office must be leased, a secretary must be hired, books and supplies have to be purchased, insurance and utilities have to be paid for, and there should be enough money left over to live on while waiting for fees to start rolling in. Lawyers already in debt for thousands of dollars to pay for their education are understandably reluctant to go deeper into debt to finance a risky venture. Getting a job with a partnership, corporation, or government means that lawyers can rely on others to give them work and income while they serve an apprenticeship and develop competence in one or more areas of the law. Solo practice requires a desire for independence that many people no longer crave.

Solo practice offers more freedom than any other practice of law, but, especially during the first few years of solo practice, that freedom may be illusory. The need to make a buck may rob the solo practitioner of any freedom to decide what cases to take and what hours to work. The solo practitioner has to drum up business by joining civic, social, and political organizations, speaking before groups, writing on legal topics, socializing in bars and restaurants, and contacting other lawyers for referrals. Solo practitioners as a group tend to make less money than people in partnerships. Solo practitioners now tend to be ethnic minorities and people from lower-income families who have trouble "fitting" into partnership practice.

Small partnerships (2-10 people) have all the advantages and disadvantages of any group of people working together in a business enterprise. If the talents of the individuals complement one another and their personalities mesh, then their collaboration will be successful. If talents do not complement each other, say, for instance, everyone is good at getting business but not so good at doing legal work or handling administrative chores, or everyone is good at doing legal work but no one has the personality to attract clients, then real success is likely to elude the partners. If personalities clash, then working conditions can be intolerable and parting can be traumatic. Like a marriage, a good partnership makes life better for the partners than they could hope to achieve on their own; life in a bad partnership can only be improved by dissolution.

Many graduating law students look on practice with a big firm as a guarantee of success. Certainly the large starting salary for an associate is a good start towards monetary success and status. People paid high starting salaries become enveloped by an aura of expertise that may be undeserved. People not getting such salaries, not because they are less competent but because they are not interested in big firm practice, can be mistakenly considered less competent.

It can be stimulating and exciting to work for a big law firm, but the picture is not all that glamorous. Big law firms have all the opportunities, pitfalls, cliques, and political maneuvering found in big corporations. Most law school graduates going to work for a big firm with the expectation of some day becoming a partner will be disappointed. After several, maybe even ten or more, years of hard and loyal service, most associates will have to face the hard reality that they are not going to be made partners. In many firms, as few as 10 to 20 percent of their brilliant law students end up as partners.

It is a heart-breaking experience to be denied advancement after so many years of devoted effort. Some of the reasons for denying partner status to a competent lawyer (the firm would not have hired the lawyer in the first place if he or she had not had excellent academic credentials, and the firm would have terminated an incompetent lawyer well before deciding whether to grant or deny partner status) include: not "fitting" into the firm "concept," whatever that means, perhaps social standing; not having the "spirit" of the firm, whatever that means; not pulling in enough business; being too aggressive; outright discrimination of one sort or another, perhaps on the basis of race, religion, or sex; and, of course, conflict with the personalities of supervising partners. In short, a long career of law practice with job security and increasing income and status is no certainty, and the sudden crack in one's vision of success with a big firm can be traumatic, especially for those accustomed to success.

Lawyers rejected as partners usually are not fired; the unwritten code is for them to quietly disappear from their firms. Finding another job with a decent future can be difficult since rejection taints them, at least as far as other big firms of similar status are concerned. Smaller law firms only want people who can bring business with them. Corporations have been recruiting recent law school graduates and promoting from within, and government jobs may be scarce. Associates also have another obstacle to finding a job: themselves. Recruited while they were still in law school, many do not know how to find a job by themselves.

The "up or out" philosophy has become less pervasive as the reasons for rejecting the promotion of an associate to partner have changed. When I started practicing law, people were not promoted to partner usually because they lacked legal skills. Now the changing economics of law practice have put a premium on the talent for bringing in business. It used to be that every firm had "finders, minders, and grinders"; now firms want everyone to be a "finder." If someone promoted to partner cannot bring in enough business to cover the cost of his or her salary (plus fringe benefits and a share of the overhead), then the other partners have to sacrifice some of their income to make up the difference. This emphasis on getting business hurts women in particular since some clients have been reluctant to deal with women, and women have not taken away as much time from parenthood as men to cultivate clients.

Inability to bring in business does not mean that an

associate lacks legal skills. Big firms know that. They also know that they need experienced associates to do their legal work. The more associates a firm has, the more money partners can make. Partners in big firms are capitalists making money from the work of associates. Hourly rates for associates are set high enough to cover the associate's salary, fringe benefits, share of overhead, plus a profit for the partners. Therefore, the more associates that partners can keep busy, the more money partners can make.

Because big firms thrive on quality work performed by associates, it is in the firms' interest to keep experienced associates for as long as possible. That is why it may now take up to ten years before a firm will decide whether an associate is partner material. To encourage people to wait that long, some firms have introduced another tier of jobs (designated by such names as "non-equity partner" or "income partner") that give people greater status in and outside the firm but do not make them full-fledged partners able to share in the firm's profits. The new job title also does not guarantee future promotion to full partner, but it is recognition that the person is heading in the right direction.

Firms are retaining good performers passed over as partners by giving them better pay and better job assignments. They remain associates—perhaps with a glorified job title, such as "senior attorney"—but with almost no chance of promotion to partner. Still they may be able to lead a more balanced life with decent pay and pleasant working conditions and without the stress of trying to become a partner. The thought of being satisfied with such a job is hard for lawyers of my generation to accept, but it is really no different than being in any dead-end job. Some people can live with the blow to their egos; others strive to prove that the blow was unjustified.

Not surprising, loyalty to the firm has been declining among associates and partners. It used to be that partners would stay with their firms through thick and thin. No more. Now more and more partners go elsewhere. Sometimes it is because they are impatient to become senior partners and get a larger share of the profits; other times it is because they are bored or do not like the way things are being run or just get a better offer. Growing competition has made firms less reluctant to "raid" other firms for talent.

It can be quite a coup for a firm to hire a partner who can bring along an important client or two. Clients have become more discerning about which lawyer they want for which task, and firms can quickly bolster a weak legal department by hiring a talented lawyer or two from another firm. They no longer feel that they have to develop their own talent from their "farm system." There are now plenty of "free agents" willing to remedy a firm's weakness for the right price. Specialization has made it clear what those weaknesses are and has made it easier for a firm to tab the right person to fill a void.

An important trend over the last decade has been a large increase in the number of lawyers working for corporations. In an effort to minimize legal costs and have people around to tell them how to avoid legal problems, corporations have been setting up their own legal departments and cutting down on the work they previously referred to legal firms. Salaries of corporate attorneys are good. Fewer hours have to be worked each week, and the job can be as secure as the financial health of the firm. The big disadvantage is that it is a corporate life with politicking for advancement, the frustration of working within a bureaucracy, and lack of freedom to make decisions. A particular risk for lawyers working within a corporation is that they can get so involved with the business side of the company that they lose the independence they need to give good legal advice.

According to a recent survey prepared by the American Bar Association's Young Lawyers Division Career Planning and Placement Committee,[4] more lawyers working for corporations were satisfied with their jobs than those working for legal firms. Solo practitioners were more satisfied than attorneys working for law firms. Legal educators expressed the most job satisfaction; people in large firms the lowest. Legal aid lawyers expressed more job satisfaction than private practitioners and corporate counsel, but other government attorneys were almost as unhappy with their jobs as those working for large firms.

Another opportunity for lawyers is public service. Lawyers are specially trained for public service and can contribute much to civic and charitable organizations, governmental commissions, and public office. Too few lawyers devote any time to public service. Most are absorbed with earning a living or accumulating wealth and consider time spent in public service just a loss of time and a waste of otherwise billable hours.

That is unfortunate, since by the very nature of their training and experience lawyers have a special responsibility to use their skills to help solve social, economic, and political problems. We live by the rule of law, not by the whim of men or women, and no one is better able than lawyers, trained in law, its formulation, interpretation, and administration, to assure that laws—and our society— reflect our desires, beliefs, and needs. Lawyers also have special competence and interest in preserving the sanctity of law in the governance of our society.

I served for eight stimulating years as a maverick alderman in the City Council of Chicago. Holding public office can be intellectually challenging and emotionally satisfying, but it is not a place for people with thin skins. The press labeled me a socialist when I urged a study of electric power rates in the thousands of cities and villages in the United States that owned power plants. The press labeled me a "capitalist" when I voted against a resolution giving the City Council control over telephone rates (no state statute gave the City Council power to do that).

My work in organizing a trust to finance Polish youngsters coming to the United States to study the American way of life and American youngsters of Polish descent going to Poland to study Polish history helped earn me a place on CIA and FBI lists of people suspected of holding liberal and radical views. I made the House Un-American Activities Committee's list because of my membership in the National Lawyers Guild, a liberal bar association organized in the 1930's to counter the conservative American Bar Association.

When I ran for re-election as an alderman in 1951, more than 10,000 leaflets were distributed by my opponent, an attorney, with the heading "House Un-American Activities Committee" and "Your alderman is a member of the National Lawyers Guild, the legal arm of the Communist Party" (which was not true). Despite that criticism, I won the election hands down. In the late 1940's and 1950's I was twice recommended to President Truman by a United States Senator for membership on the United States delegation to the United Nations and also for a federal judgeship. In later years I learned from my U.S. Senator friend and through the Freedom of Information Act that my name probably was rejected because of some of the items noted above, particularly my presence on the CIA and FBI lists. My name was deleted from those lists after I threatened to sue.

Have my experiences of being in the minority and my disappointment at not attaining judicial office soured me on public service? Not at all. My life could not have been more stimulating, exciting, and fulfilling. I am convinced that public service of some sort is an obligation of every lawyer.

Some lawyers are able to make the best qualities of law part of their lifeblood. Judge Robert Satter has described such lawyers as follows:

> Most lawyers are competent and some are exceedingly competent. There is a class of special lawyers who achieve a quality of legal service beyond excellence. These lawyers practice with a touch of artistry. They have what in musicians is called "touch" and in athletes "class." Their hallmark is that more than solving legal problems, they resolve situations; more than winning cases, they save clients; more than applying existing law, they contribute to its creative development. They have a lasting, positive influence on the relationships of the parties and on the circumstances that

gave rise to the legal problem. They are masters of the craft, and the beneficiaries of their services are not only their clients but also the legal profession and society.[5]

I like to think of these people as "compleat" lawyers. "Compleat" lawyers are prepared by education, knowledge, and experience to analyze all the implications of a legal problem—political, social, economic, and moral. Their advice is based on thorough and informed analysis; it is not "off the cuff." They are familiar with the many disciplines relevant to the resolution of legal problems and do not hesitate to call on other experts for advice or to pursue a non-legal resolution of a problem.

They are constantly aware of their responsibilities as officers of the court and members of society, and they do not ignore such responsibilities when representing a client. They are sensitive to the morality of their objective and the means of attaining it. They do not wear blinders when taking assignments from clients. They do not hesistate to reject retainers and tasks that are morally wrong. They teach clients how to comply with the highest standards of morality. They do not slough off morality as someone else's problem. Nor do they pretend to avoid moral decisions by feigning neutrality.

"Compleat" lawyers strive to improve the judicial and political systems so that all people will be better off. They are sensitive to the emotional and psychological problems of all people—including themselves—and do not pursue social goals to the detriment of personal relationships. In short, the "compleat" lawyer is human in the best sense of the word, not someone preoccupied by law but a person striving to reach his or her full potential while helping others do the same.

"Compleat" is an old-fashioned spelling of "complete," but its use is appropriate since what I have described is an old notion of what people should strive to become, a notion too often dismissed as quaint, as harking back to a mythical time when people supposedly were more virtuous. How many people are "compleat" lawyers? A good number, but not nearly enough.

The highlight of my practice was working with a world-famous chemist, Dr. Percy L. Julian, who contributed substantially to the development of synthetic hormones. In 1946, a friend in the life insurance business called to ask if I could prepare a will for one of his customers. He asked if the man could see me after work. Certainly, I said. But then my friend cautioned, "I should tell you he is a Negro. Will that make any difference?" I said, "Not at all. Tell him to have dinner with me."

We could not get into one private club of which a senior law partner was a member and two well-known Chicago restaurants since they would not serve blacks. I was shocked and ashamed at their treatment of Dr. Julian. Of course I had heard and read about discrimination. As a Jew I was sensitive to it. I grew up in the West Side of Chicago, where I had to fight with the Irish who lived on the other side of the B & O tracks. When we went to get ice for the ice box at home, we had to go in groups for self-protection. We also had to go in groups when we went from Fillmore Street and Sacramento Boulevard north to John Marshall High School. But up until then I had not experienced discrimination personally as a practicing lawyer.

Dr. Julian became one of my dearest friends and most important clients. In the more than 25 years that we worked together, I learned about chemistry (a subject I had never studied), chemical research, and application of research results to the production and marketing of chemical products. I learned how to finance business enterprises and how to put one's best financial foot forward when selling a business. From the night we first met and during my long association with Dr. Julian, I also learned the importance of being concerned about the problems of society, particularly the rights of minorities. In personal discussions and commencement addresses, Dr. Julian often emphasized the importance of making excellence a continual quest.

There are many others I worked with, some brilliant,

others ordinary, many unselfish and giving, but unfortunately many who were greedy and uncaring. I could name
many lawyers whom I respected and admired, but one
stands out: my lifelong friend, law school classmate, law
partner for thirty-five years, my confidant, and as brilliant
a lawyer as I have ever met—Bernard Savin. I have known
him intimately, starting with our law partnership in 1947
and continuing past my retirement. He is a Shakespearean
scholar. He could have been a brilliant law teacher. He is
steeped in the philosophy and understanding of the law.
Many times young and older lawyers would come to Bernie
or call him to get his analysis of a problem and his advice
how to solve it. He is a master draftsman of agreements and
pleadings. Many times judges who listened to his legal
arguments have complimented him on the excellence of his
presentation. He is an inspiration to all who cross his path.

Yes, I have found much more in the law and law practice
than I expected—some bad but mostly good. When I think
about other careers that I could have pursued, I am certain
that I am more fulfilled than I would have been as a multi-
millionaire building more and more widgets each year or as
a doctor developing skill in a specialized procedure or as a
scholar limited to one field of study or as an astronomer in a
lofty but lonely quest to understand the universe. My universe has been all knowledge and all people. I have been
able to satisfy creative urges and feelings of social responsibility and experience the reward of helping people amicably resolve disputes and the challenge of constantly learning about every subject imaginable. Law has stretched my
mind to the limits of my potential. For that, I am grateful.

Chapter 17

New Frontiers in the Law

> [W]e stand today on the edge of a
> new frontier...a frontier of unknown
> opportunities and perils—a front-
> ier of unfulfilled hopes and threats.
> John F. Kennedy[1]

Advances in science and technology change not only our physical world but also our attitudes towards that physical world, its inhabitants, and ourselves. Just as the law had to adjust to the Industrial Revolution, now it has to adjust to the information society and new developments in science. But adjustment is not always enough. Some developments, such as those involving nuclear weaponry and genetic engineering, are potentially so dangerous that they must be controlled by law if we and our world are to survive in a recognizable form. Law must develop legal concepts and legal structures to manage conflicts between science and technology and accepted mores of society. Law must keep

209

science and technology from mastering the society they are supposed to serve.

When I started studying law, I never dreamed that there would be thousands of pages of laws and judicial decisions controlling almost every facet of our lives. In law school I did not take courses in federal taxes or labor law. Federal taxes were not an important consideration in business and personal transactions, and the labor movement was still in its gestation stage. Law was considered a fairly static profession. We did not dream that practicing law would require a lifetime of continuous study, not only of law but of many other disciplines. It is impossible to imagine all the new frontiers that will be touched by law in the future, but it is safe to guess that a few of them will be the following.

Life and Death

It used to be that law was only concerned with the consequences of life and death, rather than when life and death occurred. Now that we can create (and patent) life in a test tube and prolong bodily functions beyond what used to be death, it has become necessary for the law to decide what is life and death.

Early law protected the property rights of the unborn (e.g., they could inherit property), but they could not be "legally" hurt. Someone stabbing a pregnant woman in the abdomen would not be liable for a fetus' injuries because the law did not recognize the fetus' legal existence when personal injuries were involved.

Ironically, as courts began to permit children to recover damages for injuries they suffered in the womb (e.g., from drugs such as thalidomide), they also gave women the right to abort a fetus before legal life begins (the third trimester of a pregnancy). The Supreme Court's emphasis on the "viability" of a fetus rather than the paramount privacy rights of women over the right of the government to protect the "potentiality of life" means that, as medical advances make it possible for ever and ever younger fetuses to survive premature birth, there will be a temptation for courts to further restrict women's right to abort fetuses. For example, if medicine learns how to save fetuses born six months prematurely, then fetuses may be "viable" after three months, and courts may decide to restrict women's right to abortion to the first trimester of pregnancy. A fetus may not be a "person" entitled to constitutional rights, but how long will the law permit researchers to "play God" with test-tube babies? When do dividing cells make the leap from potential life to legal life?

Whose child is that legal life? Must "parents" be "blood" relatives, or is a surrogate who carried a child to term the "real" parent? Do sperm and eggs make for parents? Can men who donate sperm (or women who donate eggs) be liable for the costs of rearing children resulting from those sperm or eggs (perhaps from Nobel prize winnings)? Who has the right to decide whether children born with health problems should be left to die? The parents? The government? How much control should parents have over their children's upbringing?

As medical advances have made it possible for the body to function beyond the life of the conscious individual, people have begun to say enough is enough and demand "death with dignity." This has forced the law to decide not only when a person is dead but also who can make that determination—relatives, physicians, the court, or the individual, through a "living will." It is easy to say that courts should err on the side of caution, but too much hesitation can deprive others of organ transplants vitally needed to preserve lives. Too much hesitation can be very costly for survivors responsible for paying the decedent's medical bills.

For years I was horrified when I heard of the taking of a life, whether it was by way of capital punishment for murder, war, euthanasia, or "pulling the plug" on someone who was brain dead. But as I grew older I realized that there are *extreme* circumstances under which it is more merciful to take a life. "Negotiated deaths," hundreds, perhaps even thousands, of which quietly take place each day, should be legalized and appropriate laws formulated to set forth the circumstances under which such deaths may be arranged.

Medical advances allure people with the prospect of squeezing out precious extra seconds of life, but they are expensive, beyond the financial reach of most persons, and a costly burden on society. Unless law intervenes to apportion these benefits to all people, then we will have a society where a select few can buy not only material things but life itself.

GENETIC ENGINEERING

Genetic engineering, which eventaully may allow people to change the "blueprint" for human development, offers the promise of "defect-less" human beings and the prospect of less-than-human humans.

Proponents of genetic engineering scoff at people who worry that we may soon have humans made-to-order. They label as "science fiction" predictions that "parents" someday may be able to choose the physical, emotional, and intellectual characteristics of their "offspring." Proponents rightly emphasize the difficulty of eliminating single-gene defects (e.g., sickle cell anemia, albinism, Tay-Sachs disease, and phenylketonuria), let alone controlling complex traits, such as intelligence and aggressiveness, which apparently are affected by the interaction between many different genes and the environment. They also point out that genetic engineering is applied to individuals, not societies, which means that deleterious results can be caught before massive social damage is done. They argue that there is plenty of time before we have to worry about the implications of current research.

The practical difficulties of genetic engineering are apparent. Of more concern is the attitude that we should "perfect" human beings. It is intriguing to think that we may be able to eliminate "defects." But shouldn't we question whether "defects" really are defects? For example, the same gene that causes sickle cell anemia can protect people from malaria. Before we eliminate "defects," shouldn't we know the consequences? Should we blithely ignore the risk that, by eliminating "defects," we are also sapping the strength of the human species by cutting down diversity in our genetic pool? We should remember how "super" wheat, which was developed in the 1950's, was destroyed by a new strain of disease that "ordinary" wheat had the strength to resist. Laws need to be developed to reflect society's informed judgment about which changes are desirable and which are not.

Even if genetic engineering is not an immediate threat, the attitude that humans should be "perfected" is. We already try to "perfect" plants and animals by using selective breeding, and attempts have been made to use the same techniques on humans. Nazis did it with their Lebensborn ("well of life") program, which was an attempt to "purify" the Aryan race by selectively mating people. Now we are doing it with our "banks" of "selected" sperm and our screening of unborn children for "undesirable" characteristics. Methods developed to increase the probability that a child of a particular sex will be born also have been used by parents.

The attitude that humans should be "perfected" is dangerous because it decreases our tolerance for human differences. Who will determine perfection? What is perfection? An Einstein? A Mother Theresa? A Willie Mays? A Harvard-educated lawyer? A black man, white man, or yellow man? A woman? Perhaps a human who is submissive to the leaders of a totalitarian state? Will there be someone or state agency deciding the specifications of the perfect human being?

Lack of tolerance for human differences has caused much of the strife in our world. Whites think blacks are inferior. Men think women are inferior. Communists think all people should believe as they do. Medieval Catholics offered

Jews the choice of conversion or death. Our history is filled with atrocities committed to eliminate differences among people.

Fulfillment of the "promise" of genetic engineering may be decades away, but now is the time to make decisions about genetic engineering and develop laws reflecting our consensus. Otherwise it may be too late to make a choice. As Horace Freeland Judson, a defender of genetic engineering, wrote in *The New Republic*:

> If such enhancements are ever possible, surely they are decades away. A friend who is a molecular biologist said to me recently that by that time, people may be more used to the application of genetic engineering. The boundary may be crossed psychologically before it is crossed technologically.[2]

Judson argued that future generations may welcome genetic engineering and that "[w]e have no reason to foreclose their choices."[3] But if we give no thought to the matter now, while we still recognize it as a potential problem, then we may be foreclosing their choice by inculcating the attitude that it is no problem.

Scientists like to disassociate themselves from the consequences of "pure" research (e.g., they did not drop the nuclear bomb; they will not use genetic engineering to breed the subhuman Epsilons of Aldous Huxley's *Brave New World*). But society cannot afford to let science run wild. There must be some restraints.

If research is dangerous to society, then it should not be allowed to proceed without limitations. It may be "pure" research to experiment on humans to decide what helps people survive gunshot wounds, but society does not permit scientists to satisfy their craving for "pure" research by shooting people. It might advance scientific knowledge to expose people to varying levels of radiation, but society does not permit it.

Too often, dedication to "pure" science is used by scientists to abdicate moral responsibility. Ironically, the same scientists who criticize lawyers for immoral behavior may not give a second thought to treating animals cruelly in experiments. How long a leap is it from believing that animals can be mistreated to believing that "lower" levels of humans can be sacrificed for the greater good of "better" humans? Justice Oliver Wendell Holmes, Jr., a noted civil libertarian, had no difficulty upholding the right of the state to sterilize people with low IQ's:

> We have seen more than once that the public welfare may call upon the best citizens for their lives. It would be strange if it could not call upon those who already sap the strength of the state for these lesser sacrifices, often not felt to be such by those concerned, in order to prevent our being swamped with incompetence.[4]

What other sacrifices can be demanded of people "who already sap the strength of the state"?

Genetic engineering already has stopped being "pure" science and is fast becoming a big business. Genetic engineers have asked lawyers and the law to protect the proprietary value of their work and to tailor governmental regulations, designed for an academic setting, for businesses. Now it is time for lawyers and the law to lead the way to make certain that genetic engineering is used to benefit individuals and society.

COMPUTER SOCIETY AND PRIVACY

Computers have helped us greatly to increase our knowledge about the world we live in. But the information society has also chipped away at our individual privacy. Computers know our physical characteristics, our age, our marital status, how many children we have, our health, our education, how much money we earn and save, what books we read, what television programs we watch, what purchases we make, sometimes even our attitudes about specific issues. There is not much more to be learned about us than

is now recorded in the computers of the Internal Revenue
Service, charge card companies, credit bureaus, the banks
we patronize, and various agencies of local, state, and federal governments.

Too much information is exchanged and utilized for purposes never intended by individuals when they volunteered
it. If people want the names and mailing addresses of
environmentalists, they can get mailing lists from envi-
ronmentalist groups. If they want the names of people
interested in science, they can get mailing lists of subscrib-
ers to science magazines. If they want lists of people practicing a particular religion, they can get a list of people
belonging to a particular religious organization. Commercial organizations sell lists of people having X number of
dollars or earning a living in occupation Y. Such information is used by businesses to sell us commercial goods and
by politicians to make sure they are telling us what we want
to hear.

Laws need to be developed to protect the privacy of individuals, who deserve to get as much protection as their
proprietary rights. Laws also need to be developed to deter
and penalize the criminal use of computers. The home computer has been called the burglary tool of the electronics
age. Computers have become a threat to military security.
Knowledge is power, and we must develop the law to make
sure that knowledge is not misused.

MEDIA, FREEDOM OF SPEECH, AND PRIVACY

The right of privacy sounds like an idea our Founding
Fathers should have included in the Constitution, but it
was not until 1965 that the Supreme Court discovered it in a
"penumbra" of the Constitution. Since then it has increasingly been used to keep the government and press out of
people's private lives. Freedom of speech and press have
been around since the Bill of Rights was first adopted, but it
was not until 1969 that the Supreme Court made it clear

that the purpose of those freedoms was to make sure the public has access to a free flow of information, not to let people say or write or broadcast whatever they like.

Although the media like to identify their interests with the public's, the public distrusts the media as much as it does other institutions in society. In the 18th century, individuals could protect themselves from lies published in the press by telling their neighbors the truth or printing their own newspapers. Now that the media are controlled by a small number of people and serve a national—sometimes even an international—audience, individuals have to be protected from abuse by the media, and the public's right to information has to be assured. The increasing concentration of newspapers—most areas of the country are served by only one newspaper—makes the public increasingly dependent on journalists' integrity to make sure they get all the information they need.

Broadcasters have been obligated to air opposing viewpoints on controversial issues of public importance, to provide air time for people to respond to personal attacks, and to afford political candidates equal opportunity to use the broadcasters' facilities. Similar restrictions have been rejected for newspapers, but as cable television and direct satellite broadcasting multiply the number of broadcasters and the number of one-newspaper towns continues to multiply, the justification for such restrictions on broadcasters is lessening and the need to impose such restrictions on newspapers is increasing.

The public's right to privacy and information also has been threatened by a growing government, which gathers more and more information about individuals and society. There is always the possibility that government will misuse the information it has about individuals. We already have seen that happen. There is also the possibility that government will withhold information that the public needs to make informed decisions about social issues. The public needs laws to limit the use of private information that individuals are required to give the government. Voters need rules requiring the government to release information they need if they are to intelligently debate and shape public policy. Attempts by the federal government to limit the scope of the Freedom of Information Act, censor foreign speakers and films, censor governmental officials, classify information that is not vital to the national security, and intimidate university researchers (making them reluctant to use even *un*classified information) must be resisted if we are to have an informed electorate.

WAR, PEACE, AND WORLD CONFLICT RESOLUTION

Most people agree that the gravest and most immediate danger to humanity is the prospect of an intentional or accidental nuclear confrontation between the superpowers. Nuclear war knows no national boundaries or limits on its destructive potential.

Since the end of World War II, valiant, and some not so valiant, attempts have been made to put the genie back in the bottle, or at least to get nations to control the use of nuclear power. Despite agreements to limit the proliferation of nuclear weapons among lesser-developed nations and limit the weaponry of the superpowers, the world inventory of nuclear weapons is bigger than ever, and the destructive power of the stockpile has become incalculable.

Because conflict between the superpowers risks the ignition of a nuclear confrontation, it behooves all nations and people of the world to cool down "hot spots" and resolve disputes without war. Since World War II, the United Nations and World Court of International Justice have been established, but neither these organizations nor ad hoc attempts to resolve international disputes have reduced the number of hot spots around the world.

Conflict resolution, one of the prime goals of the law, will be needed for as long as there is diversity and competition among people and nations—probably as long as humanity survives. Just as individuals coexist more peacefully when they live by the rule of law, so will nations if they ever agree to be governed by laws. Problems involving the threat of war, pollution, and the economy are global in scope and demand global solutions. Perhaps the need to solve these problems will convince nations that it is in their best interest to be ruled by law.

If world conflict resolution fails and there is a nuclear holocaust, there still may be a place for law in this world. One's imagination can run wild visualizing the plight of survivors, many near death from radiation, all pillaging for food, water, and diminishing medical supplies. Instantaneous decisions about who shall live and who shall die may have to be made, and law will be necessary to prevent life in the rubble from becoming chaos. If there are no survivors, let us hope that the law of natural selection develops a successor better able to tolerate and perhaps enjoy life on this planet in all its diversity.

LAW OF THE SEAS

When the world was big and the seas endless, there was not much occasion for conflict among nations over rights to the sea. Now control over certain sea lanes is vital for national security. Access to oil in the Mideast depends on free passage through the Persian Gulf. Access to other essential raw materials, food, and manufactured goods depends on free passage elsewhere around the world. As land supplies of many of the world's resources become exhausted, the competition for the riches of the ocean will intensify.

The Law of the Seas was developed to resolve such conflicts, but the United States and other nations have been slow to ratify the agreement, the result of many years of negotiations. It will be a challenge for lawyers and others interested in effective international law to resolve differences among nations and make the Law of the Seas universal.

OUTER SPACE

Where humans go, conflicts follow, and space is no exception. An international treaty forbids the use of space to test nuclear weapons, but space already is being used for other military purposes. Satellites are used to spy on other countries and may be used to launch attacks against other nations and even other satellites.

Once space is colonized, there will be a need for laws to govern the colonists. Property rights will become a particularly sensitive problem. Can someone or some country own a planet? How should water and air be divvied up? Who has the right-of-way when spacecrafts cross paths? Developing laws applicable to life in space should become one of the most exciting and challenging tasks of the legal profession.

SURVIVAL OF DEMOCRACY

American democracy has continued for more than 200 years, a record unmatched in the history of civilization. Nothing in the history of the governance of human beings compares to the rights and freedoms guaranteed by democracy, yet democracy is on the wane. The tenets of democracy appeal to millions of people but have been adopted by few nations.

In crisis after crisis in recent decades, our government has responded slowly and with weakness. Congress and the president too often have been deadlocked and unable to respond effectively to serious problems confronting the nation. Sometimes it seems that our leaders cater to special interests instead of promoting the best interests of our people.

This is not the place to catalogue the shortcomings of our system of government. The point is that the brains, skills, and dedication of all people, particularly lawyers, will be needed during the balance of this century and in future centuries to modify the basic underpinnings of our society so that it can cope with a changing world and still maximize the rights and freedom of future generations. Lawyers dominated the first Constitutional Convention. I am confident that they will be able to lead this country past the temptation to resolve problems by trammeling human liberties.

Chapter 18

Future of the Law World

My interest is the future because I am going to spend the rest of my life there.

Charles Kettering[1]

The world of law and law practice has changed radically since the 1930's, when I started practicing law. "Modern" technology in those days meant electric instead of horse-drawn street cars, and eight bits meant a dollar, not a measurement of how fast computers can process information.

We researched law in those days by burying ourselves in the musty caverns of the Chicago Law Institute's law library on the 10th floor of the Cook County Building at Clark and Washington Streets. Piles of law books, some open, others with important pages marked, surrounded us

222

as we worked late into the night. We spent hours hoping to find that one case—or perhaps those few cases—that would tell us what the rule of law was in our client's case. But when our search was successful, we felt the time had been well spent. We had met the challenge.

Today, more than 50 years later, a lawyer can get on a computer in a law office and do research by using one of the many legal and business data bases. Given proper instructions, the computer can list all the court cases and many books and articles dealing with a particular point of law. It can provide summaries of what each of the courts has said and can display the full text of court opinions and books on its screen. No longer does a lawyer need to run around a library gathering up all the books containing what may or may not be pertinent cases. If I need a copy of a court's opinion, I can get one by instructing the computer to print one for me. I was overwhelmed at first at the thought of using computers for research, but I grew to love them because they shortened the time necessary for research.

When I started practicing law, "mechanized" practice meant use of an L.C. Smith or Remington typewriter—manual, not electric—and possibly an Edison dictaphone or the more conventional dictating machine with wax cylinders. Nowadays law offices, which can occupy several floors of a building, have electric typewriters, photocopying machines, and computers with word processing and data processing capabilities.

As a former stenographer, word processing has been of special interest to me. Word processing programs speed production of documents by making it easier to type them (there is no need to wait for a carriage to return, and margins, pagination, and headings can be handled automatically by the computer) and to correct mistakes (whole pages do not have to be retyped; instead the corrections can be made on the computer screen). Commonly used documents do not have to be retyped. Instead the document can be copied from one file to another, where necessary changes can be made.

What would we do without fast photocopying machines? Complex litigation, which now takes years, might take decades. And what would law firms do without computers to record time, keep books, bill clients, and docket pending matters? Many large law offices now have lawyers dictate directly to a central office in their suites, where a bank of secretaries transcribe their messages.

Back in the old days, if you had a case that was going to take considerable time and involved hundreds of documents and exhibits, much of the trial preparation was done by assistants. The lawyer trying a case would be backed up by a bank of assistants, ready to hand the lawyer whatever material was necessary to examine a witness. Today, computers have simplified the mechanical part of a trial. Documents are fed into a computer, organized, summarized, indexed, and made available on a moment's notice. Computers store all material needed to examine witnesses, and, by the close of evidence, the computer has helped the trial lawyers organize the points to be made during closing arguments. It sometimes seems amazing that we were able to practice without computers. But we did, and effectively, too.

Life for the practicing lawyer in the 1930's was comparatively simple. The only books you needed when you started practice were the state statutes (a single volume), perhaps a practice guide book, and a good forms book. After making a few fees you could splurge and buy a set of annotated statutes for your office so that you could cut down your trips to the library. There simply was no need for an extensive office library. You were confident that you knew the law affecting your client. You felt you were in control of your case and knew all the law you needed to know. That is not necessarily true today. With the multiplication of state laws and the monstrous growth of federal law and adminstrative regulations since the 1930's, it may be impossible for even the most aggressive lawyer to have all that needs to be known at his or her fingertips, even with considerable research.

Computers have become an indispensable aid for researching the law, which changes more rapidly today than ever before. But computers are expensive, which means that wealthy individuals and big businesses have a decided advantage in complicated litigation—they can afford the cost of thoroughly researching the law. Big law firms have more lawyers available for their cases, but the extra labor is not cheap. The average person may find that it costs too much to seek justice in the courts.

Finding a law job during the 1930's was very difficult. Lawyers had to look for non-law jobs to support their families. I was fortunate during the Depression. While other lawyers could not earn $15 or $20 a week, I was earning $100 and more—but as a court reporter and typist, not as a lawyer. One sizeable law firm offered me a job for $30 a week, but the money was not entirely for my legal talent—I was to help the stenographic pool in my spare time.

Few women and minorities practiced law in the 1930's; now they are a growing presence. I never thought much about why there were not more women and minorities practicing law with me. I also did not give it much thought why over the years more and more women and minorities began practicing law, but I have always enjoyed meeting brilliant lawyers of any sex or race. I think women and minorities have brought to the law profession a greater sensitivity to the needs of women, children, and minorities.

In 1979, Manuel P. Galvan, then editor of the *Chicago Daily Law Bulletin*, asked lawyers, writers, and people of science to predict what the law profession would be like 125 years later.[2] Here are some of the things he learned:

> By the year 2104, attorneys will have increased greatly. Instead of one lawyer for every few hundred people, there will be one attorney for every 50 persons.
>
> Sole practitioners will be an extinct breed. The majority of the lawyers at that time will be employees of the government or huge corporations or mammoth law firms. Some 60,000 of the seven million lawyers will serve as judges, and about half of those will be on the federal bench.

Litigation will be massive. Lawsuits will become as much of one's life as making a major purchase.

....

Law schools will not change drastically because they will always look to the past for foundation blocks. Specialized law degrees will be commonplace, but smaller law schools will still emphasize a broad curriculum and general law degree.

While many basic courses will be taught through video-taped lectures and computer programmed learning sequences, the Socratic method will still be the most trusted teaching approach.

....

Approximately 44 percent of the students in law school will be on corporate scholarships.

Law itself will not change, but it will enter new areas in which man has increased his domain. These will include energy regulation, DNA experimentation, weather regulating, thought scanning, space exploration and space treaties.

In an article celebrating the 50th anniversary of the Bureau of National Affairs, Inc. (BNA), John A. Jenkins, a member of the publisher's editorial staff, speculated about how law practice will change by 2029.[3] "FutureLaw," according to Jenkins, may be dominated by prepaid legal insurance plans. Like prepaid medical insurance plans, payment of an annual fee guarantees access to legal services. "As prepaid plans proliferate, there will be greater practice of 'preventive law.' People will seek advice before they get into trouble, rather than retaining a lawyer afterward." As a result, "[m]ost lawyers will spend less time practicing law, and more time acting as counselors on personal problems that have become legal problems." The cost of such programs will be strictly controlled "because those who organize prepaid plans in the future will take pains to assure that the deliverers of legal services—the lawyers—don't control the costs. Instead, lawyers will be placed on salaries that are set by the dues-paying clients. In addition, large plans will operate...with sophisticated computers that keep track of time to assure that time—and money—isn't wasted."

In Jenkins' "FutureLaw," those who do not belong to a prepaid legal plan will be able to go to low-cost legal clinics, which have been proliferating since advertising restrictions for lawyers were removed. "As Americans, helped by legal clinics and prepaid plans, learn in the future how to use the law to their advantage, they may find they have little or no use for lawyers as we know them today." University of Hawaii professor James Dator, quoted by Jenkins, believes that lawyers will be replaced by "conflict-resolving entrepreneurs trained in the 'people treating' business—meaning most certainly not lawyers as presently trained, but rather social workers, psychologists, public health workers, spiritual counselors, and the like." Thomas Ehrlich, former president of the Legal Services Corporation, suggested to Jenkins that "all lawyers might be civil servants" in this "de-lawyered" future.

The 500-lawyer firm of today will become the 2,000-lawyer firm of the future, sometimes by merging with other firms. As a result of this increased size, according to Jenkins, "the superfirms will have to pay far closer attention to modern management concepts or risk becoming lethargic, unprofitable giants," and "each new client...will bring with it the possibility of a conflict of interest." "[W]hat I see," Donald I. Baker, former assistant attorney general in charge of the Justice Department's Antitrust Division, explained to Jenkins, "is firms paying a lot more attention to their product mixes and how they relate to each other. They will say, 'By God, we are willing to spend the money to have the capacity to be good at A, B, and C, but we aren't going to try to do X, Y, and Z.' The reason being that every new area you add creates a new conflict of interest"—and the possibility that a firm will lose more clients because of a conflict of interest than it can gain.

Traditional corporate ties to one firm are breaking down, according to Baker, because "the kind of work the corporate law firms were doing 20 years ago is increasingly being done in house, by corporate law departments. They are becoming a much larger and more substantial part of the world. And it makes a lot of sense, because the corporate law department can handle repetitive work—like leases, financing agreements, pre-merger notification work." "Corporate general counsels," Baker predicts, "are going to shop around more for legal services. They'll be considering price and quality, whereas in the old days a business might send most of its work—corporate, tax, antitrust, and so forth—to its traditional firm. A corporation will go to Firm A for tax, Firm B for antitrust, Firm C for labor, and so forth."

This assumes, of course, that there still will be lawyers. Dator, according to Jenkins, envisions a day when computers will replace judges, and lawyers will be replaced by technicians able to give computers all the information they need to decide a case: "What is the judiciary anyway but a gigantic, pre-industrial computer? That is the essence of the sanctity, secret words and procedures which only those learned in the law can understand and know how to utter; the massive reports which take up so much room and to which all parties to the process must appeal. This is what the robes, and wigs, and elevated bench, and 'oyez, oyez' and all the other mumbo-jumbo which is part of our 'government of laws and not men' is meant to bring about: the very fairness, impartiality, and equity that is so easy for a properly-programmed and accessed computer, and so difficult, not to say impossible, for a human judge, jury, attorney, and clerk. So why not design a physical technology to replace our present, obsolete social technology?"

Now I would like to make some of my own predictions about what lawyers and law practice will be like fifty years from now—if democracy survives and the rule of law prevails.

I doubt that lawyers will proliferate in the next fifty years as they have in the past half century. Law has become less attractive as a profession since a law degree no longer is perceived as a guarantee of wealth. Despite public fears that "surplus" lawyers will "manufacture" employment for themselves, the huge increase in the number of lawyers in recent years has brought market forces into play and forced many lawyers to price their services more competitively. Moreover, individuals and many businesses are replacing lawyers with do-it-yourself programs. Larger businesses are developing their own in-house legal departments and are using fewer lawyers that way. Many controversies that once led to litigation no longer will involve lawyers since individuals and businesses are rapidly learning that they can save money and time by settling controversies by themselves or through arbitration or mediation. More and more people will be able to take their disputes to small claims courts, making the law readily available to the public without the need for lawyers.

The near monopoly that lawyers have enjoyed in providing legal services will be broken as the sometimes self-imposed mystique of the law is dispelled. Many matters now handled by lawyers for high fees, such as simple probates, uncomplicated real estate deals and closings, leases, simple wills, and uncontested divorces involving little property, can be handled by reasonably intelligent lay persons and certainly can be handled by paralegals. Already there is a movement toward using paralegals, simplifying laws, and making certain legal matters routine enough for lay persons to handle by themselves.

Although lawyers will not proliferate, I believe women lawyers will. Minority lawyers will have more problems in establishing a foothold, but their percentage of the legal profession also will increase.

At the same time that certain legal matters become simple enough for lay persons to handle, law in general will become more complex and will require many lawyers to become specialists. This does not mean that the general practitioner will disappear, any more than the family doctor vanished in this age of medical specialization. There always will be a place for someone prepared to handle the most common legal problems for the average family, such

as buying or selling a home or family business, preparing a
will, filling out income tax returns, handling simple probate
matters, defending against evictions, and getting children
out of scrapes with the law. General practitioners also will
be needed to tell people what specialists they should
consult.

More people should be able to take advantage of legal
services as more and more businesses provide prepaid legal
insurance plans for their employees and shopping center
legal clinics make routine matters more affordable.
Increased advertising will give a Madison Avenue sheen to
lawyers, but it will help inform people about their legal
rights.

Advertising probably will not reduce legal fees in non-
routine matters because legal research will become more
difficult, time-consuming, and costly. As society rapidly
changes, old laws will need to be modified and new ones
adopted to accommodate changing economic and social
conditions. Lawyers will not only have to keep abreast of
these changes but also will have to keep up with proliferous
court decisions and analyses of court decisions and statutory changes. Keeping up with this deluge of information
will cost clients plenty of money. It also will require lawyers
to become proficient in using computers. Few small firms
and libraries will be able to afford "hard copy" (once known
as books and articles) of all the information needed to practice law—or even find space to store it all. Nor will there be
time to peruse books. In fact, law books may become a
rarity. Not only can a computer locate volumes and turn
pages faster than a human, but its data bases can be
updated more quickly. It takes months to publish new
information in book form; computer files can be updated in
minutes. Computers will have to be used to keep up with the
Joneses, but using them is costly and will continue to be so
since proprietors of data bases—which they usually mon-
opolize—are not likely to sell access cheaply.

There are bound to be major changes in our adversary
system of justice, which is time consuming, costly, waste-

ful, and frequently unjust, since "justice" may depend more on the skills of the lawyer than the merits of the case. As Chief Justice Warren Burger has said, "We should get away from the idea that a court is the only place in which to settle disputes. People with claims are like people with pains. They want relief and results, and they do not care whether it is in a courtroom with lawyers and judges or somewhere else."[4] More and more disputes will be resolved by arbitration and mediation instead of by costly and time-consuming litigation.

Personal injury cases have gotten completely out of hand. A few lawyers are still "ambulance chasers." Many accept unconscionable contingent fee arrangements, giving the lawyer a financial stake of up to 50 percent (occasionally even higher) in the recovery. Grossly inflated jury verdicts have increased insurance costs, and the multitude of personal injury cases have clogged the court calendars. Surely a more sensible and practical procedure for handling personal injury cases needs to be developed. It could very well be a system comparable to workers' compensation.

For some time the jury system has been increasingly criticized as a means of deciding disputes. Jurors have been criticized as incompetent to sift and judge facts, particularly in complex litigation and technical matters, and ill-equipped to comprehend the law. Jury trials are costly, time consuming, and frequently unproductive since many jury verdicts are rejected by trial judges and overturned on appeal. Constitutional guarantees will make it difficult to radically change the jury system, but some changes will have to be made. I believe that the traditional 12-member jury will become a rarity (it will be replaced by six-member juries) and so will unanimous verdicts in civil suits. Money and time will be saved by having judges choose jurors instead of lawyers.

There will be substantial changes in the criminal justice system. Americans have become upset about criminals avoiding jail on legal technicalities and insanity pleas. Increasing crime, particularly violent crimes such as murder and rape, has made the public less tolerant of many of the constitutional rights of the accused that permit the guilty to go scot-free. Certainly strict rules of evidence will be eased to make it easier to convict people.

Law schools will modify their curricula to reflect changing social, economic, and legal conditions. Probably the first year of law school will still be devoted to basic courses such as contracts, torts, real property, sales, procedure, and legal research (including instruction in computer research). After the first year, students will be permitted to specialize in certain areas of the law. Specialties could include such areas as international trade, U.S. and foreign taxation, intellectual property (patents, copyrights, and trademarks), matrimonial law, trial advocacy, perhaps even war and peace. The Socratic method will continue to be used in the first year of law school, but lecturing will be used in later courses because that is a more effective way of giving students the information they need to know. Law schools will expand the number of courses providing practical advice how law is practiced (e.g., how to start a law practice, how to run a law office, how to negotiate settlements and contracts, how to deal with clients, how to deal with judges) and will encourage students to apprentice with practicing attorneys—just as they did in the old days.

I believe that the foregoing constitutes a realistic and conservative forecast of what law practice and the law world will be like fifty years from now. It is interesting to speculate about how many lawyers practicing today would want to practice in the law world I have described. I suspect that most will react to the changes over the next fifty years as I reacted to the changes over the past half century—by adjusting to them but not taking any time to think about their implications. It was not until I cut back my practice that I began thinking about where we had been and where we are now.

I doubt that I would find the practice of law in the future as exciting and stimulating as my fifty years have been. For my taste, practicing law has already become too computerized, too impersonal, and too compartmentalized. I have enjoyed the variety of intellectual challenges presented by the law, but I fear that variety may be reduced by growing specialization. For me there is no thrill in using a computer to pigeon-hole legal problems instead of working on them from scratch. I have enjoyed the people contact, but that is being lost as law becomes more of a business.

Still, it is exciting to think of all the challenges people face and to imagine the world that could be created if ever we could work together to eliminate war, hunger, poverty, and pollution and assure ourselves of a world in which freedom and the rule of law prevail. If only to be involved in such challenges, I wish I were starting over again. Law has been all I hoped it would be. I hope future lawyers find their own measure of satisfaction in the practice.

Chapter 19

Law in a Changing Society

> *Law cannot stand aside from the*
> *social changes around it.*
> Justice William J. Brennan, Jr.[1]

For America's bicentennial, members of the American Bar Association were asked to choose milestones in America's legal history. Not surprising, twelve of the eighteen milestones they chose occurred within the past fifty years.[2] It is not surprising, not because memories are short, but because our lives are so much more controlled by law now than they were fifty years ago.

It is trite to say that we live in a changing society, but the significance is lost on many. For the average person, change is a new job, a different lifestyle, different attitudes toward government and toward other people. For the lawyer, changes in society are much more significant because change requires adjustment of the legal and informal relationships between people and institutions in society. For example, divorced persons and singles living together have special financial needs, personal relationships, and re-

234

sponsibilities with which the law must deal. The sudden emergence of AIDS as a serious threat to public health has required new laws and court decisions to determine who shall bear the costs of the disease and to balance the rights of individuals to employment, education, and privacy against the needs and fears of the many.

The Depression greatly changed our world. I cannot forget the hopelessness of people on the bread lines. These were people who wanted to work, who needed to work, but who had no bootstraps to grab onto. Americans have had the romantic notion about themselves that they are self-reliant (the lone cowboy myth), but the Depression belied that notion. People were forced to recognize that economic and social interrelationships had become complex and that it was no longer possible for most people to go it alone. Individuals could not successfully battle the devastating economic forces arrayed against them. "Go West!" proved to be merely an empty phrase. Only government had the muscle to wage war against the Depression.

Greater interdependence and greater expectations of what society should do for the individual have led to greater governmental intrusion into our lives, and this intrusion—as well as efforts to shield a sphere of privacy from this intrusion—has been sanctioned by a multitude of laws and popular will. By the end of Roosevelt's presidency, people began to expect the government to solve major social problems, and by the 1960's many people began to expect the government to solve all of their problems. Some still do (e.g., parents who blame the federal government for not preventing their child's suicide), but others have begun to see a more limited role for government.

Many people decry governmental intrusion. They say that they want to get government off their backs. But they do not want to forego the benefits of governmental regulation. They want government to help the sick and elderly. They want consumer safety laws. They want the environment protected. They want the government to help them get jobs. They just do not want what they think are unnecessary regulations. Some pundits find an inconsistency in these attitudes and feel that people do not really know what they want. These same pundits like to view the problem as either-or—either people should want governmental regulation or they should want to go it alone. What they do not seem to understand is that people want to strike a balance between too little governmental intervention in their lives and overregulation of their lives. Gradually the pendulum is swinging back to a point where government will have a significant role but where individuals will be expected to show enough self-reliance to maintain their self-respect.

As we have become more interdependent, we have had to take another look at what our civil liberties are and should be. Unfortunately, most people take our civil liberties for granted and do not analyze what freedoms they want our society to guarantee. People approve the notions of freedom of speech, freedom of the press, freedom of association, and freedom of religion—in the abstract. But when asked to apply these principles to specific factual situations, they tend to be less tolerant. For example, the same people who approve the idea of freedom of speech may approve bans on certain expressions of opinion, say by a communist or a Nazi.

Too many people think that civil liberties are static. But there have been few times in American history when there were no demands to extend or restrict civil liberties. Fundamental liberties such as freedom of speech, freedom of association, freedom of religion, and freedom of press have been enshrined in the Constitution, according to Supreme Court Justice Robert Jackson, to:

> withdraw certain subjects from the vicissitudes of political controversy, to place them beyond the reach of majorities and officials and to establish them as legal principles to be applied by the courts. One's right to life, liberty, and property, to free speech, a free press, freedom of worship and assembly, and other fundamental rights may not be submitted to vote; they depend on the outcome of no elections.[3]

When is the right of another or others recognized as superior to an individual's right? Does freedom of speech entitle one to yell "fire" in a crowded theater? Do women have the freedom to have an abortion? Does a terminally ill person have the right to refuse food and starve to death? Does a governmental employee have the right to publicly disclose the contents of governmental documents relating to the security of the nation? Must the separation between church and government be complete, or may the government take action that encourages all religion?

In our frontier society, civil liberties meant freedom from others' interference. Millions of people came to this country to escape certain limits on their liberty. My parents were among them. When the frontier closed and people no longer could move to escape restrictions on their liberties, we had to get away from the notion of civil liberties merely as the opportunity to live as one wishes, free from all restraints except those necessary to protect the freedom of others. As people have become more interdependent, the definition of *civil liberties* has evolved to include not only the negative notion of freedom from restraint but also the positive ideas of a right to have opportunities and a right to receive help to take advantage of opportunities. At one time it was considered sufficient—and "liberal"—to remove all barriers, such as discrimination, that keep people from participating in the race we call life. Now it is also considered important to assure people equal training for that race. Some have even gone so far as to redefine the goal from assuring equal opportunity to win to assuring equal results at the finish line (e.g., quotas).

Much of my thinking has been shaped by the Depression, a time that showed the limits of the old definition of *civil liberties*. Social and economic interdependence has required governmental intrusion to curtail certain rights in order to protect what have become fundamental liberties, such as the right to food and shelter. The right to discriminate has been sharply curtailed. No longer can people discriminate with impunity regarding employment, housing, and public accommodations. People are expected to devote a larger share of their earnings to the care of those less fortunate. Only through law and, ironically, through governmental regulation can people be guaranteed freedom from government and other individuals and freedom to reach their full potential.

In the last century, Alexis de Tocqueville observed that "[s]carcely any question arises in the United States which does not become, sooner or later, a subject of judicial debate."[4] Never has that been more true than today. In what the late Earl Warren considered the most significant decision during his almost sixteen years as Chief Justice of the United States Supreme Court,[5] the court decided that it could order reapportionment to make sure each person would have one—and only one—vote. In a later case, the Supreme Court reshaped political institutions by declaring that the traditional state practice of electing representatives by geographical region, such as counties, was illegal because, as Chief Justice Warren argued, "[l]egislators represent people, not trees or acres."[6]

It is ironic—and a little frightening—that federal judges, who are not elected by the people and who are given lifetime employment to isolate them from the will of the people, increasingly have been deciding how political institutions should be run. More and more disputes between different branches of the government (e.g., over executive privilege and legislative vetoes) are being settled by courts, which have been increasingly relied on to keep representative democracy running smoothly. Courts have also taken over political functions (e.g., they have started spending taxpayers' money for such things as prison reform and school desegregation). Courts even have been asked to approve agreements between the United States and foreign governments (e.g., the agreements made to release Americans held hostage in Iran). When elected representatives have abdicated their responsibility to cope with changing social conditions, courts have stepped in to fill the void (e.g., courts earned the respect of thoughtful Americans for standing up to sentiment against busing). Fortunately, considering the power they wield, judges have been committed to our democratic institutions.

The law recognizes that people are not economically independent and need to be protected. Sellers once hid behind caveat emptor—let the buyer beware—but more and more they are being held accountable for poor quality goods and services. Laissez faire once ruled the country; now people expect—and laws demand—that businesses be socially responsible. Chemicals may not be dumped in the air or water with impunity. Harm caused by defective products must be redressed. Employees may not be exposed to occupational hazards. Society feels that businesses should not be too big—so it cuts them down in size.

Businesses no longer can hire and fire whomever they please. They may not discriminate on the basis of race, sex, age, religion, handicap, or national origin, and it will not be long before all decisions made regarding employees must be related to job performance. Already courts are moving in that direction in job termination suits. The traditional rule has been that employers may fire people "at will," but courts have been carving out exceptions that eventually will overwhelm the rule. Society expects people to be treated fairly, and courts are enforcing that value by prohibiting employers from firing employees without good cause.

People traditionally have had no obligation to help others—even when they were in distress. In fact, the law has encouraged people not even to attempt to help others. For example, a person can get into trouble for botching a rescue but does nothing legally "wrong" by standing by and watching someone drown. Most states have adopted "Good Samaritan" laws to hold blameless people who try to render emergency assistance, and recently there have been some attempts to impose affirmative obligations on people to do what they can to help those in distress.

Another attitude that is not appropriate for an interdependent society is the traditional legal principle—certainly contrary to common sense—that the government can do no wrong (*sovereign immunity*). The practical effect of this principle is that state and federal governments cannot be sued unless they consent to be sued. The required consent has been given in many situations, but the doctrine still is an obstacle to suits against the government.

Ironically, an important benefit of increasing governmental regulation is that people have been gaining the right to be themselves. Fetters have been removed from blacks and women; now they have the opportunity to assert themselves as individuals. So do children; they no longer are treated as their parents' property. Gays are coming out of the closet. Illegitimate children no longer are nonpersons—the United States Supreme Court finally said so in 1968.

Society no longer is willing to take the chance that interpersonal conflict can be worked out by individuals and that those with power will wield it benevolently. Each technological advance is followed by a flurry of lawmaking. So is each new social development. Cohabitation by unmarried persons has spawned all sorts of "love suits"—palimony, even galimony—which courts have accepted. Rampant divorce has led to new rules about division of property and custody of children. Society has decided that interdependence requires strict regulation to keep the social fabric from tearing.

That changes in our social, economic, and political lives have been accommodated by the law within our democratic system is one of the wonders of our century. The law may fear chance resolutions of conflict and abuse of power, but it also recognizes people's need to carve out individual identities for themselves. The right to privacy from governmental intrusion fortunately was discovered in a "penumbra" of the Constitution. Protection from a ravenous information industry has been guaranteed by laws regulating what information can be gathered about people and who can see it. Much has been done to protect the dignity of the individual, but much more has to be done and will be done. People once had no right to die and no right to choose whether or not to bring a child into this world; now responsibility for those choices has been placed where it belongs.

While it is clear that law changes as society changes, it also is true that changes in the law can change society. A remarkable example of this has been the change in society brought about by court decisions and legislation promoting the civil rights of minorities and women. Those changes in the law have not eliminated prejudice and discrimination, but they have challenged people's prejudices by allowing women and minorities to occupy positions where they have been able to disprove stereotypes.

Laws are not neutral. They reflect change, but they also promote change. They promote the rights of one group at the expense of another. Employers do not have the right to hire only people who love Shakespeare—not if that decision has the effect of discriminating against a protected class of people. One person's freedom ends where another's begins. One person's freedom may be another's oppression. This we cannot allow. But it is a delicate balancing act to decide where to draw the line. What business decisions should not be scrutinized by the government? What can people do to change their environment?

Too many people think of law as carved in stone and not as a tool that can be shaped to meet people's changing needs. Until the public assume responsibility for determining which laws will govern them, it is up to lawyers to do so. Since lawyers work on the front lines of human conflict, they must learn to recognize actual and potential conflict. They must devise new laws and revise old laws to reduce the negative social and economic effects of conflict. They must advocate changes that will help all people fulfill their potential as human beings. But they should not limit their role to advocacy. Lawyers also should use their persuasive skills to smooth the path for needed changes. Laws have become the lifeblood of society. Lawyers must be the doctors ministering to society's health.

NOTES

Chapter 1

Our System of Civil Justice

[1]   Derek C. Bok, "A Flawed System," *Harvard Magazine* (May-June 1983), p. 41.

[2]   Remarks of Warren E. Burger at the Midyear Meeting of the American Bar Association, February 12, 1984.

[3]   Quoted in John P. Bradley, Leo F. Daniels and Thomas C. Jones (eds.), *The International Dictionary of Thoughts* (Chicago: J.G. Ferguson Publishing Company, 1969), p. 415.

[4]   Lenore L. Cahn (ed.), *Confronting Injustice: The Edmond Cahn Reader* (Boston: Little, Brown, and Company, 1966), p. 383.

[5]   Quoted in *ibid.*, p. 384.

[6]   Quoted in *ibid.*

[7]   Henry Ward Beecher, *Proverbs from Plymouth Pulpit*, ed. William Drysdale (New York: D. Appleton and Company, 1887), p. 63.

[8]   Jerome Frank, *Courts on Trial* (Princeton, New Jersey: Princeton University Press, 1950), p. 7.

[9]   Aleksandr I. Solzhenitsyn, *Gulag Archipelago*, trans. Harry Willetts (New York: Harper & Row, Publishers, 1976), Vol. 3, p. 517.

[10]   Quoted in Robert Wayne Pelton, *Loony Laws* (New York: Walker Publishing Company, 1981), pp. 39, 40.

243

[11]   Southern Pacific Co. v. Jensen, 244 US 205, 222 (1917).

[12]   Northern Securities Co. v. United States, 193 US 197, 400 (1904) (dissent).

[13]   Speech at Elmira, New York before the Elmira Chamber of Commerce, May 3, 1907.

[14]   Harlan F. Stone, "The Common Law in the United States," 50 *Harvard Law Review* 4, 10 (1936).

[15]   *Reader's Digest* (January 1963), p. 25.

[16]   Cited by Robert Wayne Pelton, *Loony Laws, op. cit.*, pp. 3, 45; *Pets 'n' People* Vol. 2, No. 2.

[17]   Richard Neely, *How Courts Govern America* (New Haven, Connecticut: Yale University Press, 1981).

[18]   Jerome Frank, *Courts on Trial, op.cit.*, p. 85.

[19]   Quoted in Patrick Young, "The American Judge: What Qualities for Greatness?" *The National Observer* (March 17, 1969), p. 22.

[20]   William Shakespeare, *Hamlet*, Act III, Scene I.

[21]   Quoted in John B. Bradley, Leo F. Daniels and Thomas C. Jones (eds.), *The International Dictionary of Thoughts, op.cit.*, p. 415.

[22]   H.L. Mencken, *Prejudices: Third Series* (New York: Alfred A. Knopf, 1922), p. 101.

[23]   Art Wortman (ed.), *Will Rogers—Wise and Witty Sayings of a Great American Humorist* (Kansas City, Missouri: Hallmark Editions, 1969), p. 47.

[24]   Remarks of Warren E. Burger at the Midyear Meeting of the American Bar Association on February 12, 1984.

[25]   Notes for a law lecture, July 1, 1850. Roy P. Basler (ed.), *The Collected Works of Abraham Lincoln* (New Brunswick, New Jersey: Rutgers University Press, 1953), Vol. 2, p. 81.

[26]   Remarks of Warren E. Burger at the Midyear Meeting of the American Bar Association on February 12, 1984.

[27]   Quoted in Marc Galanter, "Reading the Landscape of Disputes: What We Know and Don't Know (And Think We Know) about Our Allegedly Contentious and Litigious Society," 31 *UCLA Law Review* 4, 10 (1983).

[28]   Victor E. Flango and Mary E. Elsner, "The Latest State Court Caseload Data: An Advance Report," *State Court Journal* (Winter 1983), p. 16.

[29]   *Ibid.*, p. 18.

[30]   Marc Galanter, "Reading the Landscape of Disputes: What We Know and Don't Know (And Think We Know) about Our Allegedly Contentious and Litigious Society," *op. cit.*

[31]   Charles D. Breitel, "The Quandary in Litigation," 25 *Missouri Law Review* 225 (1960).

[32]   Marc Galanter, *op. cit.*

[33]   Derek C. Bok, "A Flawed System," *op. cit.*, p. 41.

34 *Ibid.*
35 Barbara A. Curran, *The Legal Needs of the Public: The Final Report of a National Survey* (Chicago: American Bar Foundation, 1977), pp. 186, 190.
36 Michael Zander, "How To Explain the Unmet Need for Legal Services?" *American Bar Association Journal* (November 1978), pp. 1676-1679.
37 Remarks of Jimmy Carter at the 100th Anniversary Lunch of the Los Angeles Bar Association on May 4, 1978.
38 Derek C. Bok, "A Flawed System," *op. cit.*, pp. 38, 39.
39 Quoted in Edwin Chen, "The Poor Still Go Begging for Legal Help," *Los Angeles Times*, February 19, 1984, Part I, p. 8.
40 Learned Hand, "Thou Shalt Not Ration Justice," 9 *The Legal Aid Brief Case* No. 4 (April 1951), p. 5.
41 Cited in Edwin Chen, "The Poor Still Go Begging for Legal Help," *op. cit.*, p. 8.
42 Thomas Ehrlich, "Save the Legal Services Corporation," *American Bar Association Journal* (April 1981), p. 435.
43 Edwin Chen, "The Poor Still Go Begging for Legal Help," *op. cit.*, p. 8.
44 Stephen Wermiel, "Government-Paid Legal Services for the Poor Stir Local Contention and a Growing National Debate," *The Wall Steet Journal*, June 12, 1981, p. 38.
45 Thomas S. Johnson, "Legal Services for the Average Citizen," *American Bar Association Journal* (July 1978), p. 979.
46 Cited in Andrea Pawlyna, "Judging Legal Clinics," *Family Weekly*, January 3, 1982, p. 9.
47 Cited in Michael Kinsley, "Fate and Lawsuits," *The New Republic* (June 14, 1980), p. 21.
48 *Business Week*, October 13, 1980, p. 168.
49 David Ranii, "Summary Jury Trials Gain Favor," *The National Law Journal*, June 10, 1985, p. 30.
50 Remarks of Warren E. Burger at the Midyear Meeting of the American Bar Association on February 12, 1984.

Chapter 2

Criminal Justice

1 Walter V. Schaefer, "Federalism and State Criminal Procedure," 70 *Harvard Law Review* 1, 26 (1956).
2 Alan M. Dershowitz, *The Best Defense* (New York: Random House, 1982), p. xviii.

[3] U.S. Department of Justice Bureau of Justice Statistics, *Report to the Nation on Crime and Justice* (October 1983), p. 24.

[4] American Medical Association Committee on Medicolegal Problems, Report of Conclusions and Recommendations Regarding the Insanity Defense, p. 3.

[5] *Ibid.*

[6] *Ibid.*, p. 1.

[7] Joseph P. Fried, "Insanity Plea with Faked Illness Upheld," *The New York Times*, June 24, 1984, Section 1, p. 28.

[8] Wayne R. LaFave and Austin W. Scott, Jr., *Criminal Law* (St. Paul, Minnesota: West Publishing Company, 1972), pp. 58, 59.

[9] Alan M. Dershowitz, *The Best Defense, op. cit.*, p. xiv.

[10] Quoted in Stephen Wermiel, "Lawyer's Public Image Is Dreadful, Spurring Concern by Attorneys," *The Wall Street Journal*, October 11, 1983, p. 20.

[11] Quoted in Murray Teigh Bloom, *The Trouble with Lawyers* (New York: Simon and Schuster, 1968), p. 110.

[12] Alan M. Dershowitz, *The Best Defense, op. cit.*, p. xix.

[13] *The Los Angeles Daily Journal*, October 19, 1983, p. 4.

[14] *Chicago Tribune Magazine*, November 6, 1983, p. 6.

[15] Walter V. Schaefer, *The Suspect and Society* (Evanston, Illinois: Northwestern University Press, 1967), p. 61.

[16] James Fitzjames Stephen, *A History of the Criminal Law of England* (London: Macmillan and Co., 1883), Vol. 1, p. 441.

[17] Leonard W. Levy, *Origins of the Fifth Amendment: The Right Against Self-Incrimination* (New York: Oxford University Press, 1968).

[18] Henry J. Friendly, "The Fifth Amendment Tomorrow: The Case for Constitutional Change," 37 *University of Cincinnati Law Review* (Fall 1968), p. 696.

[19] Criminal Justice Research Report—The Effects of the Exclusionary Rule: A Study In California, cited in Bruce Fein, "Why the Exclusionary Rule Is Ripe for Revision," *The National Law Journal*, March 5, 1984, p. 13.

[20] James A. Cramer, Henry H. Rossman and William F. McDonald, "The Judicial Role in Plea Bargaining," *Plea Bargaining*, eds. William F. McDonald and James A. Cramer (Lexington, Massachusetts: Lexington Books, 1980), p. 139.

[21] Malcolm M. Feeley, *The Process Is the Punishment* (New York: Russell Sage Foundation, 1979), pp. 30, 31.

[22] Albert W. Alschuler, "Implementing the Criminal Defendant's Right to Trial: Alternatives to the Plea Bargaining System," 50 *The University of Chicago Law Review* (Summer 1983), p. 948.

[23] *Ibid.*, p. 964.

Chapter 3

Public Image of Lawyers
and the Law Profession

1   Carl Sandburg, *Complete Poems* (New York: Harcourt, Brace and Company, 1950), p. 189.
2   Charles Lamb, "The Old Benchers of the Inner Temple," *The Complete Works and Letters of Charles Lamb* (New York: The Modern Library, 1955), p. 80.
3   Quoted by Irving R. Kaufman, "Utopia without Lawyers?" *The New York Times,* August 14, 1983, Section 4, p. 19.
4   Quoted in Herbert Thurston and Donald Attwater (eds.), *Butler's Lives of the Saints* (New York: P. J. Kennedy & Sons, 1956), Vol. 2, p. 352.
5   Benjamin Franklin, *Poor Richard's Almanacks* (New York: The Heritage Press, 1964), p. 48.
6   Alexis de Tocqueville, *Democracy in America*, trans. Henry Reeve (New York: Schocken Books, 1974), Vol. 1, pp. 329, 330.
7   *Time* (April 10, 1978), p. 56.
8   *The Wall Street Journal,* June 7, 1984, p. 22.
9   *The New York Times,* August 20, 1979, Section 1, p. 21.
10   *The New York Times,* May 3, 1977, Section 1, p. 1.
11   *The New York Times Magazine,* February 12, 1984, p. 56.
12   William Shakespeare, *Henry VI*, Pt. 2, Act IV, Scene II.
13   Editorial, "Dreaming the Impossible Dream," *The Wall Street Journal,* February 10, 1976, p. 24.
14   Bryan B. Sterling, *The Best of Will Rogers* (New York: Crown Publishers, Inc., 1979), pp. 212, 213.
15   Quoted in Dick Griffin, "Top Execs Give Verdict on Lawyers," *Chicago Daily News,* August 10, 1977, p. 47.
16   Jacob M. Braude, *Complete Speaker's and Toastmaster's Library: Business and Professional Pointmakers* (Englewood Cliffs, New Jersey: Prentice-Hall, 1965), p. 81.
17   Jack Anderson and Les Whitten, "Burger Warns about Lawyers," *Chicago Daily News,* June 23, 1977, p. 11.
18   Quoted in Dick Griffin, "Top Execs Give Verdict on Lawyers," *op. cit.,* p. 47.
19   Art Buchwald, *The Buchwald Stops Here* (New York: G.P. Putnam's Sons, 1978), p. 243.
20   Quoted in Dick Griffin, "Top Execs Give Verdict on Lawyers," *op. cit.,* p. 47.
21   Jack Anderson and Les Whitten, "Burger Warns about Lawyers," *op. cit.,* p. 11.

22　Quoted in Dick Griffin, "Top Execs Give Verdict on Lawyers," *op. cit.*, p. 47.

23　Quoted in *ibid.*

24　Warren E. Burger, "The Special Skills of Advocacy: Are Specialized Training and Certification of Advocates Essential to Our System of Justice?" 42 *Fordham Law Review* 227, 234 (1973).

25　Elbert Hubbard, *Roycroft Dictionary and Book of Epigrams* (East Aurora, New York: The Roycrofters, Roycroft-Town, 1923), p. 35.

26　Jonathan Swift, *Gulliver's Travels* (New York: Harcourt, Brace and Company, 1920), p. 254.

27　Ben Jonson, *Volpone*, Act IV, Scene 5.

28　Quoted in Murray Teigh Bloom, *op. cit.*, p. 83.

29　Oscar Wilde, "The Decay of Lying," *The Works of Oscar Wilde* (Roslyn, New York: Black's Readers Service, 1927), p. 598.

30　Quoted in "Those #*X!!! Lawyers," *Time* (August 1, 1978), p. 66.

31　J.B. Handelsman cartoon, *The New Yorker* (December 24, 1973), p. 52.

32　Remarks of Jimmy Carter at the 100th Anniversary Lunch of the Los Angeles Bar Association on May 4, 1978.

33　Jack Anderson and Les Whitten, "Burger Warns about Lawyers," *op. cit.*, p. 11.

34　Derek C. Bok, "A Flawed System," *op. cit.*, pp. 38, 39.

35　Barbara A. Curran, *The Legal Needs of the Public: The Final Report of a National Survey, op. cit.*, pp. 229-231.

36　*Ibid.*, p. 232.

37　*Ibid.*, p. 210.

Chapter 4

Legal Reasoning and Analysis

1　Max Lerner (ed.) *The Mind and Faith of Justice Holmes* (New York: The Modern Library, 1948), pp. 51, 52.

2　Edward H. Levi, "An Introduction to Legal Reasoning," 15 *The University of Chicago Law Review*, 501, 502 (1948).

3　Max Lerner (ed.), *The Mind and Faith of Justice Holmes, op. cit.*, p. 368.

4　Quoted in Emilie Tavel, " 'A Bright Lamp of Learning,' " *The Christian Science Monitor*, April 24, 1963, Section 2, p. 1.

5　Lon L. Fuller, *The Morality of Law* (New Haven, Connecticut: Yale University Press, 1964), p. 96.

⁶ Richard Neely, *Why Courts Don't Work* (New York: McGraw-Hill Book Company, 1983), p. 109.

⁷ Benjamin N. Cardozo, *The Nature of the Judicial Process* (New Haven, Connecticut: Yale University Press, 1921), p. 28.

⁸ Edgar Bodenheimer, *Jurisprudence: The Philosophy and Method of the Law* (Cambridge, Massachusetts: Harvard University Press, 1962), p. 156.

⁹ Benjamin N. Cardozo, *The Nature of the Judicial Process, op. cit.*, p. 177.

Chapter 5

The Adversary System and Trial Advocacy

¹ Jerome Frank, *Courts on Trial, op. cit.*, p. 85.

² Quoted in John P. Bradley, Leo F. Daniels and Thomas C. Jones (eds.), *The International Dictionary of Thoughts, op. cit.*, p. 432.

³ Quoted in Tryon Edwards (ed.), *The New Dictionary of Thoughts* (Rev. ed., C. N. Catrevas; New York: Classic Publishing Company, 1931), p. 329.

⁴ Felix S. Cohen, "Modern Ethics and the Law," 4 *Brooklyn Law Review* 33, 34 (1934).

⁵ Jerome Frank, *Courts on Trial, op. cit.*, p. 86.

⁶ Marvin E. Frankel, "The Search for Truth: An Umpireal View," *University of Pennsylvania Law Review*, 1031, 1037 (1975).

Chapter 6

The Jury System

¹ Letter to Thomas Paine, July 11, 1789. Andrew A. Lipscomb and Albert Ellery Bergh (eds.), *The Writings of Thomas Jefferson* (Washington, D.C.: The Thomas Jefferson Memorial Association, 1905), Vol. 7, p. 408.

² Quoted in Jonathan Green (ed.), *Morrow's International Dictionary of Contemporary Quotations* (New York: William Morrow and Company, Inc., 1982), p. 312.

³ For the history of juries, see Morris J. Bloomstein, *Verdict: The*

Jury System (Rev. ed.; Dodd, Mead & Co., 1972); Dale W. Broeder, "Jury," *Encyclopaedia Britannica* (Chicago: Encyclopaedia Britannica, Inc., 1972), Vol. 13, pp. 159, 160.
  4 Williams v. Florida, 399 US 78, 90 (1970).
  5 *Ibid.*, p. 100.
  6 Warren E. Burger, "Is Our Jury System Working?" *Reader's Digest* (February 1981), p. 126.
  7 Winston S. Churchill, *A History of the English Speaking People* (New York: Dodd, Mead & Company, 1956), Vol. 1, p. 219.
  8 Quoted in Samuel W. McCart, *Trial by Jury* (Philadelphia: Chilton Books, 1964), p. 10.
  9 G.K. Chesterton, *Tremendous Trifles* (New York: Dodd, Mead and Company, 1917), pp. 86, 87.
  10 Michigan Standard Jury Instructions (2nd ed.) Sections 15.01, 15.03, 15.04.
  11 Jerome Frank, *Courts on Trial, op. cit.*, p. 116.
  12 Irving R. Kaufman, "The Media and Juries," *The New York Times*, November 4, 1982, Section 1, p. 27.
  13 Irving Goldstein and Fred Lane, *Goldstein Trial Technique* (2nd ed.; Mundelein, Illinois: Callaghan & Company, 1969), Section 9.03.
  14 *Ibid.*, Sections 9.29, 9.31.
  15 Samuel W. McCart, *Trial by Jury, op. cit.*, p. 35.
  16 Philip Hager, "Burger Opposes Role for Lawyers in Selecting Jurors," *Los Angeles Times*, January 1, 1985, Section 1, p. 10.
  17 Morton Hunt, "Putting Juries on the Couch," *The New York Times Magazine*, November 28, 1982, p. 72.
  18 *Ibid.*, p. 82.

Chapter 7

Arbitration and Mediation and the Resolution of Conflict

  1 Remarks of Warren E. Burger at the Midyear Meeting of the American Bar Association, January 24, 1982.
  2 Jerome Frank, *Courts on Trial, op. cit.*, p. 378.
  3 Robert Farmer & Associates, Inc., *The Last Will and Testament* (New York: Arco Publishing Company, Inc., 1968), p. 174.
  4 Wording recommended by American Arbitration Association.
  5 American Almond Products Co. v. Consolidated Pecan Sales, 144 F2d 448, 450 (1944).
  6 Quoted in Jerome Frank, *Courts on Trial, op. cit.*, p. 378.

⁷ Elwood M. Rich, "An Experiment with Judicial Mediation," *American Bar Association Journal* (May 1980), p. 530.
⁸ *Ibid.*

Chapter 8

United States Supreme Court and the Constitution

¹ Fred Rodell, *Nine Men: A Political History of the Supreme Court of the United States from 1790 to 1955* (New York: Random House, 1955), p. 33.
² *Ibid.*, p. 10.
³ Quoted in Leonard Baker, *John Marshall: A Life in Law* (New York: Macmillan Publishing Co., Inc., 1974), p. 352.
⁴ *Congressional Quarterly's Guide to the U.S. Supreme Court* (Washington, D.C.: Congressional Quarterly, Inc., 1979), p. 678.
⁵ Alexander Bickel, *The Least Dangerous Branch* (Indianapolis, Indiana: Bobbs-Merrill Co., 1962), p. 1.
⁶ John Randolph quoted in Leonard Baker, *John Marshall: A Life in Law, op. cit.*, p. 414.
⁷ Marbury v. Madison, 5 US 137, 178 (1803).
⁸ Jacob E. Cooke (ed.), *The Federalist* (Middletown, Connecticut: Wesleyan University Press, 1961), No. 78, p. 525.
⁹ *Ibid.*
¹⁰ Letter to Judge Spencer Roane, September 6, 1819. Andrew A. Lipscomb and Albert Ellery Bergh (eds.), *The Writings of Thomas Jefferson, op. cit.*, Vol. 15, p. 213.
¹¹ United States v. Butler, 297 US 1, 79 (1936).
¹² Speech at the University of Minnesota College of Law, October 19, 1984.
¹³ *Congressional Quarterly's Guide to the U.S. Supreme Court, op. cit.*, p. 685.
¹⁴ *Ibid.*
¹⁵ Bob Woodward and Scott Armstrong, *The Brethren: Inside the Supreme Court* (New York: Simon and Schuster, 1979), p. 233.
¹⁶ *Ibid.*, pp. 205-220.
¹⁷ Introduction to *Congressional Quarterly's Guide to the U.S. Supreme Court, op. cit.*, p. vii.
¹⁸ Raoul Berger, *Government by Judiciary: The Transformation of the Fourteenth Amendment* (Cambridge, Massachusetts: Harvard University Press, 1977), p. 333.

[19] Quoted in Robert Yates, "Goldberg Blames Court for Its Own Problems," *Chicago Daily Law Bulletin,* October 21, 1983, p. 1.
[20] *Ibid.*
[21] *Ibid.,* p. 7.

Chapter 9

Divorce Merry-go-round

[1] Quoted in A. Alvarez, *Life after Marriage* (New York: Simon and Schuster, 1981), p. 105.
[2] For summary of history of divorce, see Homer H. Clark, Jr., *Law of Domestic Relations* (St. Paul, Minnesota: West Publishing Company, 1968).
[3] Lenore J. Weitzman, *The Divorce Revolution: The Unexpected Social and Economic Consequences for Women and Children in America* (New York: The Free Press, 1985), p. 323.
[4] *Ibid.,* p. xi.
[5] Nilda R. Weglarz, "Divorce Becomes a Big Business as Cases Grow in Size, Complexity," *The Wall Street Journal,* August 28, 1985, Section 2, p. 19.
[6] Robert Coulson, *Fighting Fair: Family Mediation Will Work for You* (New York: The Free Press, 1983), p. 5.

Chapter 10

Estate Planning—A Growth Business

[1] Art Wortman (ed.), *Will Rogers: Wise and Witty Sayings of a Great American Humorist, op. cit.,* p. 46.
[2] Quoted in Terry Atlas, "He's Out To Stop the Probate Plunder," *Chicago Tribune,* June 10, 1980, Section 4, p. 3.
[3] For a summary of the history of death transfer costs, see Robert A. Esperti and Renno L. Peterson, *The Handbook of Estate Planning* (New York: McGraw-Hill Book Company, 1983), pp. 4-9.
[4] *Ibid.,* p. 4.

Chapter 11

Morality and Professional Responsibility for the Lawyer

¹ Jean Giraudoux, *The Madwoman of Chaillot, Masters of Modern Drama*, eds. Haskell M. Block and Robert G. Shedd (New York: Random House, 1962), p. 750.

² Charles Dickens, *The Old Curiosity Shop* (New York: Dodd, Mead & Company, 1943), Chap. 56, p. 421.

³ H.L. Mencken (ed.), *A New Dictionary of Quotations on Historical Principles* (New York: Alfred A. Knopf, 1942), p. 668.

⁴ Felix S. Cohen, "Modern Ethics and the Law," *op. cit.*, p. 40.

Chapter 12

Lawyers' Competence (Or Incompetence?)

¹ Warren E. Burger, "The Special Skills of Advocacy: Are Specialized Training and Certification of Advocates Essential to Our System of Justice?" *op. cit.*, p. 234.

² Quoted in Norman Krivosha, "Lawyer Competence from Another Perspective," *American Bar Association Journal* (July 1982), p. 828.

³ Rule 1.1 of the American Bar Association's Model Rules of Professional Conduct.

⁴ Dorothy Maddi, *Trial Advocacy Competence: The Judicial Perspective* (Chicago: American Bar Foundation, 1978), cited in Russell Burris, "Testing in Practice Skills," *ALI-ABA CLE Review*, April 24, 1981, p. 1.

⁵ Anthony Partridge and Gordon Bermant, *The Quality of Advocacy in the Federal Courts: A Report to the Judicial Conference of the United States To Consider Standards for Admission to Practice in Federal Courts* (Washington, D.C.: Federal Judicial Center, 1978), cited in *ibid.*, p. 2.

⁶ Remarks of Warren E. Burger at the Midyear Meeting of the American Bar Association on February 12, 1978.

⁷ *Ibid.*

⁸ Norman Krivosha, "Lawyer Competence from Another Perspective," *op. cit.*, p. 828.

⁹ *Ibid.*, p. 829.

¹⁰ *Ibid.*

¹¹   Task Force of the ABA Section of Legal Education and Admissions to the Bar, *Lawyer Competency: The Role of the Law Schools* (Chicago: ABA Press, 1979), p. 9.

Chapter 13

Client-Lawyer Relationships

¹   Jacob M. Braude, *Complete Speaker's and Toastmaster's Library: Definitions and Toasts* (Englewood Cliffs, New Jersey: Prentice-Hall, Inc., 1965), p. 109.

²   Jeremy Bentham, *The Works of Jeremy Bentham* (Edinburgh: William Tait, 1843), Vol. VII, p. 474.

³   Editorial, "For Lawyers, No Double Role," *Los Angeles Times*, February 16, 1983, Section 2, p. 4.

⁴   Upjohn Co. v. United States, 449 US 383, 389 (1981).

⁵   Editorial, "For Lawyers, No Double Role," *Los Angeles Times*, op. cit., Section 2, p. 4.

⁶   Rule 1.6 of the American Bar Association's Model Rules of Professional Conduct.

⁷   Rules 3.3 and 4.1 of the American Bar Association's Model Rules of Professional Conduct.

⁸   Elizabeth Loftus, "Reconstructing Memory, the Incredible Eyewitness," *Psychology Today* (December 1974), p. 119.

⁹   See, e.g., survey by Missouri Bar cited in Thomas P. Brown, III, "Practicing Defensive Law," *Law Office Economics and Management* (Mundelein, Illinois: Callaghan & Company), Section 30.0, Article E, p. 8.

Chapter 14

Legal Fees—Too High?

¹   Adam Smith, *An Inquiry into the Nature and Causes of the Wealth of Nations* (New York: P.F. Collier & Son Corporation, 1937), p. 107.

²   Quoted by Murray Teigh Bloom, *The Trouble with Lawyers*, op. cit., p. 306.

³   Rule 1.5 of the American Bar Association's Model Rules of Professional Conduct.

⁴   *Ibid.*

5 *Ibid.*
6 *Ibid.*
7 Timothy Harper, "A Rare Look into Soviet Courts," *American Bar Association Journal* (October 1983), p. 1495.

Chapter 15

Legal Education

1 Anton-Hermann Chroust, *The Rise of the Legal Profession in America* (Norman, Oklahoma: University of Oklahoma Press, 1965), p. 176.
2 *Ibid.*, p. 177.
3 *Ibid.*, p. 195.
4 Nathaniel E. Gozansky, "The Growing Significance of Professional Responsibility Considerations," *Maximizing the Law School Experience*, eds. Michael I. Swygert and Robert Batey (St. Petersburg, Florida: Stetson University College of Law, 1983), p. 44.
5 *Ibid.*
6 Robert Stevens, *Law School: Legal Education in America from the 1850s to the 1980s* (Chapel Hill, North Carolina: The University of North Carolina Press, 1983), p. 209.
7 *Ibid.*, p. 53.
8 *Ibid.*, p. 38.
9 *Ibid.*, p. 37.
10 *Ibid.*, p. 38.
11 *Ibid.*
12 Jerome Frank, *Courts on Trial, op. cit.*, p. 227.
13 Task Force of the ABA Section of Legal Education and Admissions to the Bar, *Lawyer Competency: The Role of the Law Schools, op. cit.*, p. 3.
14 *Ibid.*, p. 14.
15 Ivan E. Bodensteiner, "An Explanation of Clinical Education," *Maximizing the Law School Experience, op. cit.*, p. 163.
16 Robert Stevens, *Law School: Legal Education in America from the 1850s to the 1980s, op. cit.*, p. 243.
17 Herbert L. Packer and Thomas Ehrlich with the assistance of Stephen Pepper, *New Directions in Legal Education* (New York: McGraw-Hill, 1972), p. 80.
18 Thomas L. Shaffer and Robert S. Redmount, *Lawyers, Law Students and People* (Colorado Springs, Colorado: Shepard's, Inc., 1977), p. 128.
19 *Ibid.*, pp. 4, 5.

[20] Charles W. Joiner, "Teaching Professional Responsibility," *American Bar Association Journal* (April 1978), p. 553.
[21] Jon W. Bruce, "A Critique of the Litigation Emphasis of Legal Education," *Maximizing the Law School Experience, op. cit.*, p. 36.
[22] Derek C. Bok, "A Flawed System," *op. cit.*, p. 45.
[23] Robert Stevens, *Law School: Legal Education in America from the 1850s to the 1980s, op. cit.*, p. 58.
[24] Warren E. Burger, 1983 Year-End Report on the Judiciary.

Chapter 16

Legal Profession as a Way of Life

[1] Survey was prepared by subcommittee of the American Bar Association's Young Lawyers Division Career Planning and Placement Committee and was cited in an article by two members of that committee. See Gary A. Munneke and N. Kay Bridger-Riley, "Singing Those Law Office Blues," *Barrister* (Fall 1981), p. 50.
[2] Max Lerner (ed.), *The Mind and Faith of Justice Holmes, op. cit.*, p. 29.
[3] *Ibid.*, p. 31.
[4] Cited by Gary A. Munneke and N. Kay Bridger-Riley, "Singing Those Law Office Blues," *op. cit.*, p. 51.
[5] Robert Satter, "Practicing Law with a Touch of Artistry," *American Bar Association Journal* (April 1981), p. 392.

Chapter 17

New Frontiers in the Law

[1] Speech accepting nomination as Democratic candidate for the presidency, July 15, 1960.
[2] Horace Freeland Judson, "Thumbprints in Our Clay," *The New Republic* (September 19 & 26, 1983), p. 17.
[3] *Ibid.*
[4] Buck v. Bell, 274 US 200, 207 (1927).

Chapter 18

Future of the Law World

¹ John P. Bradley, Leo F. Daniels and Thomas C. Jones (eds.), *The International Dictionary of Thoughts, op. cit.*, p. 315.
² Manuel P. Galvan, "A Future Glimpse of the Law World," *Chicago Daily Law Bulletin*, November 17, 1979, p. 1.
³ John A. Jenkins, *FutureLaw* (Washington, D.C.: Bureau of National Affairs, Inc., 1979).
⁴ Quoted in *ibid.*, p. 5.

Chapter 19

Law in a Changing Society

¹ Gaston Lecture at Georgetown University, November 25, 1957; quoted in George Seldes (ed.), *The Great Quotations* (New York: Pocket Books, 1967), p. 564.
² Jethro K. Lieberman, *Milestones! 200 Years of American Law* (New York: Oxford University Press and St. Paul, Minnesota: West Publishing Company, 1976), p. vii.
³ West Virginia State Board of Education v. Barnette, 319 US 624, 638 (1943).
⁴ Alexis de Tocqueville, *Democracy in America, op. cit.*, Vol. 1, p. 330.
⁵ Jethro K. Lieberman, *Milestones! 200 Years of American Law, op. cit.*, p. 295.
⁶ Reynolds v. Sims, 377 US 533, 562 (1964).

Suggestions for Further Reading

Edmond Cahn, *The Moral Decision: Right and Wrong in the Light of American Law* (Bloomington, Indiana: Indiana University Press, 1956).

Benjamin N. Cardozo, *The Growth of the Law* (New Haven, Connecticut: Yale University Press, 1924).

Benjamin N. Cardozo, *The Nature of the Judicial Process* (New Haven, Connecticut: Yale University Press, 1921).

Palmer D. Edmunds, *Law and Civilization* (Washington, D.C.: Public Affairs Press, 1959).

Jerome Frank, *Courts on Trial* (Princeton, New Jersey: Princeton University Press, 1950).

W. Friedmann, *Legal Theory* (5th ed.; New York: Columbia University Press, 1967).

Carl Joachim Friedrich, *The Philosophy of Law in Historical Perspective* (Chicago: The University of Chicago Press, 1958).

Lon L. Fuller, *The Morality of Law* (New Haven, Connecticut: Yale University Press, 1964).

259

Karl N. Llewellyn, *Jurisprudence: Realism in Theory and Practice* (Chicago: The University of Chicago Press, 1962).

Richard Neely, *How Courts Govern America* (New Haven, Connecticut: Yale University Press, 1981).

Roscoe Pound, *An Introduction to the Philosophy of Law* (New Haven, Connecticut: Yale University Press, 1922).